Multicultural Books for PreK–Grade Three

Multicultural Books for PreK–Grade Three

A Guide for Classroom Teachers

Edited by
Xiufang Chen and Susan Browne

ROWMAN & LITTLEFIELD
Lanham • Boulder • New York • London

Published by Rowman & Littlefield
An imprint of The Rowman & Littlefield Publishing Group, Inc.
4501 Forbes Boulevard, Suite 200, Lanham, Maryland 20706
www.rowman.com

86-90 Paul Street, London EC2A 4NE

Copyright © 2023 by Xiufang Chen and Susan Browne

All rights reserved. No part of this book may be reproduced in any form or by any electronic or mechanical means, including information storage and retrieval systems, without written permission from the publisher, except by a reviewer who may quote passages in a review.

British Library Cataloguing in Publication Information Available

Library of Congress Cataloging-in-Publication Data

Names: Chen, Xiufang, 1971- editor. | Browne, Susan, 1956- editor.
Title: Multicultural books for preK-grade three : a guide for classroom teachers / edited by Xiufang Chen and Susan Browne.
Description: Lanham, Maryland : Rowman & Littlefield, 2023. | Includes bibliographical references. | Summary: "A practical guide for teachers seeking to use multicultural literature in the early grades"—Provided by publisher.
Identifiers: LCCN 2022048606 (print) | LCCN 2022048607 (ebook) | ISBN 9781475865820 (cloth) | ISBN 9781475865837 (paperback) | ISBN 9781475865844 (epub)
Subjects: LCSH: Reading (Primary) | Multicultural education. | Children—Books and reading.
Classification: LCC LB1525 .M79 2023 (print) | LCC LB1525 (ebook) | DDC 372.64/044—dc23/eng/20221206
LC record available at https://lccn.loc.gov/2022048606
LC ebook record available at https://lccn.loc.gov/2022048607

Contents

List of Figures and Tables	ix
Acknowledgments	xi
Foreword: "I *Don't* Want To Read About Princesses": The Awesome Responsibility of Inviting Young Children into the Literacy Community *Shanetia P. Clark*	xiii

1 Overview of Multicultural Literature for Younger Children in Classrooms ... 1
Xiufang Chen and Susan Browne
   Purpose and Scope ... 1
   Overview of Chapters ... 5

2 Our Stories, Our Voices: Native Children's Literature ... 9
Tim Swagerty
   Understanding Native American Culture ... 9
   Evaluating and Selecting Native Children's Books ... 12
   Using Authentic Native Literature in the Classroom with Young Children ... 13
   Resources on Native Culture and Literature for Children ... 22

3 The Power and Possibilities of African American Children's Literature ... 31
Susan Browne
   Understanding African American Culture ... 31

	Evaluating and Selecting African American Literature for Young Children	34
	Using African American Literature with Young Children in Classrooms: Strategies and Activities	38
	Resources	42
4	**Asian American Children's Literature**	**47**
	Xiufang Chen	
	Understanding Asian American History and Culture	47
	Evaluating and Selecting Asian American Children's Books	51
	Using Authentic Asian American Literature in the Classroom with Young Children	54
	Resources on Asian American Culture and Literature for Children	65
5	**Jewish Children's Literature**	**69**
	Melanie D. Koss and Deborah Greenblatt	
	Understanding Jewish Culture	69
	Evaluating and Selecting Jewish Children's Books	71
	Using Authentic Jewish Literature in the Classroom With Young Children	76
	Resources on Jewish Culture and Literature for Children	88
6	**Latinx Children's Literature: Why Latinx Children's Literature Is Essential for All Classrooms**	**95**
	Julia López-Robertson	
	Authenticity	98
	Book Selection	101
	Latinx Children's Literature in the Classroom	103
	Classroom Activities	106
	Closing Thoughts	110
7	**Middle Eastern–North African (MENA) Children's Literature**	**115**
	Zeynep Isik-Ercan	
	Understanding MENA Cultures	115
	Evaluating and Selecting Children's Books on MENA Cultures	119
	Using Authentic Middle Eastern and North African Literature in the Classroom with Young Children	121
	Children's Books on Middle Eastern Cultures to Start With	124

Contents vii

	Children's Books Cited in the Chapter	129
	Resources on MENA Cultures and Literature for Children	129
8	Caribbean Children's Literature	131
	Melissa García Vega	
	Understanding Caribbean Culture	131
	Evaluating and Selecting Caribbean Children's Books	138
	Using Authentic Caribbean Literature in the Classroom with Young Children	140
	Resources on Caribbean Culture and Literature for Children	157
9	Books, Gender, and Sexuality in the Early Grades	165
	Kate E. Kedley	
	Understanding and Defining LGBTQ+ in Education: Individuals, Communities, and the Law	165
	Evaluating and Selecting LGBTQ+ Children's Books	167
	Using Authentic LGBTQ+ Literature in the Classroom with Young Children	168
	LGBTQ+ Children's Books to Start With	169
	Resources on LGBTQ+ Culture and Literature for Children	173
10	Sharing Lived Dis/ability Experiences with Young Children through Picturebooks	177
	Monica C. Kleekamp	
	Understanding Lived Dis/ability Experiences	177
	Evaluating and Selecting Children's Books Featuring Dis/ability	179
	Sharing Authentic Literature Featuring Dis/ability in the Classroom with Young Children	183
	Humanizing Children's Books Featuring Dis/ability	188
	Resources on Dis/ability Advocacy and Literature for Children	192

About the Editor and Contributors 195

List of Figures and Tables

FIGURES

Figure 2.1	A Story of Survival: The Wampanoag and the English	14
Figure 2.2	From Trails to Truth: Oklahoma History from a Native Perspective	16
Figure 2.3	The Blue Roses	17
Figure 2.4	Giveaways: An ABC Book of Loanwords from the Americas	18
Figure 2.5	Powwow's Coming	19
Figure 2.6	Powwow Day	20
Figure 2.7	From FRY BREAD by Kevin Noble Maillard	21
Figure 2.8	Native American Lessons and Activities	24
Figure 4.1	Criteria for Analyzing Asian American Literature	52
Figure 4.2	A Blank Copy of Concept Map	57
Figure 7.1	Two Girls Reading Stories	118
Figure 8.1	Map of the Caribbean	132
Figure 8.2	Under the Mango Tree	144

TABLES

Table 3.1	Culturally Conscious Themes Found in African American Literature	35
Table 3.2	Questions to Assist in Evaluating Illustrations and Text in African American Literature for Young Children	38
Table 3.3	Historically Responsive Literacy Planning	42

Table 5.1	Common Jewish Apparel, Objects, Places, Holidays, and Foods	72
Table 5.2	Jewish Values	75
Table 6.1	Triple Entry Journal	108
Table 8.1	Languages Associated with the Caribbean Region	133
Table 8.2	Guiding Tools for P–3 Classroom Teachers to Evaluate and Select Authentic Children's Books	141
Table 8.3	Lesson Plans for Implementing with Children: Activities and Strategies	146

Acknowledgments

Many people made this book happen. First of all, we want to thank the thousands of pre- and in-service teachers we have worked with over the past decades. It is their honest sharing of willingness, joys, struggles, and frustration when using multicultural children's literature in their practice that inspired us to write this book. Without them, this book would not exist. Therefore, this book is mainly for them; our appreciation presents to guide them through the critical and complex process of using multicultural children's literature in the classroom. We are also grateful for the opportunity to share this book with classroom teachers, undergraduate and graduate students, and those working to incorporate multicultural literature in preschools, centers, professional development, and workshops. Especially, we appreciate our contributors for their authentic insider perspectives in writing each chapter and Shanetia Clark for writing the foreword.

We would also like to thank those educators who attended our presentation sessions and provided invaluable feedback at the Literacy Research Association and American Educational Research Association's annual conferences. Their experiences of working with teacher candidates and classroom teachers have helped us refine the focus of this book. We thank Susanne Canavan at Rowman & Littlefield for inviting us to start this book project and Carlie Wall at Rowman & Littlefield for helping us complete this journey.

I, Xiufang Chen, would like to thank the many children of immigrants of color I knew or worked with during the last two decades and other children whose cultures have been underrepresented and/or misrepresented in literature and school curriculum in the United States. I thank them for sharing their racial, ethnic, cultural, and/or social hardships and for their efforts to embrace this diverse world. I hope this book can help children like them to become better understood and at the same time gain new perspectives of understanding themselves and others with support from their teachers and caregivers. I thank authors who write authentic multicultural literature for our children and scholars who keep exploring issues related to multicultural education and multicultural literature. I thank my parents for teaching me the importance of reading and Holly Johnson for exposing me to US children's literature. I am indebted to my husband Yongjun Rong and friends, especially Connie Tang, for their support and encouragement during this journey. Finally, I would like to thank my daughter, Vivian Rong, an avid reader and writer, who shares her stories with me and extended my understanding of the importance of children's literature and multicultural literature.

I, Susan Browne, would like to acknowledge the many children I taught over the years who embraced the diverse literature read in the classroom. Unlike my youth, there were books that had authentic representations of their lives that allowed us to engage in rich cultural explorations. On library days, it was common for my students to return with books about Black characters and by Black authors that they were eager to read on their own. This was not only an affirmation but equally an important reminder of the potential of multicultural literature in the lives of young readers. I am grateful for my undergraduate and graduate students who are working to ensure that students across the grades have diverse books in their hands or on their devices. I would like to acknowledge the work of scholars such as Rudine Sims Bishop, Violet Harris, Wanda Brooks, Michelle Martin, and the late Lawrence Sipe for opening and continuing to provide spaces for scholarship on literature for Black children and youth. I thank the remarkable writers who write diverse literature and give voice to important stories. Finally, I thank my family for their enduring love and support and give special thanks to my husband Al Simpkins, daughter Lydia Peace, and grandson Brandon Hampton.

Foreword

"I *Don't* Want To Read About Princesses"

The Awesome Responsibility of Inviting Young Children into the Literacy Community

Shanetia P. Clark

A few years ago, I supervised a student teaching intern in a kindergarten classroom. This classroom was filled with color, bright posters, and examples of students' work and drawings on the walls. The desks were in groups of four, so students would be able to collaborate and learn from one another. The mentor teacher was attentive and supportive of my student teaching intern. The children appeared to get along and seemed to enjoy being at school. I always felt a positive energy each time I set foot in that room.

One morning while I was there, this dynamic group of kindergarteners were engaged in language arts center rotations. One center, which was led by my student teaching intern, focused on word study; the mentor teacher worked with another group of children in their writing journals; and finally, the third set of children ventured to the classroom library for a center. The young children traveled from center to center without incident. During the third and final rotation, a young Black boy named Jamal[1] walked to the classroom library space. Jamal was one of two Black boys in this class of twenty

---

[1] "Jamal" is pseudonym.

kindergarteners, which had seven other children of color and nine boys. (My eyes naturally sought him, for I have been in classrooms in which the only time the teacher spoke to Black boys was to reprimand or scold them for being wiggly five-year-olds. Luckily, this was not the case.) Jamal was a bright, energetic, and curious little Black boy. I enjoyed conversing with him; I looked forward to our chats.

On this particular day when Jamal went to the classroom library for the third rotation, I initially saw an eager boy. He moved quickly to the space and dug through the books. I watched his entire demeanor slowly shift from eager to dejected. His shoulders hunched. He scowled. I asked him, "What's wrong, Jamal? Are you ok? Did you find a book that you want to read?" He looked me directly into my eyes and whispered, "I *don't* want to read about princesses. There are only princess books over there!" He walked away from the classroom library and moved to play with the alphabet games. His teacher looked at me, and I told her that he didn't find any books that interested him and that he was now creating words with the alphabet game. (I think that if I wasn't there, she would have told Jamal to go back to read the "princess books.")

This moment has stayed with me for a long time. I witnessed the moment that he realized that he was not a part of the classroom literacy community. There were no books that spoke to him. Upon closer inspection, none of the books had characters of color. None had characters of color experiencing joy. The only books were Disney books, non-multicultural retellings of fairy tales, and books about animals. Jamal transformed from a little Black boy who felt that he belonged to one who felt alone and abandoned. It demonstrated how *each* space in the classroom has to represent all of the children; it reaffirmed that the classroom library—a place for young children to be welcomed into the literacy community—must be inviting, representative, and inclusive.

I am excited about *Multicultural Books for PreK–Grade Three: A Guide for Classroom Teachers*. There is finally a resource for in-service (as well as pre-service) teachers to introduce and critically analyze a wider collection of high-quality literature—ranging from board books to chapter books—for this early childhood age group. It is imperative that teachers present and share books with young children that are appropriate, that spark a passion for reading, and that celebrate beautiful cultural diversities. I appreciate the scholars who contributed to this book because they, as cultural insiders, are intimately invested in illuminating children's literature that honors and uplifts their cultures.

Readers can trust the chapters, the scholars' suggestions of literature selections, and how to navigate discussions about different cultures in ways appropriate for young children. These chapters provide resources to locate, integrate, and interrogate literature for young children. As an added bonus, being able to shine a light on various cultures that are woefully underrepresented in children's book publishing will also ignite publishers to seek out children's books written by, about, and for these cultures.

As teachers, especially those who teach the youngest students, we must realize the awesome responsibility we have. We must bring young children into the literacy community. We must increase *access* to literature that showcases characters who positively represent the cultures of our students. We must be mindful of—and disrupt—harmful stereotypes. A way to do so is to authentically integrate high-quality literature into teaching and learning that enables young children to be excited about reading and feel connected to their classmates and classroom. That way, no other child will feel dejected and disconnected as Jamal did that day when he walked away from his classroom's library.

Shanetia P. Clark,
Chair of Department of Early and
Elementary Education at Salisbury University

Chapter 1

Overview of Multicultural Literature for Younger Children in Classrooms

Xiufang Chen and Susan Browne

PURPOSE AND SCOPE

This book is a guide for teachers seeking to use multicultural literature in the early grades. It also serves as a valuable resource for classroom teachers who routinely use multicultural literature as part of their practice. In addition, the book is written for both undergraduate and graduate children's literature and multicultural literature courses as well as for workshops or seminars focusing on teaching preschool–grade 3 children with multicultural books.

Nieto (1992) has long asserted that the broad function of multicultural education (a precursor to multicultural literature) is found in its ability to provide knowledge and information, to change the way children look at the world by offering new perspectives, to promote and/or develop appreciation for those different than oneself, and to illuminate the human experience. She describes basic characteristics of multicultural education that affirm diversity as: (1) antiracist education, (2) basic education, (3) important for all students, (4) pervasive, (5) education for social justice, (6) a process, and (7) critical pedagogy. Nieto guides understandings of culture that are rooted in a democratic stance toward education that acknowledges ethnic, racial, linguistic, religious, economic, and gender differences. Using critical pedagogy as its underlying philosophy, multiculturalism is committed to empowering students with voices geared toward their unique decision-making and social action skills. Banks' (2015) five dimensions of multicultural education are widely used in framing a knowledge base around multicultural education. He offers conceptually distinct, yet interrelated categories related to multiculturalism for schools to consider: (1) content integration, (2) the knowledge construction process, (3) prejudice reduction, (4) an equity pedagogy, and (5) an empowering school culture and social structure. Banks' work speaks to culturally grounded pedagogical approaches that seek to transform school environments.

Multiculturalism remains increasingly significant as recent projections suggest that the United States will consist of primarily minority populations in the next twenty-five years (Colby & Ortman, 2015; Hernandez & Napierala, 2013; Lichter, 2013; U.S. Census Bureau, 2012). Iwai (2019) points to the importance of teachers in both developing and utilizing a wide range of instructional approaches to incorporate multiculturalism into the curriculum to foster diversity awareness, respect for others, and meaningful connections to our global society. National factors such as the increasing diversity in classrooms, the lack of a diverse teaching force, the prevalence of racial unrest, mass shootings of targeted populations, and the rise of other acts of hate and violence toward racial and ethnic groups point to the use of multicultural literature in the classroom as a model for what Grobman (2007) refers to as reconfiguring understandings around difference. Multicultural literature offers opportunities to explore commonalities across cultures and explorations of differences. Bishop (1990) describes multicultural literature as a mirror, window, or sliding glass door. As a mirror, multicultural literature in some way reflects the reader's life. As a window, the literature is a lens through which readers can explore the lives of those different from themselves and as sliding glass doors it allows the reader to step into the imaginary world the author sets forth. In discussing the potential of multicultural literature with adolescent readers, Linder (2021) says that multicultural literature not only serves as mirrors or windows but also presents opportunities to connect with social emotional learning skills such as social awareness and thereby enable learning about the hopes, trepidations, challenges, and successes of others within authentic geographic and societal contexts. These ideas represent curricular opportunities that are relevant, appropriate, and transferable to Pre-K through third-grade classrooms as well.

Multicultural literature in this book is defined as texts about racial and ethnic groups that are culturally and socially different from the white majority in the United States, who see their perspectives widely presented in American literature (Norton & Norton, 2003). This literature reimagines the books selected by teachers for enjoyment, instruction, and inclusion in classroom libraries. Multicultural literature authentically makes differences such as gender and physical ability visible in explorations of diversity. Multicultural literature is rich in cultural detail. The literature uses authentic dialogue and presents cultural issues in enough depth such that young children can talk about them. The inclusion of cultural groups is purposeful and never simply fulfills a quota (Yokota, 1993). Multicultural literature accurately reflects a group's culture, language, history, and values and is concerned with exploring human conditions (Bishop, 1992) and reversing stereotypes (Howard, 1991).

For young children, books with multicultural characters and themes clearly allow readers to take the perspective of others and realize their experiences. Robinson (2013) points out that for many students the possibilities to explore connections or disconnections with people having experiences, culture(s), social and economic situations, and heritages different from their own might only be possible through the multicultural literature they are exposed to in the classroom.

Osario (2018) argues that while it is important to have multicultural literature in the classroom, it is equally important to examine how it is utilized. She goes on to suggest that it is used to (1) promote or develop an appreciation for diversity, (2) honor students' voices, (3) connect to students' rich linguistic and cultural backgrounds, and (4) promote critical consciousness. Multicultural texts enable empathy through transactions in which readers think about the circumstances of others. These books are worlds rich with spaces to share emotions and/or react to the feelings of others. Multicultural books can help young readers step away from a self-centered stance to consider the beliefs and values of others. In these ways, literature about diverse populations and experiences can transform images that have been presented inaccurately or omitted historically.

Multicultural literature is also seen as having major subsets that can be examined through the nuances of racial, ethnic, and cultural identity. One primary example is what Harris (1997) describes as culturally conscious literature that illustrates through text that literature cannot stand apart from culture by emphasizing extraordinary events, unlikely heroes/heroines, and themes of ancestry and identity.

Critical texts are often multicultural in nature. These books are concerned with what bell hooks (1993) calls the privileged act of naming. Critical texts are deliberate in expressing inequalities in society and the pursuit of social justice. These books enable young readers "to develop knowledge around the inherent nature of texts and to become readers from critical perspectives" (Albers et al., 2011). Critical texts examine the existence of difference. They support understandings of history and life by providing a voice for traditionally silenced or marginalized people. The literature shows how to take action on important social issues. The literature examines dominant systems and structures in society that work to position people and groups of people. The literature sometimes does not end happily because of the complex issues it presents (Leland et al., 1999).

This book is a practical guide for educators on the use of multicultural literature in preschool through third grade. This book is significant for early childhood educators because of the potential during the early years when the major portions of a young child's intellect, social skills, and personality are developing, which offers this time as ripe for exploring cultural knowledge about oneself and others. The National Association for the Education of Young Children in their 2009 Quality Benchmark for Cultural Competence Project reports that for the "optimal development and learning of all children, educators must acknowledge culture." Multicultural literature for young children provides an array of opportunities for immersion in cultural differences. We know that when students from diverse backgrounds read literature that highlights the experiences of their cultural group, they learn to feel pride in their identity and heritage. They become confident in writing about and valuing their own experiences. Meanwhile, an introduction to difference is important for children in preschool to third grade. It provides a representative view of the diversity in the United States and helps to foster respect for others at an early age. By the upper elementary grades, teachers who favor a critical perspective are able to guide students to explore issues of power relations. Thus, the foundation for these later discussions should be established in the primary grades. According to Norton (2013), engaging with multicultural literature supports imagination and creativity and has the potential to improve reading scores. Multicultural literature allows for a reimagining of how emergent literacy unfolds when issues of justice and equity are explored at an early age. "Teaching criticality humanizes instruction and makes it more compassionate" (Muhammad, 2020, p. 117). Early literacy experiences and the development of critically thoughtful students can be meaningfully intertwined.

There is a growing body of work that addresses the significance of multicultural literature and its use in the classroom. As this guide will address, careful attention should be given to multicultural books used with young children for the ideas they reflect and the possibilities of those ideas. Donna Norton's (2013) *Multicultural Literature: Through the Eyes of Many Children* (4th edition) has been an often used text in courses devoted to multicultural literature. Although it offers a comprehensive examination of African American, Native American, Asian American, Latino, Jewish, and Middle Eastern cultures, the book is limited in its focus on early grades and it does not address the literature on differences connected to physical, mental, and economical abilities and gender identification as well. At this time, *Using Multiethnic Literature in the K-8 Classroom* published in 1997 by Christopher-Gordon Publishers and edited by Violet J. Harris remains one of the only texts to address multiethnic literature in the early grades. While it is a seminal text, the book is nearly twenty years old and its focus spans grades K–8 with limited emphasis on the early years. In addition, as indicated by the title, the text looks at multicultural literature solely through the lens of race and ethnicity.

Potential audiences include pre-service teachers (primarily early childhood and early elementary pre-service teachers), early childhood educators, early elementary teachers, curriculum coordinators (early childhood and school level), and teacher educators. Courses where the book could be used include but are not limited to Multicultural Literature, Early Literacy Development, and Children's Literature.

OVERVIEW OF CHAPTERS

Chapter 1 is an overview of the book. It discusses the context and rationale of this book, namely, the significance of multicultural literature for younger children. Chapters 2 to 10 unfold in the same structure. Each chapter focuses on a culture that is visible in the United States, yet remains underrepresented in the literature. Some cultural groups might be represented in more children's books than the others. For example, more children's books are accessible to Latinx families than to Vietnamese, Indonesian, or Pakistani families. Even within a cultural group, there are differences among and between subgroups. For instance, there exist differences between and among Asian Americans in terms of regional dialect, religion, class background, educational level, and political perspective as well as distinctions based on generation, gender, and lifestyle orientation. This book will help educators teach young children that these differences exist and thus avoid essentializing any "category" of culture. This book is especially unique in that each chapter is written by an author or authors representing the culture discussed, which thus provides authentic insider perspectives.

Starting with exploring that particular culture, each chapter includes a guide on how to select and evaluate the literature on the culture. The classroom examples then showcase strategies and activities for classroom teachers to use children's literature on that culture with young children. Finally, each chapter provides suggested children's books and resources for understanding the culture.

Readers are reminded that multicultural books, while powerful tools, can only do so much. Educators need to continually hone their capacity for cross-cultural functioning beyond the mere use of multicultural books in the classroom. Some examples include cultural training workshops for teachers, the use of caregivers and family members as learning resources in the classroom, and cultural self-assessment.

REFERENCES

Albers, P., Harste, J. C., & Vasquez, V. (2011). Interrupting certainty and making trouble: Teachers' written and visual responses to picturebooks. In P. Dunston, L. Gambrell, K. Headley, S. Fullerton, P. Stecker, V. Gillis, & C. Bates (Eds.), *60th Yearbook of the Literacy Research Association* (pp. 179–194). Literacy Research Association.

Banks, J. A. (2015). Multicultural education, school reform, and educational equality. In The Equity Project (Ed.), *Opening the doors to opportunity for all: Setting a research agenda for the future* (pp. 54–63). American Institutes of Research.

Bishop, R. S. (1990). Mirrors, windows, and sliding glass doors. *Perspectives: Choosing and Using Books for the Classroom, 6*(3), ix–xi.

Bishop, R. S. (1992). Multicultural literature for children: Making informed choices. In V. Harris (Ed.), *Teaching multicultural literature in grades K–8* (pp. 37–53). Christopher-Gordon.

Colby, S., & Ortman, J. M. (2015). *Projections of the size and composition of the US population: 2014 to 2060*. U.S. Census Bureau.

Harris, V. (1997). *Using multicultural literature in the K-8 classroom*. Christopher Gordon Publishers.

Hernandez, D. J., & Napierala, J. S. (2013). Early education, poverty, and parental circumstances among Hispanic children: Pointing toward needed public policies. *Journal of the Association of Mexican American Educators, 7*(2), 30–39. https://eric.ed.gov/?id=EJ1.

Hogue, C. (2013). *Government organization summary report: 2012*. United States Census Bureau.

Howard, E. E. (1991). Authentic multicultural literature for children: An author's perspective. In M. V. Lindgren (Ed.), *The multicolored mirror: Cultural substance in literature for children and young adults* (pp. 91–99). Highsmith.

Iwai, Y. (2019). Culturally responsive teaching in a global era: Using the genres of multicultural literature. *The Educational Forum, 83*(1), 13–27.

Leland, C., Harste, J., Ociepka, A., Lewison, M., & Vasquez, V. (1999). Exploring critical literacy: You can hear a pin drop. *Language Arts, 77*(1), 70–78.

Lichter, D. T. (2013). Integration or fragmentation? Racial diversity and the American future. *Demography, 50*(2), 359–91.

Linder, R. (2021). Enhancing social awareness development through multicultural literature. *Middle School Journal, 52*(3), 35–43.

Muhammad, G. (2020). *Cultivating genius: An equity framework for culturally and historically responsive literacy*. Scholastic Incorporated.

National Association for the Education of Young Children (NAEYC). (2009). *Quality benchmark for cultural competence project*. http://www.naeyc.org/files/ naeyc/file/policy/state/QBCC_Tool.pdf.

Nieto, S. (1992). *Affirming diversity: The sociopolitical context of multicultural education*. Longman.

Norton, D. (2013). *Multicultural children's literature: Through the eyes of many children* (4th ed.). Pearson.

Norton, D. E., & Norton, S. (2003). *Through the eyes of a child: An introduction to children's literature* (6th ed.). Pearson.

Osorio, S. L. (2018). Multicultural literature as a classroom tool. *Multicultural Perspectives, 20*(1), 47–52.

Robinson, J. A. (2013). Critical approaches to multicultural children's literature in the elementary classroom: Challenging pedagogies of silence. *New England Reading Association Journal, 48*(2), 43–51.

Yokota, J. (1993). Issues in selecting multicultural children's literature. *Language Arts, 70*(3), 156–67.

Chapter 2

Our Stories, Our Voices: Native Children's Literature

Tim Swagerty

UNDERSTANDING NATIVE AMERICAN CULTURE

To understand Native culture, we must first look at its development from origination to complex civilization and the impact of European colonization. These stages of development have greatly influenced the stories of these people and the narratives that rose out of them.

Native American culture has existed in the Western Hemisphere since as early as 12,000 BC, stemming from ancient peoples of Siberia or beyond in Eurasia who migrated to these continents either by Beringian or by Pangean origins. Either theory is plausible and probable given substantive proof of deep DNA connections between paleo-Eurasians, paleo-Siberians, and paleo-Amerindians (Raghavan et al., 2014; Wei et al., 2018).

That being pre-established as some measure of constant, the genesis of the various and diverse Native cultures that burgeoned in these lands and between these shores unambiguously took root in areas where ice covering arable soils receded first. These cultural hearths[1] were the first to achieve the basic characteristics of civilization[2] on these American continents and serve as hubs of cultural diffusion and dissemination for those that developed in subsequent periods. From these foundational civilizations in North America stem the great Archaic cultures that served as the path to the vast and diverse Native cultures that would spread to every corner of North America (Briney, 2020; Britannica, 2021; National Geographic, 2019; Team, 2020).

By the thirteenth century, America was teaming with highly developed Native cultures that encompassed vast populations and population centers. These included Cahokia as the center of the Upper Mississippian region, the Anasazi of the Upper Southwest, the Hohokam of the Middle Southwest, the Mogollon of the Lower Southwest, and the Pataya of the Lower Pacific Coast (Anderson & Rocek, 2018; Bayman, 2002; Bey, 2022; Benson, 2009; Colton, 1938; Reed, 2002; Rinaldo, 1941; Schlanger, 1992; Shakely, 2019; Wallace, 2007; Young, 2000).

With these cultural hearths founded and the pillars of civilized society established came the intangible expressions of collective culture in the telling and recording of origin stories. These cultural narratives transferred through shared communication strategies form the progenition of collective cultural knowledge handed down for and to subsequent generations into perpetuity. Depicted on cave walls, recorded in codices, sgraffitoed on pottery, and regaled through dramatic gesture and powerful voice, these are the histories and traditions shared that document and authenticate the powerful and indomitable spirit of our ancestors (Codices, 2019; Howe, 1999; Iyer, 2001; Jansen, 1990; King, 2003; Whitely, 2009).

These cultural traditions continued unabated until contact with European explorers casting themselves westward into a vast unknown seeking fame, fortune, and fancy under the additional auspices of newly established monarchial governments' desire for God, Gold, and Glory. Contact resulted in the decimation of Native populations through exposure to foreign illnesses to which they possessed no immunity or defense and the subjugation of the surviving few to the indoctrinations of the Catholic Church. Cultural practices were forbidden in the forced deculturation of proselytized neophytes, thus retarding or eliminating the continuance of cultural sustenance for any measure of survival for future generations. Changed too in this violent extermination of Native culture were traditional gender roles in favor of European expectations more in line with the male-dominated liturgy of papist Rome (Bernstein, 1959; Donnelly, 2019; European Colonization and Epidemics Among Native Peoples, 2022; Russell, 2004).

From this point in history forward, stories of Native cultures would be those told about them from the perspective of the European colonizers rather than those by them of the origins, glories, and hardships of the generations of heroes and ancestors that came before. For the next two centuries, assimilationists would work to integrate the Native regardless of the dominant country or culture. As European influences gave way in the Western Hemisphere to those more uniquely American, the strategy changed little. To survive, the Native in America would have to change or perish (Fulford, 2006; Sayre, 2000; Smith, 2000; Yeboah, 2005).

Natives forced into European education models in the new America with a strict adherence to conformity and assimilation left little room for cultural sensitivity or culturally relevant curriculum. The abolition of Native culture became the mission of the government of the United States through the late nineteenth and early twentieth centuries. The Native Boarding School became both the vehicle and solution for the assimilation of the Native into mainstream culture through the complete and abject obliteration of any recognizable remnant of Native identity. Richard Henry Pratt, founder of the Carlisle Indian School in Carlisle Pennsylvania, issued the famed statement regarding Native education as being ". . . all the Indian there is in the race should be dead. Kill the Indian in him, and save the man" (Pratt et al., 2003; Pratt, 2022; Yeboah, 2005).

The move toward a more culturally relevant and culturally sensitive representation of Natives in the curriculum began with the rise of Native cultural activism in the late 1960s and early 1970s. As with other underrepresented ethnicities of the period, Natives pushed for more autonomy and visibility. It would be a considerable period long before that was realized, but it was here that Native culturists began to start taking control and effecting change in the representation of Native culture in both school curriculum and popular media (Liu & Zhang, 2011; Equal Justice Initiative, 2019; Zinn Education Project, 2021).

The present movement and direction of Native and Indigenous education and representation in school curriculum have progressed to fostering culturally restorative and supportive depictions in classroom curricula. This is where this resource is situated, with Native and Indigenous stories being told by Native and Indigenous authors. Where best applied, they are being presented by Native and Indigenous educators for the betterment of Native and non-Native students alike. Even without the last measure accomplished, the paradigm and narrative have shifted from stories told about Native and Indigenous culture by colonizing agents bent on assimilation into annihilation. Now, they are being told and represented by authentic voices of resiliency and strength and by individuals of knowledge and experience (Lomawaima & McCarty, 2006; Stanton, 2014).

The common themes in the diverse Native and Indigenous cultures of stewardship and conservation of the gifts of Mother Earth, kinship and connection to family, honoring of the matriarchal and patriarchal models, storytelling and the passing on of tradition, remembrance of the ancestors, reverence of the Unseen, and the value and importance of our little ones are once again being discussed and shared with respect and relevance. This rich heritage of Native and Indigenous culture is once again being told by those best suited to represent the people: Our Stories, Our Voices.

EVALUATING AND SELECTING NATIVE CHILDREN'S BOOKS

As a teacher educator with a specialization in Social Studies and having worked with Early Childhood–6th grade clinical teacher candidates, I have had many opportunities to make suggestions for culturally sensitive material and culturally sustaining pedagogy for the teaching of Native American history and culture. My very first evaluative criteria for any resources brought to me for review are:

Does a Native American author the work? This question complicates the consideration because of the varied definitions of who is deemed "Native American." For the sake of clarity, the standard definition for Native American is a member[3] of any of the Indigenous Peoples of the forty-eight contiguous United States of America and Alaska. Native Hawaiians have only recently been reclassified from Aboriginals to Native Americans (U.S. Government Printing Office, 2012).

The issue for some is the deliberation that only those Native, Indigenous, and Aboriginal peoples residing in the continental United States are considered Native American in the same way that only residents of the fifty states of the United States of America, the District of Columbia, and it's incorporated territories (except Samoa) are called American. My personal definition includes anyone who maintains tribal membership or tribal affiliation[4] in any of the Native, Indigenous, and Aboriginal peoples of North, Central, and South America (HUD Exchange, 2022; Pewewardy, 1998).

Does the work portray Native culture in a positive and supportive representation? Numerous works exist that have been used since time immemorial in American classrooms to depict and represent Native American culture. Most of these are only resorted to in the month of November while Thanksgiving is observed, which is deemed Native American Heritage Month. These typically involve picking "Indian" names, making and decorating paper grocery bag, making "Indian" vests, paper feathers, and headbands, and reading books that may or may not enhance these culturally inappropriate representations (Swagerty, 2022).

The North Carolina State Advisory Council on Indian Education has compiled a list of titles they do not recommend on this subject, and most are accompanied by reviews written by parents of Native American students in the Chapel Hill-Carrboro School District. "American Indians in Children's Literature" likewise regularly reviews Native children's books and publishes those that they do not recommend and offers suggestion for replacement texts in the review (American Indian Children's Literature, 2022; North Carolina State Advisory Council on Indian Education, 2022).

My determination after that is to review the work myself to evaluate if it effectively presents a story, a message, a moral that highlights Native American peoples and culture in non-colonial,[5] non-prejudicial depictions that are culturally supportive and culturally informative. This applies to both Native students and non-Native students alike, as it is just as important for non-Native students to "unlearn" some of the cultural fallacies put forth by American popular culture and media about Native Americans as it is for Native students (Meyer, 2011; Ouimet, 2011).

USING AUTHENTIC NATIVE LITERATURE IN THE CLASSROOM WITH YOUNG CHILDREN

One of the very first suggestions I would like to make concerning informed choices about culturally relevant and culturally supportive classroom curricula is to offer the materials made available to me for dissemination through this article by the Oklahoma City Public Schools (OCPS). Native American Student Services (NASS) through the OCPS has created a factually representative and culturally relevant Thanksgiving lesson plan booklet called *A Story of Survival: The Wampanoag and the English* (OCPS, 2022).

This booklet in figure 2.1 includes facts about the Wampanoag of Massachusetts Bay, the English, and general facts of the period (1600s). They include common myths, stereotypes, and activities to avoid, some of the

Figure 2.1 A Story of Survival: The Wampanoag and the English. *Source*: Native American Student Services of Oklahoma City Public Schools. Permission arranged with Native American Student Services of Oklahoma City Public Schools. https://www.okcps.org/domain/130.

exact same I mentioned previously. The remainder of the booklet is lesson, activity, and craft suggestions that are suited for preschool–grade 3 students and easily differentiated for equity and appropriateness of diverse learners. The booklet also includes a list of fifteen additional book titles on the celebration of Thanksgiving and other stories recommended by the NASS and OCPS. Resources can be accessed at https://www.okcps.org (OCPS, 2022).

Included in this resource are lesson plans to be used with this booklet and others for book titles recommended by authors through the NASS and the OCPS.

They have also been made available for use by teachers specifically in Oklahoma (Muskogean for "Red People") resources of *From Truth to Trails: Oklahoma History from a Native Perspective* (OCPS, 2022).

This booklet in figure 2.2 gives an overview of Oklahoma's history and the Native peoples who lived there in its earliest days. These include the Wichita (Kitikiti'sh), Caddo (Kadohadacho), Apache (Inde), and Quapaw (Ogaxpa) peoples. Most of the work deals with the forced removal of the tribes from the southeast United States to Oklahoma, I.T. (Indian Territory as it was called from 1830 to 1890) during the Jackson Administration. These include the Tsalagi (Cherokee), Chahta (Choctaw), Mvskoke (Muskogee, formerly Creek), Chikasha (Chickasaw), and Seminole Nations. It includes the names and tribal agency contacts of the thirty-nine tribes now residing in the state. This booklet is formatted similarly to the first and includes common myths, misconceptions, and stereotypes to avoid, as well as helpful tips for creating your own Native American lesson units. It also offers culturally supportive Native American lessons and activities, with vocabulary and additional recommended readings. The resources can be accessed at https://www.okcps.org (OCPS, 2022).

Additionally, they included an informational sheet suitable for sharing during the season associated with dress-up days, for example, Halloween, All Hallows Eve, All Saints Day, Day of the Dead, or Harvest Festival (a popular sectarian alternative). It provides information about cultural appropriation by non-Natives of any culture, not their own, and how Native students may be allowed during this time to wear traditional regalia, and the opportunity is opened for dialogue and discussion about the fact that Native American culture is alive and living in the present (OCPS, 2022).

Figure 2.2 From Trails to Truth: Oklahoma History from a Native Perspective. *Source*: Native American Student Services of Oklahoma City Public Schools. Permission arranged with Native American Student Services of Oklahoma City Public Schools. https://www.okcps.org/domain/130.

Native Children's Books to Start With

An amazing author's work I wish to offer first for consideration is by Linda Boyden (Cherokee/Lumbee). Linda is an award-winning author with numerous credits to her name, including Writer of the Year (2002–2003) by the *Wordcraft Circle of Native Writers and Storytellers*. Her book *Blue Roses* (ISBN-10 1600606555) received Wordcraft's Book of the Year for Children's Literature in 2007. This book also received the 2003 Paterson Prize for Books for Young People in the pre-kindergarten–grade 3 division (Lee & Low, 2022).

This debut work, seen in figure 2.3 was beautifully illustrated by Amy Córdova-Boone (Tsegi Diné), which tells a story from Boyden's childhood dream and deals with the difficult topic of the death of a loved one. In tribal lore, death is considered but a step in the journey of life and not to be feared or the discussion of avoided. Although speaking ill of those passed is considered inappropriate in Native and Indigenous culture, honoring the memory of someone and celebrating their life after they are gone is one of the most cherished ways to hold on to the memory of a loved one. Lee and Low Publishers provides a teacher's resource guide to accompany this title at *leeandlow.com*. This book is recommended for ages six to nine (1–3 grades) (Lee & Low, 2022; Teachers Guide, 2022).

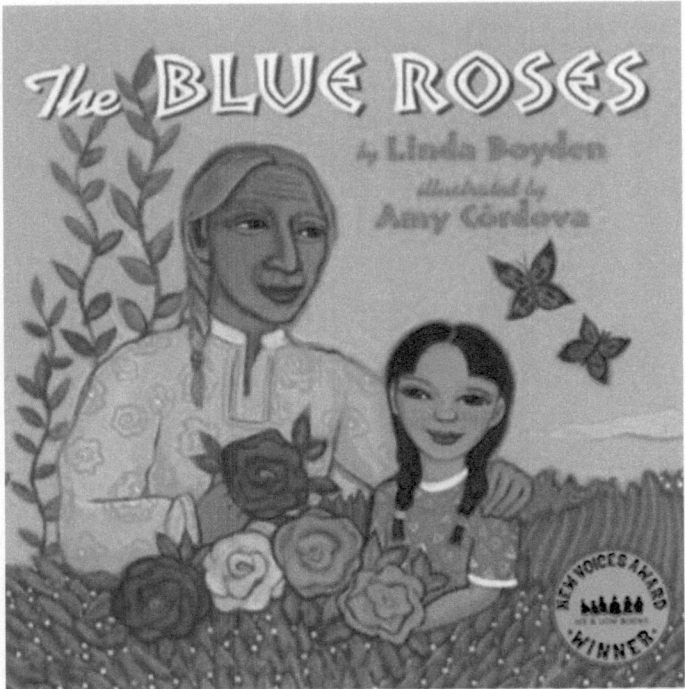

Figure 2.3 **The Blue Roses.** *Source*: Text copyright © 2002 by Linda Boyden. Illustrations copyright © 2002 by Amy Córdova. Permission arranged with LEE & LOW BOOKS Inc., New York, NY 10016. All rights reserved. Learn more at leeandlow.com/books/the-blue-roses.

Another work that I wish to share of Mrs. Boyden's is the book entitled *Giveaways: An ABC Book of Loanwords from the Americas* (ISBN-10 100826342655). This book, shown in figure 2.4, both written and illustrated by her, creates a wonderfully colorful alphabet list of words originating in the Western Hemisphere with the Native and Indigenous peoples of North, Central, and South America. These words have found their way into common usage either regionally or nationally. Each word is accompanied by a beautiful illustration and descriptive tale of the origin of the word, the people who used it, and an informative back-story about their culture. Her bibliography for the book, rather than a traditionally bland recitation of sites and sources, is an additional resource of "extra cool" facts and acknowledgments. It is recommended for ages six to nine (1–2 grades), but the colorful and engaging illustrations would make it easily applicable and relatable to preschool age as well (UNM Press, 2022).

The last of Mrs. Boyden's book, seen in figure 2.5, is *Powwow's Coming* (ISBN-10 0826342655), again written and illustrated by her.

Figure 2.4 Giveaways: An ABC Book of Loanwords from the Americas. *Source*: Text and illustrations copyright © 2010 by Linda Boyden. Permission arranged with University of New Mexico Press, Albuquerque, NM. All rights reserved. Learn more at unmpress.com/books/powwows-coming/9780826342652.

Our Stories, Our Voices: Native Children's Literature 19

This colorful depiction of traditional Native practice centers on the cultural and social function of powwow and the heartbeat of the occasion, the drum. Held to celebrate a family event, honor someone, or commemorate a time of year, Native powwows are how cultural traditions are remembered, celebrated, and passed down to future generations. The bibliography is again atypical in that it supports the work by detailing powwow etiquette and giving information about Native games popular at powwow in the Notes to the Reader. These could be incorporated into a lesson after the reading of the book to involve bodily kinesthetic students and still retain the focus of the lesson. Additional teacher resources for this title can be accessed at Reading is Fundamental website, *rif.org/literacy-central/book/powwows-coming*. This book is recommended for ages four to eight (P–3 grades) (Reading is Fundamental, 2022).

On the same subject of family gathering is the recently published work seen in figure 2.6 titled *Powwow Day* (ISBN-10 158089948X) by Traci Sorell

Figure 2.5 Powwow's Coming. *Source*: Text and illustrations copyright © 2007 by Linda Boyden. Permission arranged with University of New Mexico Press, Albuquerque, NM. All rights reserved. Learn more at unmpress.com/books/giveaways/9780826347268.

Figure 2.6 Powwow Day. *Source*: Illustration copyright © 2022 by Madelyn Goodnight. Used with permission of the publisher. Learn more at charlesbridge.com/products/powwow-day.

(Cherokee) and illustrated by Madelyn Goodnight (Chickasaw). This author has been awarded for other titles by the American Indian Library Associations (AILA)'s the American Indian Youth Literature Honor Award. These include *We are Still Hear!; Native American Truths Everyone Should Know* (2021, honored in 2022) and *We are Grateful, Otsaliheliga* (2018, honored in 2020). Resources for these last two titles can be accessed at *cdn.shopify.com/we-are-still-here-teachers-guide* and *cdn.shopify.com/we-are-grateful-teachers-guide*, respectfully (Reading is Fundamental, 2022).

Powwow Day is about a young Native girl, River, coming out of illness and wishing to dance again. It is an uplifting story about moving from isolation to the healing power of community that is powwow. It likewise provides information about history and function of powwow traditionally, but also its function in modern Native culture. Teacher resources for this book can be found at *teachingbooks.net*. This book is recommended for ages four to eight (P–3 grades) (Charlesbridge, 2022).

Figure 2.7 From FRY BREAD by Kevin Noble Maillard. *Source*: Illustrated by Juana Martinez-Neal. Text copyright © 2019 by Kevin Noble Maillard. Illustrations copyright © 2019 by Juana Martinez-Neal. Used by permission of Roaring Brook Press, a division of Holtzbrinck Publishing Holdings Limited Partnership. All rights reserved.

Another recommended title is shown in figure 2.7 titled *Fry Bread: A Native American Family Story* (ISBN-10 1626727465). This work is by Kevin Noble Maillard (Seminole) and illustrated by Juana-Martinez-Neal (Peruvian). This work was awarded, among numerous others, the Robert F. Sibert Medal (2020) and the AILA's American Indian Youth Literature Honor Award (2020) (Macmillan, 2022).

This hardback picture book tells the story a family spanning three generations participating preparing a cultural staple at Native tables. The vivid descriptions and colorful illustration make it an excellent addition to a preschool–grade 3 reading resource list. It includes in the end papers a traditional fry bread recipe and numerous resource contacts to tribal nations in the United States. Teacher resources for this book can be found at *learningtogive.org/resources/fry-bread-literature-guide*. It is recommended for ages three to six (P–1 grades) (Learning to Give, 2022).

On a topic of recent political issue is the children's book *We are Water Protectors* (ISBN-10 1250203554) written by Carole Lindstrom (Anishinaabe, Métis) and illustrated by Michaela Goade (Tlingit/Haida). Awarded both the Caldecott Medal and Golden Kite Award for Picture Book Text in 2021, this work is a rallying cry inspired by Native- and Indigenous-led protest events at the Standing Rock Reservation (Lakota) against the Dakota Access Pipeline in 2016. It conveys the message of conservation and stewardship of the gifts of Mother Earth and highlights the position in Anishinaabe (Ojibwe) culture that women hold a special kinship to the water and are charged with its protection. Teacher resources for this book can be found at *macmillan.com/we-are-water-protectors-activity-kit.pdf*. It is recommended for ages three to six (P–1 grades) (Macmillan, 2022).

Another engaging title for children on Native culture is *Bowwow Powwow* (ISBN-10 1681340771) written by Brenda J. Child (Red Lake Ojibwe) and illustrated by Jonathan Thunder (Red Lake Ojibwe). The work has been translated into Ojibwe language by Gordon Jourdain (Lac La Croix First Nation). This book is a story of the power of storytelling and imagination and how the spoken word has been used for eons of time to convey cultural knowledge and inspire future generations. It was awarded the American Library Association's Notable Children's Book Award in 2018. Teacher resources for this title can be accessed at *teachingbooks.net/bowwow powwow*. It is recommended for ages three to seven (1–2 grades) (TeachingBooks, 2022).

The last book I will recommend is one entitled *The Forever Sky* (ISBN-10 168134098) by Thomas Peacock (Fond du Lac Band, Lake Superior Chippewa) and illustrated by Annette S. Lee (Ojibwe/Lakota). It is a story of two brothers and their love for their departed grandmother. The older brother tells his younger brother stories told by their grandmother of the ancestors looking down from the stars. This work was awarded the AICL's Best Picture Book Award and the Northeastern Minnesota Book Award for Children's Literature, both in 2019. Teacher resources for this title can be found at *teachingbooks.net*. This book is recommended for ages three to seven (P–2 grades) (TeachingBooks, 2022).

RESOURCES ON NATIVE CULTURE AND LITERATURE FOR CHILDREN

A number of amazing resources have been compiled and made available to preschool to Grade 3 pre-service and in-service teachers to aid them in the selection of culturally supportive and culturally relevant Native children's literature.

Native American Student Services of the Oklahoma City Public Schools has included in their publication, "A Story of Survival: The Wampanoag and the English," a list of recommended titles complied as a teacher resource. There are lesson plans for this booklet and lesson plans for other recommended titles included in the publication (OCPS, 2022).

A similar list is likewise included in the NASS publication of "From Trails to Truth: Oklahoma History from a Native Perspective." While there are a few repetitions between the publications, both include relevant titles with lesson plans, tips for culturally relevant Native American units, and lesson planning suggestions (OCPS, 2022).

On the two books referenced dealing with the subject of Native American powwows, Powwows.com has powwow-related lesson plans that can be accessed at powwows.com/native-american-pow-wow-lesson-plan/ (Gowder, 2022).

One of the most applicable lessons of this publication lends itself well to use in/around Thanksgiving/Harvest celebrations in November, Native American Heritage Month.

This lesson shown in figure 2.8 gives teachers a way to introduce a difficult topic to teach in a way that resembles the imagery of the season but presents a much more relevant interpretation of the topic of Native and Indigenous culture. The booklet has other suggestion on this topic on additional pages (OCPS, 2022).

The *American Indians in Children's Literature* website (https://americanindiansinchildrensliterature.blogspot.com), founded by Dr. Debbie Reese (Nambé Pueblo) in 2006 and joined in 2016 by Dr. Jean Mendoza, publishes lists of recommended works on culturally relevant Native children's literature and reviews of titles both positive and negative. Dr. Reece has also contributed to *embracerace* (https://www.embracerace.org/resources/how-to-choose-excellent-childrens-books-by-and-about-american-indians) with a list of selection criteria for teachers to use when selecting Native children's literature and additional recommended titles (Reece, 2022).

Read in Color "Recommended Reading" by Little Free Library (https://littlefreelibrary.org/indigenous-read-in-color-recommended-reads) has a vast library of source information on children's titles of varied ethnicities, but

NATIVE AMERICAN LESSONS AND ACTIVITIES

The Three Sisters

Native Americans called corn, beans, and squash the Three Sisters because they grew so well in a small space. The corn provided a stalk to support the beans while they grew. The beans provide nutrients to help squash and corn so they can grow. The squash vines provided shade to prevent weeds from growing. The three sisters were the primary food source for many Native American tribes.

Lesson #1

Learning Goal
1. I can describe the Three Sisters.

Supplies
- Beans
- Corn kernels
- Small squash

Question: How do you think the food was prepared without a stove like we use today?

Activity: Use the sentence started, "I observed ____.", as needed.

Teacher will lead a discussion on beans, corn and squash. Ask the students if they have eaten the food and if so, how was it prepared. Talk about how these three were staples for the Native American tribes. After showing the good whole group, put items into a science/sensory tub for the students to explore. Encourage the students to use their 5 senses to describe the corn, beans and squash. Teacher can provide samples to taste or concentrate on sight, smell and touch.

Students will record what they observed. This can be done in small groups or as a whole group. Teachers may put out magnifying glasses and color word cards to help record observations

Figure 2.8 Native American Lessons and Activities. *Source*: Native American Student Services of Oklahoma City Public Schools. Permission arranged with Native American Student Services of Oklahoma City Public Schools. https://www.okcps.org/domain/130.

most notably on Indigenous for not only early readers but middle and adult as well (Littler Free Library, 2022).

Colours of Us (https://coloursofus.com/32-native-american-childrens-books) publishes a list of 100 Native American Children's books (updated 2021), some of which I have highlighted in this chapter (Colours of Us, 2022).

First Nations Development Institute (https://www.firstnations.org/wp-content/uploads/2018/11/Revised_Book_Insert_Web_Version_March_2018.pdf) is a non-profit organization that assists Native tribal communities with a focus on education. The educational resource they produce is suggested reading list that covers a variety of levels and topics (First Nations Development Institute, 2022).

NOTES

1. There are eight recognized cultural hearths worldwide; for example, Huang Valley of China, Ganges Valley of Southeast Asia, Indus Valley of Pakistan, Tigris and Euphrates Valley of Iraq, Nile Valley of Egypt, Niger Valley of West Africa, Andes Mountains of South America, and Mesoamerica of North America. Two significant examples are recognized in the Western Hemisphere as the centers of the development of civilization and progenitors of Native culture: the Andes Mountains of Chile and Peru and Mesoamerica at the tip of Mexico.

2. While some discrepancy exists as to this list of characteristics, for the purpose of this reference they include (1) large population centers, (2) monumental architecture and unique art styles, (3) shared communication strategies, (4) systems for administering territories, (5) a complex division of labor, and (6) the division of people into social and economic classes.

3. "Member" is generally thought of as legally registered in a federally recognized Native American tribe in the United States with the required level of certified "Indian blood" determined by the respective tribal government to qualify for membership. It varies by tribe.

4. Tribal affiliation denotes someone who maintains a cultural connection or community attachment through active association and participation in a recognized Native, Indigenous, or Aboriginal population in the Americas.

5. Non-colonial refers to the absence of references and chronological framing of Native culture in terms of European colonization.

REFERENCES/BIBLIOGRAPHIES

American Indians in Children's Literature. (n.d.). https://americanindiansinchildrensliterature.blogspot.com.

Anderson, A. L., & Rocek, T. R. (2018). GIS modeling of agricultural suitability in the highlands of the Jornada branch of the Mogollon culture of southcentral New Mexico. *Journal of Archaeological Science: Reports*, 22, 142–53.

Bayman, J. M. (2002). Hohokam craft economies and the materialization of power. *Journal of Archaeological Method and Theory*, 9, 69–95. https://doi.org/10.1023/A:1016132225354.

Benson, L., Pauketat, T., & Cook, E. (2009). Cahokia's boom and bust in the context of climate change. *American Antiquity*, 74(3), 467–83. https://doi.org/10.1017/S000273160004871X.

Bernstein, M. D., & Blum, A. A. (1959). Spaniards and Englishmen: A reconsideration of the causes of new world colonization. *The Journal of General Education*, 12(4), 222–34. http://www.jstor.org/stable/27795652.

Bey, Lee. (2016, August 17). Lost cities #8: mystery of Cahokia – Why did North America's largest city vanish? *The Guardian*. ISSN 0261-3077. Retrieved March 3, 2022.

Briney, A. (2020, January 23). The culture hearths of past and present. *ThoughtCo*. Retrieved March 29, 2022, from https://www.thoughtco.com/culture-hearths-and-cultural-diffusion-1434496.

Britannica, T. Editors of Encyclopedia (2021, August 30). Archaic culture. *Encyclopedia Britannica*. https://www.britannica.com/topic/Archaic-culture.

Codices. Indigenous Peoples of the Americas - UC Santa Barbara Library. (2019, August 15). Retrieved March 29, 2022, from https://spotlight.library.ucsb.edu/starlight/indigenous-peoples-of-the-americas/feature/codices.

Colours of Us (n.d.). https://coloursofus.com/32-native-american-childrens-books.

Colton, H. S. (1938). Names of the four culture roots in the Southwest. *Science*, 87(2268), 551–52.

Donnelly, M. (2019). *The Sacrifice of God's Glory for the Sake of Gold: Bringing Christianity & Humanity to the New World* (Unpublished Doctoral Dissertation or Master's Thesis). University of Prince Edward Island, Canada.

Embracerace. (n.d.). https://www.embracerace.org/resources/how-to-choose-excellent-childrens-books-by-and-about-american-indians.

European Colonization and Epidemics Among Native Peoples (n.d.). Retrieved March 29, 2022, from https://daily.jstor.org/european-colonization-and-epidemics-among-native-peoples/.

Fry Bread. Macmillan. (2021, July 20). Retrieved April 28, 2022, from https://us.macmillan.com/books/9781626727465/frybread.

Fry Bread Literature Guide. Fry Bread Literature Guide|Learning to Give. (n.d.). Retrieved April 28, 2022, from https://www.learningtogive.org/resources/fry-bread-literature-guide.

Fulford, T. (2006). *Romantic Indians: Native Americans, British Literature, and Transatlantic Culture 1756–1830*. Oxford University Press.

Giveaways. University of New Mexico Press. Retrieved April 28, 2022, from https://unmpress.com/books/giveaways/9780826347268.

Gowder, P. (2017, March 18). Native American pow wow lesson plan. *PowWows.com*. Retrieved April 28, 2022, from https://www.powwows.com/native-american-pow-wow-lesson-plan/.

Howe, L. Fall (1999). Tribalography: The power of native stories. *Journal of Dramatic Theory and Criticism*, XIV(1), Fall 1999. https://journals.ku.edu/jdtc/article/view/3325.

Iyer, L. (2001). Cave paintings and wall writings: Blanchot's signature. *Angelaki: Journal of Theoretical Humanities*, 6(3), 31–43.

Jansen, M. (1990). The search for history in Mixtec codices. *Ancient Mesoamerica*, 1(1), 99–112. Retrieved March 30, 2022 from http://www.jstor.org/stable/44478198.

King, T. (2003). *The Truth About Stories: A Native Narrative.* House of Anansi.

Little Free Library. (n.d.). *Read in color recommended reading.* https://littlefreelibrary.org/indigenous-read-in-color-recommended-reads.

Liu, K., & Zhang, H. (2011). Self-and counter-representations of native Americans: Stereotypical images of and new images by native Americans in popular media. *Intercultural Communication Studies*, 20(2), 105–18.

Lomawaima, K. T., & McCarty, T. L. (2006). *"To Remain an Indian": Lessons in Democracy From a Century of Native American Education.* Teachers College Press.

Meyer, N. (2011). Selecting diverse resources of native American perspective for the curriculum. *Education Libraries*, 34(1), 23–32. https://files.eric.ed.gov/fulltext/EJ937211.pdf.

National Geographic Society. (2012, October 9). Key components of civilization. *National Geographic Society.* Retrieved March 10, 2022, from https://www.nationalgeographic.org/article/key-components-civilization/.

Native American activism: 1960s to present. Zinn Education Project. (2021, November 19). Retrieved March 30, 2022, from https://www.zinnedproject.org/materials/native-american-activism-1960s-to-present/.

Native American activism. Equal Justice Initiative. (2019, November 11). Retrieved March 30, 2022, from https://eji.org/news/history-racial-injustice-native-american-activism.

Native American Children's Literature Recommended Reading List. (n.d.). First Nations Development Institute. https://www.firstnations.org/wp-content/uploads/2018/11/Revised_Book_Insert_Web_Version_March_2018.pdf.

North Carolina State Advisory Council on Indian Education. (n.d.). *Books about, or featuring, American Indian that are not recommended.* Retrieved April 8, 2022, from https://files.nc.gov/dpi/documents/americanindianed/resources/not-recommended.pdf.

Oklahoma City Public Schools. (2022a). *A story of survival: He Wampanoag and the English.* https://www.okcps.org/cms/lib/OK01913268/Centricity/Domain/130/2021%20OKCPS%20NASS%20Thanksgiving%20Booklet.pdf.

Oklahoma City Public Schools. (2022b). *From truth to trails: Oklahoma history from a native American perspective.* https://www.okcps.org/cms/lib/OK01913268/Centricity/Domain/130/OK%20History%20Booklet%202019%20From%20Trails%20to%20Truths.pdf.

Ouimet, A. (2011). *Culturally relevant literature: How to identify and use culturally relevant literature* (Doctoral Dissertation or Master's Thesis). St. John FisherCollege, New York.

Pewewardy, C. (1998, April). Fluff and feathers: Treatment of American Indians in the literature and the classroom. *Equity and Excellence in Education.* http://www.hanksville.org/storytellers/pewe/writing/Fluff.html.

Powwow day. Charlesbridge. (n.d.). Retrieved April 28, 2022, from https://www.charlesbridge.com/products/powwow-day.

Pratt, R. H. (n.d.). Series I: General Correspondence and Official Papers, 1867-1924. Series I: General Correspondence and Official Papers, 1867–1924 | Archives at Yale. https://archives.yale.edu/repositories/11/archival_objects/435399.

Pratt, R. H., Utley, R. M., & Adams, D. W. (2003). *Battlefield and classroom: Four decades with the American Indian, 1867–1904.* University of Oklahoma Press.

Public Law 101-343—Aug. 3, 1990 104 stat. 391 public law (n.d.). Retrieved April 8, 2022, from https://www.congress.gov/101/statute/STATUTE-104/STATUTE-104-Pg391.pdf.

Raghavan, M., Skoglund, P., Graf, K. E., Metspalu, M., Albrechtsen, A., Moltke, I., Rasmussen, S., et al. (2014). Upper Palaeolithic Siberian genome reveals dual ancestry of Native Americans. *Nature*, 505(7481), 87–91. https://doi.org/10.1038/nature12736.

Read in color recommended reading. Little Free Library. (2022, January 10). Retrieved April 15, 2022, from https://littlefreelibrary.org/read-in-color-recommended-reading/?gclid=Cj0KCQjwr-SSBhC9ARIsANhzu14h1UmuQqadMJP08KnQ0an1JY9ndFYqhs6z21i49t9fn9uyx5F5Z1gaAubYEALw_wcB.

Reed, P. F. (Ed.). (2002). *Foundations of Anasazi Culture: The Basketmaker Pueblo Transition.* University of Utah Press.

Reese, D. (2006). American Indians in Children's Literature (AICL). Revised and withdrawn. [Web blog post]. Retrieved April 8, 2022, from https://americanindiansinchildrensliterature.blogspot.com/p/revisions-to.html.

Rinaldo, J. (1941). Conjectures on the independent development of the Mogollon culture. *American Antiquity*, 7(1), 5–19.

Russell, L. M. (2004). God, gold, glory and gender: A postcolonial view of mission. *International Review of Mission*, 93, 39–49.

Sayre, G. M. (2000). *Les sauvages américains: Representations of Native Americans in French and English Colonial Literature.* University of North Carolina Press.

Schlanger, S. H. (1992). Recognizing persistent places in Anasazi settlement systems. In *Space, Time, and Archaeological Landscapes* (pp. 91–112). Boston, MA: Springer.

Shackley, M. S. (2019). The Patayan and Hohokam: A view from Alta and Baja California. *Journal of Arizona Archaeology*, 6(2), 83–98.

Smith, S. L. (2000). *Reimagining Indians: Native Americans Through Anglo Eyes, 1880–1940*. Oxford University Press.

Stanton, C. R. (2014) The curricular Indian agent: Discursive colonization and indigenous (dys)agency in U.S. history textbooks. *Curriculum Inquiry*, 44(5), 649–76. https://doi.org/10.1111/curi.12064.

Swagerty, T. (2022). Digital access to culturally relevant curricula: The impact on the native and indigenous student. In E. Reeves & C. McIntyre (Eds.), *Multidisciplinary Perspectives on Diversity and Equity in a Virtual World* (pp. 99–113). IGI Global. https://doi.org/10.4018/978-1-7998-8028-8.ch006.

Teacher's guide - The Blue Roses: Lee & Low Books. (n.d.). Retrieved April 28, 2022, from https://www.leeandlow.com/books/2365/teachers_guide.

TeachingBooks. (2022a). *Teaching resources for bowwow powwow*. Retrieved April 28, 2022, from https://www.teachingbooks.net/tb.cgi?tid=62080.

TeachingBooks. (2022b). *Teaching resources for the forever sky*. Retrieved April 28, 2022, from https://www.teachingbooks.net/tb.cgi?tid=68989.

Team, S. G. (2020, August 20). Cultural hearths - Major cultural hearths of the world. *SarkariGuider.com*. Retrieved March 10, 2022, from https://sarkariguider.com/major-cultural-hearths-of-the-world/.

The Blue Roses. Native American | Nature | coping with death | Lee & Low Books. (n.d.). Retrieved April 28, 2022, from https://www.leeandlow.com/books/the-blue-roses.

U.S. Government Printing Office. (2012). *Senate report 112-251 - To express the policy of the United States regarding the United States relationship with Native Hawaiians and to provide parity and a process for the recognition by the United States of the Native Hawaiian governing entity*. Retrieved April 7, 2022, from https://www.govinfo.gov/content/pkg/CRPT-112srpt251/html/CRPT-112srpt251.htm.

Wallace, H. D. (2007). *Hohokam Beginnings*. The Hohokam Millennium (pp. 12–21).

We are grateful teachers guide-Shopify. (n.d.). Retrieved April 28, 2022, from https://cdn.shopify.com/s/files/1/0750/0101/files/we-are-grateful-teachers-guide.pdf?v=1603827629.

We are still here guide-Shopify. (n.d.). Retrieved April 28, 2022, from https://cdn.shopify.com/s/files/1/0750/0101/files/we-are-still-here-teachers-guide.pdf?v=1620938220.

We are water protectors activity kit v3 - Macmillan Publishers. (n.d.). Retrieved April 28, 2022, from https://static.macmillan.com/static/macmillan/2020-online-resources/downloads/we-are-water-protectors-activity-kit.pdf.

Wei, L. H., Wang, L. X., Wen, S. Q., Yan, S., Canada, R., Gurianov, V., Huang, Y. Z., et al. (2018). Paternal origin of Paleo-Indians in Siberia: Insights from Y-chromosome sequences. *European Journal of Human Genetics*, 26, 1687–1696. https://doi.org/10.1038/s41431-018-0211-6.

What Constitutes "Tribal Affiliation or Community Attachment" F. HUD Exchange. (n.d.). Retrieved April 8, 2022, from https://www.hudexchange.info/faqs/reporting-systems/hmis/data/data-standards/what-constitutes-tribal-affiliation-or-community-attachment/.

Whitley, D. S. (2009). *Cave Paintings and the Human Spirit: The Origin of Creativity and Belief*. Prometheus Books.

Wilson, J. (1998). *The Earth shall Weep: A History of Native America*. Grove Press.

Yeboah, A. (2005, February). Education among Native Americans in the periods before and after contact with Europeans: An overview. In *Annual National Association of Native American Studies Conference*, Houston, TX.

Young, B. W., Fowler, M. L., & Fowler, M. J. (2000). *Cahokia, the Great Native American Metropolis*. University of Illinois Press.

CHILDREN'S BOOKS CITED IN THIS CHAPTER

Boyden, L. (2007). *Powwow's Coming*. University of New Mexico Press.

Boyden, L. (2010). *Giveaways: An ABC Book of Loanwords From the Americas*. University of New Mexico Press.

Boyden, L. (2011). *The Blue Roses*. Lee and Low Publishers.

Child, B. J., Jourdain, G., & Thunder, J. (2018). *Bowwow Powwow*. Minnesota Historical Society.

Lindstrom, C. (2020). *We Are Water Protectors*. Roaring Brook Press.

Maillard, K. N. (2019). *Fry Bread: A Native American Family Story*. Roaring Brook Press.

Peacock, T. (2019). *The Forever Sky*. Minnesota Historical Society Press.

Sorel. T. (2018). *We Are Grateful: Otsaliheliga*. Charlesbridge.

Sorel, T. (2021) *We Are Still Here! Native American Truths Everyone Should Know*. Charlesbridge.

Sorel, T. (2022). *Powwow Day*. Charlesbridge.

Chapter 3

The Power and Possibilities of African American Children's Literature

Susan Browne

UNDERSTANDING AFRICAN AMERICAN CULTURE

When thinking about the story of African Americans in this country, the human enslavement of the Trans-Atlantic Slave trade has historically served as an origin story. Indeed, the capture of Africans from the interiors of West Africa and the trek to the coast represent the beginnings of African American enslavement.

The 1619 Project: Born on the Water picturebook by Nikole Hannah-Jones and Renée Watson and illustrated by Nikkolas Smith is a children's text derived from the Pulitzer Prize-winning 1619 Project: A New Origin Story, by Hannah-Jones. The picturebook shows that African Americans "had a home, a place, a land before they were sold . . . and that there was a time when they did not pray for freedom" (Hannah-Jones & Watson, 2021, np). The authors were intentional in depicting that the story of African Americans does not begin with slavery. Told through poetry, the book uses a young girl's homework assignment to construct experiences of Black people in Africa, on the Middle Passage and in America. The book leaves readers with the understanding that although African Americans were born on the water it is not where they are from.

Throughout this chapter, the compound word "picturebook" is used to express the bond between text and art that creates something beyond what each form might contribute separately (Wolfenbarger & Sipe, 2007). In the picturebook, *Your Legacy: A Bold Reclaiming of our Enslaved History*

(Williams, 2021), children are again introduced to a historical legacy that began in Africa before 1619. The book further portrays the ways African Americans survived 400 years of enslavement and acknowledges the sacrifices and accomplishments that can be evidenced in future generations of Blacks in America. Tracey Baptiste's nonfiction book for children, *African Icons: Ten People Who Shaped History* (2021), introduces Black history that originated on Africa's continent with portraits of ten leaders who changed the world.

Picturebooks such as the aforementioned offer counter-storytelling as they embrace thinking and feelings that embody other subjectivities in ways that storytelling shaped by dominant narratives centering slavery as the African American origin story does not (Taliaferro Baszile, 2015). According to Costello and Reigstad (2014), counter-storytelling narratives disrupt common narratives that alone can serve as misconceptions and misrepresentations of Blackness and Black people. By no means does this suggest that slavery is no longer of the utmost significance to chronicling African American life in the United States. It does however insist on a humanizing lens toward Blackness.

Historian Henry Loius Gates and Kwame Anthony Appiah created Africana (2005), a scholarly encyclopedia that examines the history of Africa and the African Diaspora in five volumes indicating the immense culture of African Americans. Gates' 2013 six-part documentary series, *The African Americans: Many Rivers to Cross*, further offers a comprehensive view of five centuries of African American history and culture starting on the continent of Africa and continuing to 2013 America. The episodes unfold as: (1) *The Black Atlantic* (1500–1800), (2) *The Age of Slavery* (1800–1860), (3) *Into the Fire* (1861–1896), (4) *Making a Way Out of No Way* (1897–1940), (5) *Rise!* (1940–1968), and (6) *A More Perfect Union* (1968–2013). It could be suggested that the title for content from 2013 to the present day might be *The Criticality of Race: Black Lives Matter*. Other recommended adult texts for educators that support deeper understandings of African American culture include: *On Juneteenth* (Gordon-Reed, 2021), *Wake: The Hidden History of Women-Led Slave Revolts* (Hall, 2021), *Caste* (Wilkerson, 2020), *How to Be an Antiracist* (Kendi, 2019), and *The New Jim Crow: Mass Incarceration in the Age of Colorblindness* (Alexander, 2012). Engaging in work to understand African American history and culture works toward becoming better equipped to teach African American students.

African American Literary Traditions

Characteristics of African American culture have been influential in the development of African American literature. A prominent aspect of African American literature has been the emphasis on moving away from the white mainstream by exploring new themes and forms. The Harlem Renaissance of the 1920s and 1930s furthered the development of a Black aesthetic that emerged from a spirit of cultural self-identification and self-determination. During the 1940s and 1950s, African American literature emphasized social issues and the social and political climate of the 1960s had a major impact on literary and cultural movements. Writers drew their literary inspiration from the Black community and wrote powerfully in what could be described as a collective voice.

A Black aesthetic continued to grow literarily and guide attention to new standards of beauty, cultural pride, and nationalism. Feelings (1995) describes this aesthetic focused on Black traditions as committed to providing entertainment, passing on messages, communicating fears, hopes, dreams, and fantasies, and explaining the world along with visions of reality and a sense of truth. As a feminine voice made a space in literature, the multiplicity and complexity of African American identities continued to take shape (Appiah & Gates, 2005). The literary landscape expanded to include African American narratives and what would result in a reframing of literary history in the nation.

The genesis of African American children's literature stems from the features of adult African American literary traditions. Early periodicals such as *Fay* (1887) and *Ivy* (1888) were developed for young African American readers followed by the twentieth-century periodical, *The Brownies Book* published from January 1920 through December 1921. *The Brownies Book* began through the collaborative work of W. E. B. Du Bois, Augustus Dill, and Jessie Fauset with a monthly publication that included stories, biographies, poetry and plays to foster racial pride and intellectual excellence.

Culturally relevant, culturally conscious or diverse African American literature is primarily written by African American authors and about African American characters. These writers illustrate through text that literature cannot stand apart from culture through themes that lend an authentic voice to Black people with roots in Africa and America. These stories challenge dominant narratives in expressing to rising generations that they have a history and a literature (Dunbar Nelson, 1922).

Zeely (Hamilton, 1967) is considered to be among the first highly regarded novellas for young readers. The book tells the story of siblings, Elizabeth and John Perry's summer visit to their uncle's farm. While there, the two become the imaginary Geeder and Toeboy. Geeder experiences an awakening of self when she meets Zeely whom she believes is a Watusi Queen. The book embodies themes that Harris (1993) says are often present in literature that seeks to be conscious about African American culture such as questions of identity and intragroup color differences. Since that time, books have continued to be published for young readers with African American characters who address the themes Harris identified as seen in table 3.1.

> By the end of the century, especially during the 1990s, there was also an influx of newer writers and artists, whose work is shaping the African American literature of the 21st century. Writers like Jacqueline Woodson, Angela Johnson, and Rita Williams-Garcia and artists like Kadir Nelson, Christopher Myers, and Bryan Collier are broadening the scope of African American children's literature. They are, for example, addressing topics that had rarely been addressed in the literature before, both controversial ones such as homosexuality, and contemporary life experiences such as teenage parenting. (Sims Bishop, 2012, p. 12)

The cultural themes noted in specific picturebooks provide a guide for teachers when considering the text selection. Also, significant are the ways the books can function to support knowledge and/or information, which might change the way children look at the world by offering new perspectives. The books serve as a reflection of varying African American experiences. They can promote and/or develop appreciation for those different from one's self and provide enjoyment while illuminating the human experience.

EVALUATING AND SELECTING AFRICAN AMERICAN LITERATURE FOR YOUNG CHILDREN

When selecting literature to read with young children, considerations around quality require texts: (1) that are accurate representations/depictions, (2) that are literarily well-crafted, (3) that promote student engagement and

Table 3.1 Culturally Conscious Themes Found in African American Literature

Culturally Conscious Themes (Harris, 1993, pp. 73–74).	Picturebooks Addressing Each Theme
1. The effect of racism and legal discrimination	*The Proudest Blue: A Story of Hijab and Family* (Muhammad, 2019) It is the first day of school for two sisters and for one the first day of hijab.
2. Information about slavery as an institution and its impact	*All Different Now: Juneteenth, the First Day of Freedom* (Johnson, 2014) The story of Juneteenth, the day freedom finally came to the last of the slaves in the South is told through the eyes of a little girl.
3. Struggles for equality	*Unspeakable: The Tulsa Race Massacre* (Boston Weatherford, 2021) The devastation of Tulsa's Greenwood district in 1921 when a white mob attacked the Black community.
4. Interracial relationships	*The Other Side* (Woodson, 2001) A Black and white little girl work to become friends in a small segregated town.
5. Families and their loyalties and obligations to each other	*All Because You Matter* (Charles, 2022) A message to Black and Brown children reminding them that they are loved and that they matter.
6. Love and its meaning and manifestations	*Hair Love* (Cherry, 2019) Family love is seen through a young girl's hair.
7. The effects of beauty standards that oppress	*Hair Like Mine* (Perry, 2015) A little girl is unhappy that her naturally curly hair looks different from others comes to realize that it is special.
8. Everyday rituals and events in life	*Freedom in Congo Square* (Boston Weatherford, 2016) Nonfiction story about African American history, hope, and joy in difficult circumstances.
9. Extraordinary events that create unlikely heroes and heroines	*Sit-In: How Four Friends Stood Up By Sitting Down* (Pinkney, 2010) Four young men following Dr. Martin Luther King Jr.'s words of peaceful protest and sit-in at a "whites only" lunch counter.
10. Struggles for the value of education	*When the Schools Shut Down* (Gladden, 2022) Autobiographical account of an African American girl's experience during the shutdown of public schools in Virginia, following Brown vs. Board of Education.

(continued)

Table 3.1 (Continued)

Culturally Conscious Themes (Harris, 1993, pp. 73–74).	Picturebooks Addressing Each Theme
11. Intragroup color differences	*Sulwe* (Nyong'o, 2019) A young girl wants her dark skin to be lighter. The book focuses on learning to love oneself, no matter the complexion.
12. Commitment to racial uplift and progress	*The Me I Choose to Be* (Tarpley, 2021) Empowering text and photography affirm the possibilities for Black children.
13. Consequences of poverty	*The Hard Times Jar* (Footman Smothers, 2003) Emma Turner loves books and dreams of having a store-bought one but money is tight for the migrant worker family.
14. Strength and resilience of African American people and culture	*The Undefeated* (Alexander, 2019) A poem that is a tribute to African Americans of the past.
15. Contributions of African Americans to US history and culture	*Heart and Soul: The Story of America and African Americans* (Nelson, 2013) A 100-year-old woman narrates African American history.
16. Strength of African American families, especially the extended family	*The Year We Learned to Fly* (Woodson, 2022) A grandmother directs siblings complaining of boredom to their history.

motivation to read, (4) that invite aesthetic evocations, (5) that invite connections, (6) that promote critical thinking, (7) that can be life-informing and life-transforming, (8) that have rich language to build vocabulary, and (9) that include opportunities for learning across the curriculum.

When addressing cultural considerations in literature for young readers, Asante (1991) points out that European culture must not be presumed as "universal" in instruction. He describes education at its best as intentional in acknowledging that all human beings have aided in the development of the world and that most human achievements exist because of communal efforts. He further insists that without a multicultural education, students are left ignorant regarding the contributions of diverse people. The use of quality multicultural literature with young children promotes literary transactions in which individual/group similarities and differences across cultures can be explored. Early exposure to multicultural literature provides windows for looking at others, mirrors for seeing oneself, and sliding glass doors to step into the world the author has created (Bishop, 1990). Hefflin and Barksdale Ladd (2001) suggest that quality in literature for African American children also has to do with liberation, a sense of feeling valued, and having power. As young readers are engaged in these ways they become prepared to embrace and navigate their own lives and place in an increasingly diverse society.

The life-informing and life-transforming potential of literature for young children has significant implications for text selection. Picturebooks such as The *Wagon* (Johnston, 1996), *A Fine Dessert* (Lockhart, 2015), and *A Birthday Cake for George Washington* (Ganeshram, 2016) have been heavily scrutinized for their inauthentic portrayals of enslaved characters. According to Howard (1991) in an authentic book the "universality" of experience pervades the story as particular characters and settings unfold. This specificity allows readers from the culture to identify with the text as they are affirmed by experiencing cultural truths in the literature. Literature nuanced in cultural specificity can provide an opportunity for new meanings and understandings to exist for cultural insiders and outsiders. A beloved picturebook by many, *The Snowy Day* (Keats, 1962), is what Sims (1982) referred to as a "melting pot" book. It was categorized as such because there are no distinguishing cultural characteristics about the main character other than his black skin. Replacing the main character in the book with another race/ethnicity would likely do little to change the overall message of the book.

Using African American literature in the classroom relates as much to its purpose as to its literary characteristics. When that purpose has been determined, it is necessary to examine both the literary and cultural elements present in the text for authenticity. If offensive language or imagery is present in a text its purpose must be examined, and critical conversations with students must take place. Table 3.2 provides questions to ask when evaluating all genres of African American literature (Norton, 2013).

In 2015, #OwnVoices arrived on Twitter from author Corinne Duyvis and brought attention to cultural insider/outsider authorship in children's literature. The hashtag has been instrumental in carving out a new category of diverse books by #OwnVoices authors. Although there has been a notable increase in books portraying Black, Indigenous, and People of Color (BIPOC) characters, the Cooperative Children's Book Center (CCBC) continues to release statistics pointing out that children's books by and about BIPOC populations continue to be insufficient. Further, according to (CCBC) data in 2021 of the 3,183 books received 307 were by Black authors with 436 about Black characters.

USING AFRICAN AMERICAN LITERATURE WITH YOUNG CHILDREN IN CLASSROOMS: STRATEGIES AND ACTIVITIES

Community Cultural Wealth

Using picturebooks with young children can promote what Yosso (2005) refers to as community cultural wealth. She describes this strengths-based approach as drawing on forms of cultural resources that operate to empower students. She further asserts that this lens is important to educational settings working to increase the number of students who remain in the p–20 academic pipeline. This approach to teaching can transform deficit views often associated with communities of color.

In *Something Beautiful* (Wyeth, 1998), an African American girl searches for and finds something beautiful in her urban community. Initially only seeing unsightliness in her neighborhood she works to seek out its beauty. *Uptown* (Collier, 2000) captures Harlem and all its rich cultural wonder through the eyes of a young boy. *Dream Street* (Elam Walker, 2021) is based on the Boston neighborhood where the author and illustrator's cousins grew up and the book is a lovely testimony to the community. Individually or as a

Table 3.2 Questions to Assist in Evaluating Illustrations and Text in African American Literature for Young Children

Evaluating Illustrations	Evaluating Text
1. Are the illustrations authentic for both the time period and geographical locations? 2. Do the characters look natural? 3. Are the characters shown as individual people with characteristics in their own right? 4. Do the illustrations perpetuate stereotypes?	1. If dialect is used, is it used appropriately? 2. Are social issues and problems addressed earnestly, accurately, and without oversimplification? 3. Are factual and historical details culturally accurate and authentic? 4. Does the author accurately describe contemporary settings and conflicts? (Norton, 2013, p. 22)

text set, the books embody the community's cultural wealth that Yosso (2005) purports. These books can be used to invite students to examine and reflect on their own communities and offer opportunities for connections with Social Studies curriculum. Students might draw maps, take photographs, interview neighbors about the beauty they see in the community, and/or develop their own writing using the book(s) as mentor texts.

Hair Stories

Singer, artist, and songwriter Solange Knowles stated, "I think many people, especially from other cultures, just don't understand the role hair plays in Black women's lives" (Corbett, 2012). She went on to write a song titled "Don't Touch My Hair," which was released on her album *A Seat at the Table* (2016). In 2009, Knowles cut her hair short and began wearing it naturally. This choice caused conversation globally as she became a face and voice for a dawning natural hair movement.

Brooks and McNair (2015) write, "One of the ways in which creators of African American children's literature help young people, particularly girls, view themselves as beautiful is through books, such as the ones examined herein, that celebrate and affirm the normalcy of Black hair" (p. 300). The authors point to scholarship examining the bearing hair has on the Black, female identity and dominant perceptions around beauty. In their content analysis, they identified six picturebooks about Black hair with female protagonists that were written by African American females. The books were *Cornrows* (Yarbrough, 1979), *I Love My Hair!* (Tarpley, 1998), *Nappy Hair* (Herron, 1997), *Crowning Glory* (Thomas, 2002), *Saturday at The New You* (Barber, 1994), and *Happy to Be Nappy* (hooks, 1999). Their analysis revealed three major themes: (1) the perspective that all hair is good, (2) the connection between Black hair and African American history, and (3) the bonding of females while hair is being combed and/or styled (p. 303). These findings offer significance as they emphasize the value of sharing children's literature addressing the realities and cultural experiences of young readers. Brooks and McNair (2015) affirm that for Black girls the books enable them to better understand the role of hair in their lives. These books further support readers who are not of color in interrogating images and representations that reject dominant European standards of beauty.

New books with story lines dedicated to themes involving African American hair continue to make their way to publication. Some of these titles include *Bedtime Bonnet* (Redd, 2020), *Hair Love* (Cherry, 2019), *Don't Touch My Hair!* (Miller, 2018), and *My Hair is a Garden* (Cabrera, 2018). All early-grade classrooms would benefit from having a collection of picturebooks focusing on Black hair. Frequent exposure to this literature works to establish an appreciation for Black hair and ensure its normalcy in its many manifestations.

An invitation to respond to the book(s) using illustrations or magazine clippings of favorite hairstyles with captions explaining the selection can be displayed in the classroom. Students can also write poems about their hair using a simile. For example, "My hair is fierce like a lion" or "My hair is as fluffy as a cloud." If using the books as a collection, students might select their favorite lines from each of the books to create a found poem that is posted in the classroom.

Black Boy Joy

Following February 26, 2012, murder of seventeen-year-old Trayvon Martin in Sanford, Florida, Bettina Love wrote the article, *I See Trayvon Martin: What Teachers Can Learn from the Tragic Death of a Young Black Male* (2013). In it, she asks how educators might examine their own race and gender perceptions to address the consistent injustices toward young Black males in classrooms. In writing that is in no way an indictment of all teachers, Love draws attention to the over-criminalization of Black males in school. Far too frequently, judgments are made about Black males based on unfounded assumptions and fear with no consideration of their intellect or personhood. Love goes on to say that it is common for educators to recognize and care about social injustices without making the necessary changes in their own practice. To "See Trayvon Martin" and Jayland Walker, Ahmaud Arbery, Daniel Prude, George Floyd, Walter Wallace Jr., Tamir Rice, and Michael Brown calls for educators to see their own "power and privilege" while disrupting practices that pathologize Black males as criminals and unteachable students.

In an analysis of books with Black male characters awarded a Caldecott Medal or Honor from 1995 to 2020, Davis et al. (2021) found:

> In the 115 Caldecott books analyzed, 38 (33%) were revealed to include any Black males. During analysis, the characters were categorized as either primary,

secondary, or background. Approximately half of these books (*n* = 18) featured Black males as the primary character(s), accounting for only 15.7% of the Caldecott books in this study. In the remaining 20 books, nine contained Black males as secondary characters and 11 as background characters. (p. 12)

This further emphasizes the need to include a purposeful emphasis on Black males in the classroom and particularly in the early grades where students are formulating so many of the qualities that shape their being.

I Am Every Good Thing (Barnes, 2020) is a picturebook offering a refrain that reads "I am" in highlighting Black boy joy. The book is an affirmation that all Black boys are worthy and to be loved.

Be Boy Buzz (2002) by bell hooks rhythmically celebrates Black boys and their beauty with dynamic words and illustrations. *Calvin* by J. R. Ford and Vanessa Ford tells the story of a transgender boy preparing for the first day of school and introducing himself to his family and friends for the first time. For these books, it will be of value for students to discuss what they like/dislike about the books and what questions they have. If read as a text set, a question could ask, What is Black Boy Joy? Students would then be invited to go back into the books to identify these themes or aspects of the text. The response could be conversation, writing, performance, or illustrations.

Family

In her 2020 book, *Cultivating Genius: An Equity Framework for Culturally and Historically Responsive Literacy* (HRL), Gholdy Muhammad provides a framework for lesson planning where identity development, skill development, intellectual development, and criticality intersect to foster genius in young learners.

The following books about family are used in table 3.3 to demonstrate how the framework can be adopted. *Me & Mama* (Cabrera, 2020) celebrates the relationship between a mother and daughter. *Daddy Speaks Love* (Henderson, 2022) is a tribute to the joy that fathers bring to their children's lives. *Max and the Tag Along Moon* (Cooper, 2015) is a moving story about a little boy and his separation from loved ones. *Sometimes Mommy Gets Angry* (Campbell, 2003) shares how sometimes Annie's mother smiles, and other days her mother gets very angry. On those days Annie knows what to do. *Visiting Day* (Woodson, 2002) presents a young girl and her grandmother as they prepare

Table 3.3 Historically Responsive Literacy Planning

FAMILY—Early Grades Read Alouds:
Me & Mama (Cabrera, 2020)
Daddy Speaks Love (Henderson, 2022)
Max and the Tag Along Moon (Cooper, 2015)
Sometimes Mommy Gets Angry (Campbell, 2003)
Visiting Day (Woodson, 2002)
Momma, Where Are You From? (Bradby, 2000)

HRL Learning Goals	What makes a family?
Identity	Who is my family? Who am I in my family?
Skill	Comparing and contrasting families
	Students will examine the ways families are the same and different.
Intellect	Students will develop knowledge and understanding of the many ways families exist.
Criticality	Students begin to consider social and cultural influences on family.

for the one day a month, they get to visit the girl's father in prison. *Momma, Where Are You From?* (Bradby, 2000) is Momma's story about the people and places from her childhood.

The nation's increasingly diverse classrooms require culturally competent approaches to instruction. This framework for planning and instruction supports advancing curriculum in humanizing ways to support all students. HRL provides an entry into supporting literacy for Black children.

RESOURCES

The African American Children's Book Project
 https://theafricanamericanchildrensbookproject.org
Just Us Books Publications
 https://justusbooks.com/pages/about-us.html
Independent Book Sellers of African American Literature:
Hakim's Books
 https://hakimsbookstore.com
Harriet's Bookshop
 https://bookshop.org/shop/harriettsbookshop
Uncle Bobbies
 https://www.unclebobbies.com

The resources below are taken from Acevedo-Aquino et al. (2020, p. 34):

Resource for analyzing a specific children's book for its cultural responsiveness and representation from Teaching Tolerance:
https://www.tolerance.org/sites/default/files/2017-11/Reading-Diversity-v2-Redesign-WEB-Nov2017.pdf

Resource for analyzing classroom library, guided reading bookroom, or scope and sequence's mentor texts from Lee & Low Books a one-page audit questionnaire:
https://www.leeandlow.com/educators/grade-level-resources/classroom-library-questionnaire

Resource for analyzing curriculum, whether it is district-made or purchased from a curriculum company. This is a Culturally Relevant Curriculum Scorecard designed and published by the Metropolitan Center for Research on Equity and Transformation of Schools (NYU Metro Center):
https://steinhardt.nyu.edu/metrocenter/ejroc/culturally-responsive-curriculum-scorecard

Diverse Book Finder
https://diversebookfinder.org/

Embrace Race
https://www.embracerace.org/resources/where-to-find-diverse-childrens-books

#DisruptTexts
https://disrupttexts.org/lets-get-to-work/

The Brown Bookshelf
https://thebrownbookshelf.com/

We Need Diverse Books
https://diversebooks.org/

Diversity Resources from the Society of Children's Book Writers and Illustrators
https://www.scbwi.org/diversity-resources/

Small Presses Owned/Operated by People of Color and First/Native Nations from the Cooperative Children's Book Center
https://ccbc.education.wisc.edu

REFERENCES

Acevedo-Aquino, M., Bowles, D., Eisenberg, J., Elliott, Z., Gainer, J., & Valdez-Gainer, N. (2020). Reflections on the #OwnVoices movement. *Journal of Children's Literature, 46*(2), 27–35.

Alexander, M. (2012). *The new Jim Crow: Mass incarceration in the age of colorblindness.* Revised edition. New Press.

Appiah, A., & Gates, H. L. (Eds.). (2005). *Africana: The encyclopedia of the African and African American experience*. Oxford University Press.

Asante, M. K. (1991). The Afrocentric idea in education. *The Journal of Negro Education, 60*(2), 170–80.

Baszile, D. T. (2015). Rhetorical revolution: Critical race counter storytelling and the abolition of white democracy. *Qualitative Inquiry, 21*(3), 239–49.

Bishop, R. S. (1990). Mirrors, windows, and sliding glass doors. *Perspectives: Choosing and Using Books for the Classroom, 6*(3), ix–xi.

Bishop, R. S. (2012). Reflections on the development of African American children's literature. *Journal of Children's Literature, 38*(2), 5–13.

Brooks, W. M., & McNair, J. C. (2015). "Combing" through representations of Black girls' hair in African American children's literature. *Children's Literature in Education, 46*(3), 296–307.

Cooperative Children's Book Center. (2019). *Data on books by and about Black, Indigenous and People of Color published for children and teens compiled by the Cooperative Children's Book Center, School of Education, University of Wisconsin-Madison*. https://ccbc.education.wisc.edu/literature-resources/ccbc-diversity-statistics/books-by-and-or-about-poc-2018/.

Corbett, C. (2012, May 31). Exclusive: Solange Knowles shares her natural hair secrets. *Essence*. https://www.essence.com/2012/05/31/exclusive-solange-knowles-shares-her-natural-hair-secrets.

Costello, A. M., & Reigstad, T. J. (2014). Approaching young adult literature through multiple literacies. *English Journal*, 83–89.

Davis, J. M., Pearce, N., & Mullins, M. (2021). Missing boys: The limited representation of black males in Caldecott books. *Journal of Children's Literature, 47*(1), 10–20.

Dunbar Nelson, A. (1922). Negro literature for negro pupils. *The Southern Workman, 51*, 59–63.

Feelings, T. (1995). Illustration is my form, the black experience, mystery and my content. In Osa Osayimwense (Ed.), *The all-white world of children's books and African American children's literature*. Africa World Press.

Ford, V., & Ford, J. R. (2021) *Calvin*. Penguin.

Gordon-Reed, A. (2021). *On Juneteenth*. Liveright Publishing.

Hall, R. (2022). *Wake: The hidden history of women-led slave revolts*. Simon and Schuster.

Hannah-Jones, N. (2021). *The 1619 project: A new origin story*. One World.

Harris, V. J. (1993). Contemporary Griots: African American writers of children's literature. In. Harris, V. J. (Ed.), *Teaching Multicultural Literature in Grades K-8*. Christopher-Gordon Publishers Inc.

Hefflin, B. R., & Barksdale-Ladd, M. A. (2001). African American children's literature that helps students find themselves: Selection guidelines for grades K-3. *The Reading Teacher, 54*(8), 810–19.

Howard, E. E. (1991). Authentic multicultural literature for children: An author's perspective. In M. V. Lindgren (Ed.), *The multicolored mirror: Cultural substance in literature for children and young adults* (pp. 91–99). Highsmith.

Kendi, I. X. (2019). *How to be an antiracist*. One World.

Love, B. L. (2014). "I see Trayvon Martin": What teachers can learn from the tragic death of a young black male. *The Urban Review, 46*(2), 292–306.

Muhammad, G. (2020). *Cultivating genius: An equity framework for culturally and historically responsive literacy*. Scholastic Incorporated.

Norton, D. (2013). *Multicultural children's literature: Through the eyes of many children* (4th ed.). Pearson.

Sims, R. (1982). *Shadow and substance: Afro-American experience in contemporary children's fiction*. National Council of Teachers of English.

Wilkerson, I. (2020). *Caste: The origins of our discontents*. Random House.

Wolfenbarger, C. D., & Sipe, L. (2007). A unique visual and literary art form: Recent research on picturebooks. *Language Arts, 84*(3), 273–80.

Yosso, T. (2005). Whose culture has capital? A critical race theory discussion of community cultural wealth. *Race Ethnicity and Education, 8*(1), 69–91.

CHILDREN'S LITERATURE

Baptiste, T. (2021). *African icons: Ten people who shaped history*. Algonquin Books.

Barber, B. (1994). *Saturday at the new you*. Lee & Low Books.

Barnes, D., & James, G. C. (2020). *I am every good thing*. Nancy Paulsen Books.

Bradby, M. (2000). *Momma, where are you from?* Orchard Books.

Cabrera, C. (2018). *My hair is a garden*. Albert Whitman & Company.

Cabrera, C. A. (2020). *Me & mama*. Simon and Schuster.

Campbell, B. M. (2003). *Sometimes my mommy gets angry*. GP Putnam's Sons.

Cherry, M. A., & Johnson, S. A. (2019). *Hair love*. Kokila.

Collier, B. (2000). *Uptown*. Henry Holt.

Cooper, F. (2015). *Max and the tag along moon*. Philomel Books.

Hamilton, V. (1967). *Zeely*. Macmillan.

Hannah-Jones, N., & Watson, R. (2021). *The 1619 project: Born on the water*. Penguin.

Henderson, L. (2022). *Daddy speaks love*. Nancy Paulsen Books.

Herron, C. (1997). *Nappy hair*. Alfred A. Knopf.

hooks, b. (1999). *Happy to be nappy.* Jump At The Sun.
hooks, b. (2002). *Be boy buzz.* Jump at the Sun.
Jenkins, E. (2015). *A fine dessert: Four centuries, four families, one delicious treat.* Schwartz & Wade.
Keats, E. (1962). *The snowy day.* Penguin.
Miller, S. (2018). *Don't touch my hair!* Little, Brown Books for Young Readers.
Redd, N. (2020). *Bedtime bonnet.* Penguin.
Tarpley, N. (1998). *I Love My Hair!* Little, Brown.
Thomas, J. (2002). *Crowning glory.* Joanna Cotler Books.
Walker, E. (2021). *Dream street.* Penguin.
Williams, S. (2021). *Your legacy: A bold reclaiming of our enslaved history.* Abrams Books for Young Readers.
Woodson, J. (2002). *Visiting day.* Puffin Books.
Wyeth, S. D. (1998). *Something beautiful.* Doubleday.
Yarbrough, C. (1979). *Cornrows.* Coward, Mccann & Geoghegan.

Chapter 4

Asian American Children's Literature

Xiufang Chen

UNDERSTANDING ASIAN AMERICAN HISTORY AND CULTURE

Asian American history dates back to 1587 when pioneering immigrants from Asia came to the United States to provide labor for plantation economy, transcontinental railroad and regional railway building, and various aspects of industrial development (Borah, 1995; Zhao, 2009). Since then, Asian Americans have played a significant role in American history (Kwoh, 2021). For example, the internment of 120,000 Japanese Americans during World War II remains a scourge of our national conscience. The ban on Asian Americans immigrating to the United States for sixty years was cited in the early twentieth century to justify denying citizenship to minorities of other races. It is because of Asian Americans that English as a Second Language education was legalized in the United States, and immigrant children can receive bilingual instruction. Asian Americans have also united with other minority groups to force lasting change and have been instrumental in advancing immigration law revisions and defending labor rights. Today, Asian Americans are often seen in solidarity with Black Americans protesting against racism and violence. In recent years, Asian Americans and Pacific Islanders have been attached in part by xenophobic anger over COVID-19. More and more Asian Americans have come together to educate Americans about Asian Americans' contributions and to launch immediate measures to reduce and eliminate hate crimes and incidents.

Asian or Asian Americans as a group have grown fast in recent years, reaching about 23 million in 2019 which makes 7 percent of the total American population (Budiman & Ruiz, 2021). This number includes not only those who identify their race as Asian alone, but also Asian in combination with other races, regardless of Hispanic origin. Among them, the three largest groups were Chinese Americans, Indian Americans, and Filipinos. According to the Pew Research Center analysis of 2019 American Community Survey (Budiman & Ruiz, 2021), 83 percent of all Asians in the United States were single-race, non-Hispanic. Aside from Hawaii, where US Asians made up 57 percent of the population in 2019, nearly half of US Asians (45 percent) lived in the West, with 30 percent in California alone. A majority of US Asians (55 percent) lived in these five states: California, New York, Texas, New Jersey, and Washington.

Asian Americans are tremendously diverse. According to the Pew Research Center report, Asian Americans "trace their roots to more than 20 countries in East and Southeast Asia and the Indian subcontinent, each with unique histories, cultures, languages, and other characteristics" (Budiman & Ruiz, 2021, para. 1). The US Census Bureau defines "Asian" as "(a) person having origins in any of the original peoples of the Far East, Southeast Asia, or the Indian subcontinent including, for example, Cambodia, China, India, Japan, Korea, Malaysia, Pakistan, the Philippine Islands, Thailand, and Vietnam" (n.d.). Their data "includes people who reported detailed Asian responses such as: 'Asian Indian,' 'Chinese,' 'Filipino,' 'Korean,' 'Japanese,' 'Vietnamese,' and 'Other Asian' or provide other detailed Asian responses" (U.S. Census Bureau, n.d.). Kiang (n.d.) however expanded this definition to represent more than thirty different nationalities and ethnic groups from the Pacific Islands, Southeast Asia, South Asia, Central Asia, and East Asia. In this chapter, I follow the definition provided by the US Census Bureau.

The diversity and complexity of Asian American populations bring various languages, cultures, and histories. According to Kiang (n.d.), even within a single nationality, significant differences exist in regional dialect, religion, class background, educational level, and political perspective, not to mention distinctions based on generation, gender, and lifestyle orientation. Other factors contributing to the diversity and complexity include biracial and/or multiracial Asian American and Amerasian children due to interracial marriage and adopted children from Asia by families in the United States who may not be Asian American themselves. Critical distinctions also exist between refugees and immigrants. Refugees who have been forced to leave their homelands because of well-founded fears or threats of persecution have typically suffered severe trauma, lost family members, and languished in refugee camps before coming to the United States. Nevertheless, once here, refugees and immigrants share many experiences, such as the language barrier, culture shock, racial discrimination, and the challenge of starting new lives.

In spite of significant socio-economic, cultural, linguistic, geographic, religious, and historical differences, Asian Americans are distinctive as a whole. They value hard work, education, family responsibility, integrity of family, interpersonal harmony, and harmony with nature (Casas & Mann, 1996; Kiang, n.d.; Kim et al., 1999; Sue & Sue, 2003). Asian culture is mostly impacted by three main Eastern philosophies: Buddhism, Confucianism, and Taoism. These philosophies view that families are hierarchically structured and paternal and that children should avoid bringing shame to their family. Traditionally, Asian culture emphasizes collectivism, conformity to norms, deference to authority figures, filial piety, hierarchical family structure, humility, emotional restraint, and maintenance of interpersonal harmony (Kim et al., 1999; Sue & Sue, 2003). The Asian philosophies also teach principles of peace, balance, and harmony, which impact the traditional Asian cultural values of interdependence, role rigidity, formality, indirect expression, and harmony with nature as described by Casas and Mann (1996). However, generational change links Asian American groups. Kim et al. (2001) state that first-generation Asian Americans adhere to Asian cultural values more strongly than Asian Americans who are several generations away from immigration. The current theories of acculturation and enculturation argue that fifth-generation Asian Americans adhere to European American cultural values more strongly than Asian Americans who are recent immigrants (Kim & Omizo, 2005).

As Kiang (n.d.) expressed, defining who are Asian Americans, in itself, is a lesson in diversity and critical thinking with social, historical, and political dimensions. Starting from 1587, long before the arrival of many European groups, pioneering immigrants from Asia settled in the United States to provide indispensable labor for plantation economy, and various aspects of industrial development (Borah, 1995; Zhao, 2009). For several decades, between 1875 and 1965, however, Asian immigrants experienced exclusion by law from the United States and were largely prohibited from naturalization (Abrams, 2005; Keely, 1971; Le, 2021b). They were deprived of their civil rights and suffered from economic hardships and segregation in education, housing, and job markets. To survive, Asian immigrants had to retreat into their own isolated communities, for example, Chinatowns. This also led to the stereotypical image of Chinese restaurants and laundry shops, Japanese gardeners and produce stands, and Korean grocery stores (Le, 2021a). In search of racial equality and social justice, they formed their own organizations and groups to use their collective strength. Even before the 1960s civil rights movement, Asian immigrants had already contributed to the development of US laws and policies, especially in areas of immigration (Zhao, 2009). After the 1965 Immigration Act (Keely, 1971), Asian American demographics changed dramatically. Unlike early Asian immigrants, they have come from all walks of life and from far more diverse regions (Zhao, 2009). Until the late 1960s, Asian Americans were generally called "Oriental" or "Asiatic" (Kang, 2002). "Orient" is basically a concept generated by the colonial experience and "Oriental" connotes rugs, spices, and other objects rather than people. Therefore, the term "Asian American" is preferable as Asia states the actual geographic location from which Asian Americans in the United States trace their origins, just like other ethnic groups (Kiang, n.d.).

Due to the historical, social, and political factors, Asian Americans have been stereotypically and distortedly depicted in movies, television, advertising, cartoons, and other media, as well as school textbooks and children's literature (Kiang, n.d.). The Asian American Journalists Association (1991) documented a wide range of stereotypic depictions of Asian Americans in print media from around the country in their study *Project Zinger: The Good, the Bad, and the Ugly*. Kiang (n.d.) argued that historic images of the treacherous Fu Manchu, the exotic/erotic Suzy Wong, and the inscrutable Charlie Chan, coupled with contemporary depictions of the dog-eating refugee on welfare, the gang member, and the violin-playing/whiz-kid/spelling bee champion, offer little of value in understanding the diverse identities and realities of Asian Americans. Similarly, Le (2021c) listed two primary stereotypes that continue to affect Asian Americans: All Asian Americans are the same and all Asian Americans are foreigners. It is problematic and sometimes disastrous to generalize certain beliefs or stereotypes about one or a few

Asian Americans to the entire Asian American population. It means prejudice and discrimination in its many forms when Asian Americans are considered as foreigners. Many Asian American families have been US citizens for several generations, and they deserve the same rights that other Americans possess but sometimes take for granted. These pervasive stereotypes should be examined as they continue to shape how many parents, teachers, administrators, and students perceive Asian Americans, and how Asian Americans often view themselves.

EVALUATING AND SELECTING ASIAN AMERICAN CHILDREN'S BOOKS

To help young students understand different cultures, it is critical to make sure the literature selected for classroom use is authentic, depicting the values, beliefs, and cultural backgrounds of various groups. Yoo-Lee et al. (2014) defined cultural authenticity as "the absence of stereotypes but also the presence of values consistent with a particular culture and the accuracy of cultural details in text and illustrations" (p. 326). Norton (2013) developed an approach that puts categories for evaluating literature (geographical and social settings, values and beliefs, major events, major conflicts, and major themes) in question format to help practitioners conduct authentication:

1. What are the geographical and social settings for the book, and are they authentic? Students should use nonfictional sources to evaluate this area. Pictures found in sources such as *National Geographic* are especially good for authenticating geographical settings.
2. What are the values and beliefs of the people in the book, and are they authentic?
3. What are the major events that make up the plot of the story? Are they possible for the time period and the culture?
4. What are the major conflicts in the book, and are they authentic for the time period?
5. What are the major themes, and are they found in other literature written about the time period or the people? (p. 8)

Besides evaluating literature for the authenticity of text and illustrations, Norton (2013) stated that it is important to evaluate books for stereotypes when selecting Asian American literature for classroom use. The Council on Interracial Books for Children (1976) provided the following criteria for analyzing Asian American books (see figure 4.1): (1) A children's book "should reflect the realities and way-of-life of an Asian American people"; (2) the

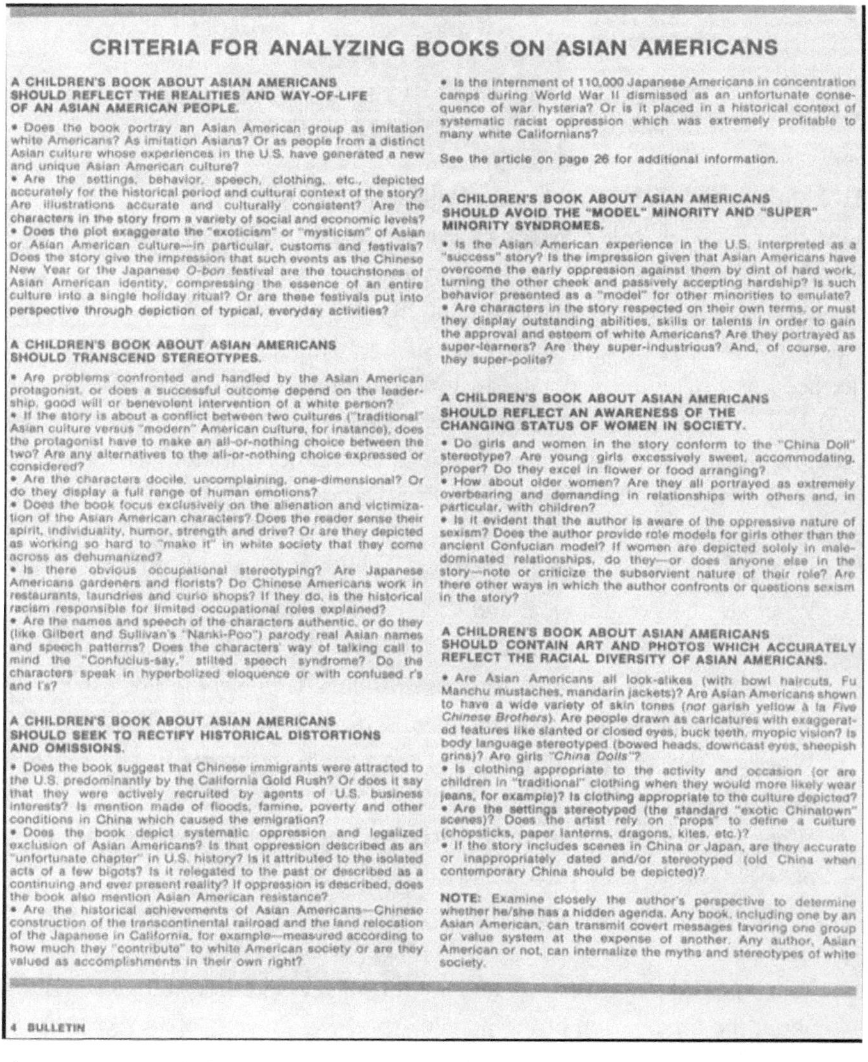

CRITERIA FOR ANALYZING BOOKS ON ASIAN AMERICANS

A CHILDREN'S BOOK ABOUT ASIAN AMERICANS SHOULD REFLECT THE REALITIES AND WAY-OF-LIFE OF AN ASIAN AMERICAN PEOPLE.

• Does the book portray an Asian American group as imitation white Americans? As imitation Asians? Or as people from a distinct Asian culture whose experiences in the U.S. have generated a new and unique Asian American culture?
• Are the settings, behavior, speech, clothing, etc., depicted accurately for the historical period and cultural context of the story? Are illustrations accurate and culturally consistent? Are the characters in the story from a variety of social and economic levels?
• Does the plot exaggerate the "exoticism" or "mysticism" of Asian or Asian American culture—in particular, customs and festivals? Does the story give the impression that such events as the Chinese New Year or the Japanese *O-bon* festival are the touchstones of Asian American identity, compressing the essence of an entire culture into a single holiday ritual? Or are these festivals put into perspective through depiction of typical, everyday activities?

A CHILDREN'S BOOK ABOUT ASIAN AMERICANS SHOULD TRANSCEND STEREOTYPES.

• Are problems confronted and handled by the Asian American protagonist, or does a successful outcome depend on the leadership, good will or benevolent intervention of a white person?
• If the story is about a conflict between two cultures ("traditional" Asian culture versus "modern" American culture, for instance), does the protagonist have to make an all-or-nothing choice between the two? Are any alternatives to the all-or-nothing choice expressed or considered?
• Are the characters docile, uncomplaining, one-dimensional? Or do they display a full range of human emotions?
• Does the book focus exclusively on the alienation and victimization of the Asian American characters? Does the reader sense their spirit, individuality, humor, strength and drive? Or are they depicted as working so hard to "make it" in white society that they come across as dehumanized?
• Is there obvious occupational stereotyping? Are Japanese Americans gardeners and florists? Do Chinese Americans work in restaurants, laundries and curio shops? If they do, is the historical racism responsible for limited occupational roles explained?
• Are the names and speech of the characters authentic, or do they (like Gilbert and Sullivan's "Nanki-Poo") parody real Asian names and speech patterns? Does the characters' way of talking call to mind the "Confucius-say," stilted speech syndrome? Do the characters speak in hyperbolized eloquence or with confused r's and l's?

A CHILDREN'S BOOK ABOUT ASIAN AMERICANS SHOULD SEEK TO RECTIFY HISTORICAL DISTORTIONS AND OMISSIONS.

• Does the book suggest that Chinese immigrants were attracted to the U.S. predominantly by the California Gold Rush? Or does it say that they were actively recruited by agents of U.S. business interests? Is mention made of floods, famine, poverty and other conditions in China which caused the emigration?
• Does the book depict systematic oppression and legalized exclusion of Asian Americans? Is that oppression described as an "unfortunate chapter" in U.S. history? Is it attributed to the isolated acts of a few bigots? Is it relegated to the past or described as a continuing and ever present reality? If oppression is described, does the book also mention Asian American resistance?
• Are the historical achievements of Asian Americans—Chinese construction of the transcontinental railroad and the land relocation of the Japanese in California, for example—measured according to how much they "contribute" to white American society or are they valued as accomplishments in their own right?
• Is the internment of 110,000 Japanese Americans in concentration camps during World War II dismissed as an unfortunate consequence of war hysteria? Or is it placed in a historical context of systematic racist oppression which was extremely profitable to many white Californians?

See the article on page 26 for additional information.

A CHILDREN'S BOOK ABOUT ASIAN AMERICANS SHOULD AVOID THE "MODEL" MINORITY AND "SUPER" MINORITY SYNDROMES.

• Is the Asian American experience in the U.S. interpreted as a "success" story? Is the impression given that Asian Americans have overcome the early oppression against them by dint of hard work, turning the other cheek and passively accepting hardship? Is such behavior presented as a "model" for other minorities to emulate?
• Are characters in the story respected on their own terms, or must they display outstanding abilities, skills or talents in order to gain the approval and esteem of white Americans? Are they portrayed as super-learners? Are they super-industrious? And, of course, are they super-polite?

A CHILDREN'S BOOK ABOUT ASIAN AMERICANS SHOULD REFLECT AN AWARENESS OF THE CHANGING STATUS OF WOMEN IN SOCIETY.

• Do girls and women in the story conform to the "China Doll" stereotype? Are young girls excessively sweet, accommodating, proper? Do they excel in flower or food arranging?
• How about older women? Are they all portrayed as extremely overbearing and demanding in relationships with others and, in particular, with children?
• Is it evident that the author is aware of the oppressive nature of sexism? Does the author provide role models for girls other than the ancient Confucian model? If women are depicted solely in male-dominated relationships, do they—or does anyone else in the story—note or criticize the subservient nature of their role? Are there other ways in which the author confronts or questions sexism in the story?

A CHILDREN'S BOOK ABOUT ASIAN AMERICANS SHOULD CONTAIN ART AND PHOTOS WHICH ACCURATELY REFLECT THE RACIAL DIVERSITY OF ASIAN AMERICANS.

• Are Asian Americans all look-alikes (with bowl haircuts, Fu Manchu mustaches, mandarin jackets)? Are Asian Americans shown to have a wide variety of skin tones (*not* garish yellow à la *Five Chinese Brothers*). Are people drawn as caricatures with exaggerated features like slanted or closed eyes, buck teeth, myopic vision? Is body language stereotyped (bowed heads, downcast eyes, sheepish grins)? Are girls "*China Dolls*"?
• Is clothing appropriate to the activity and occasion (or are children in "traditional" clothing when they would more likely wear jeans, for example)? Is clothing appropriate to the culture depicted?
• Are the settings stereotyped (the standard "exotic Chinatown" scenes)? Does the artist rely on "props" to define a culture (chopsticks, paper lanterns, dragons, kites, etc.)?
• If the story includes scenes in China or Japan, are they accurate or inappropriately dated and/or stereotyped (old China when contemporary China should be depicted)?

NOTE: Examine closely the author's perspective to determine whether he/she has a hidden agenda. Any book, including one by an Asian American, can transmit covert messages favoring one group or value system at the expense of another. Any author, Asian American or not, can internalize the myths and stereotypes of white society.

4 BULLETIN

Figure 4.1 Criteria for Analyzing Asian American Literature.

book should "transcend stereotypes"; (3) the book "should seek to rectify historical distortions and omissions"; (4) the book "should avoid the 'model' minority and 'super' minority syndromes"; (5) the book "should reflect an awareness of the changing status of women in society"; and (6) the book "should contain art and photos which accurately reflect the racial diversity of Asian Americans" (p. 4).

In a study of the images of Chinese and Chinese Americans in seventy-three picture story books, Cai (1994) found that most of the books "present quite positive images of Chinese and Chinese Americans and give the reader a sense of the Chinese culture"; many are "culturally authentic works" (p. 188). However, biased stereotypical portraits still existed, and "cultural inauthenticity is the main flaw of many books exhibited in both the content of the texts and the details of the illustrations" (p. 188).

Examining the cultural values in the authenticity of picture books, Mo and Shen (2003) echoed Cai's findings (1994) and found that some books have serious problems with cultural authenticity, while some books may portray cultural details accurately but not authentically. For example, they explained the problems of cultural authenticity in both the literary and artistic work of *Tikki Tikki Tembo* (Mosel, 1968). First of all, the book does not show the source of the folktale though the story is set in old China. In Chinese culture, full names often do not go beyond four syllables, thus the name Tikki Tikki Tembo-No Sa Rembo-Chari Bari Ruchi-PipPeri Pembo sounds quite foreign to Chinese. Meanwhile, the illustrations depict more Japanese than Chinese culture. Some books may have accurately portrayed cultural details but not authentically. For instance, Mo and Shen (2003) discussed the depiction of bound feet in the 1939 Caldecott winner book *Mei Li*. It is true that some Chinese women still had bound feet in 1939; however, after the 1911 revolution "people in China have viewed bound feet as a symbol of women's humiliated past and an emotional scar . . . people held a cultural attitude of either paying no attention or avoiding mention of them" (p. 202). This book therefore failed to meet Mo and Shen's value-based criteria for authenticity: Its artwork was "non-stereotyped" as "the scenes were depicted realistically, but . . . the book is not authentic because it does not reflect the cultural values of that time period" (p. 203). Mo and Shen (2003) found that a number of other Asian American books failed to distinguish between cultural and historical facts. Researchers have suggested that those older stereotypical books should not be used with children; rather, they should be placed in a historical section (Norton, 2013).

Yokota (2009) reported that children's books show a significant increase in the representation of Asian Americans during the past two decades and a transition away from "long ago and far away" tales to contemporary stories (p. 15). Meanwhile, the author also noted that many newly published books still perpetuate stereotypes and an assimilation ideology, and picturebooks reviewed did not represent the full range of cultural experiences, histories, themes, and descents.

Authenticating a multicultural book is a complex process. Bishop (2003) stated that it is hard to adequately and universally define cultural authenticity because variance always exists within a specific culture, but "you know it when you see it" as a cultural insider (p. 15). Authors and illustrators "who successfully write outside their own culture have had significant in-depth experiences within that culture over many years and have engaged in careful and thorough research (Cai, 1995)" (Short & Fox, 2004, pp. 237–38). Some specific strategies include checking multiple information sources, consulting an insider with expertise in the topic, hiring an insider to work with, and having readers from a range of cultural backgrounds read the book and share their responses and reflections (Moreillon, 1999). Cai (1994) pointed out that "(i)magination alone cannot help . . . to cross cultural gaps. Inexact scholarship will inevitably lead to ridiculous misrepresentation" (p. 188).

USING AUTHENTIC ASIAN AMERICAN LITERATURE IN THE CLASSROOM WITH YOUNG CHILDREN

Teachers can use authentic Asian American literature with young children in the classroom through a variety of strategies and activities. Norton (2013) illustrated several examples such as using the web to develop a unit around folklore, discussing the information from a book and investigating the influence, comparing students' retelling of a tale with the author's, and searching for evidence of the culture, researching the religions and searching for evidence of the associated cultural beliefs in folklore, interviewing someone living in the United States who originally came from an Asian country, integrating literature and geography, conducting analytical reading to critically analyze a book, identifying the symbols and the associated values in the culture, writing an author's note, comparing and contrasting tales in different cultures, and writing a survival story using the cultural beliefs in the book, and contemporary issues learned from current news. With technology, we also propose virtual field trips besides physical field trips, parallel reading using internet articles, class guests for interviews, videos, audit trail, music, food, clothing, read aloud, text set, performances, and YouTube movie-making, among many other ideas. Below is an example of how the book *Eyes that Kiss in the Corners* is selected and used in the classroom.

Eyes that Kiss in the Corners, recommended for students from preschool to grade 3, is a culturally authentic book written by Joanna Ho and illustrated by Dung Ho, published and released by HarperCollins Children's Books in January 2021. It is about a young girl of Asian heritage noticing that her eyes "kiss at the corners and glow like warm tea" and are different from those of her friends at school. At home, she shares the same eye shape and color as her Mama (mother), her Amah (grandmother), and her Mei-Mei (little sister). In those eyes, she sees love, strength, and playfulness. Through her family and their visual connection, the young girl gets a strong sense of who she is and that she is loved. It is a beautiful and lyrical picturebook that celebrates both diversity and inclusivity, with powerful, poetic language, and breathtaking landscapes from Chinese culture.

Details of Chinese cultural elements are authentically present throughout the book such as the tea set, Amah's bracelet, the flowers in Chinese folklore, the Chinese dresses, the Goddess Guanyin as a symbol of compassion or kindness, the Monkey King in Chinese folklore, the dragon and Chinese phoenix along with other characters in Chinese mythology, and clothes of the women in her stories. Too many Asian American kids have been made fun of at school because of their eye shape, food, clothes, ways they speak, and so on. *Eyes that Kiss in the Corners* expands children's ideas of what is beautiful and affirms Asian American children's identities. The author Joanna Ho stated in an interview that she wanted to help Asian American kids to "create their own counter-narrative in which they are powerful, beautiful, worthy and valuable" (Bernard-Jacobs, 2021, March 18). She continues:

> I hope when Asian kids read *Eyes that Kiss in the Corners*, they grow up knowing they are beautiful because of the special characteristics they have. I hope they see their eyes not only for their physical beauty, but also because they are

a representation of all that has been passed down to us and all that we will pass on to future generations. They are love and family and history and culture and power. I think it's important for Asian kids to see that their stories matter; this allows them to embrace their own power in the world. It's important for non-Asian kids to see these stories for the same reasons: to see that Asian stories matter, to challenge the dominant narratives about Asians, to dismantle racist beliefs and practices and systems that have existed for too long. (Bernard-Jacobs, 2021, March 18)

The following lesson guide provides an example to use *Eyes that Kiss in the Corners* in the classroom.

Before Reading

The teacher can have students in triads observe the other two students' eyes and describe the similarities and differences. Then, they will discuss what their eyes tell. To start with this activity, the teacher will explain the steps and then work with two students to model how to use descriptive words to describe and discuss.

During Reading

Using a concept map (see figure 4.2 A Blank Copy of Concept Map), students will read or listen to the book and look for the words in the text that describe the girl's eyes. The teacher will first read aloud the first couple of pages and model how to locate the descriptive words in the text. Then students will be guided to find the descriptive words or phrases on their own.

With the class, the teacher will reread the book and look for details of Chinese culture such as the tea set, Amah's bracelet, the Chinese dresses, and other elements that might require the teacher's guidance.

Finally, the teacher will guide students to discuss the ways the girl's family show love.

After Reading

The teacher can revisit the theme of loving oneself. In the book, the girl looks at herself in a mirror before leaving for school. The teacher can have students use a mirror to observe themselves and create a self-portrait. They will then

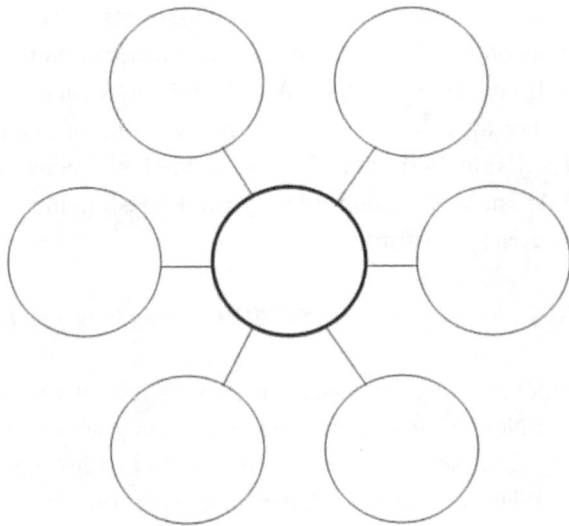

Figure 4.2 A Blank Copy of Concept Map.

describe their own eyes with descriptive words and phrases such as creative color names and comparisons to beautiful things like the author does.

The teacher will then extend to discuss who in their life makes them feel special, what they do to make them feel that way, and how they can pass that on to others. The teacher can facilitate a class discussion on Chinese culture they have learned from the book and bring more books on the culture for students to read.

It will be helpful to have a unit on Asian American culture to reinforce or further students' understanding of Asian American culture and its related issues. Teachers can introduce a set of books, movies, websites, and so on. Below are some books to start with.

Some Asian American Children's Books to Start With

Choi, Y. (2001). *The Name Jar*. Dragonfly Books.

This book explores the experience of a child immigrant, learning to accept and value her cultural identity in a new land. This book provides a window into Korean culture as well as a mirror to children who feel different because they carry a culture that differs from that of their peers. Unhei is a Korean immigrant who struggles with her identity because she doesn't feel she fits in, as she doesn't have an American name. Her classmates leave a jar filled with name suggestions on her desk but none of the American names feel right to Unhei. When a friend from her class takes the time to learn about her Korean name, he helps her to realize that she should be proud of her Korean name and she decides it's the best name for her. Grade level recommended: K–2. Awards: 2003 Arkansas Diamond Primary Book Master, and 2005 Nominee Arizona Young Readers Award.

Compestine, Y. C., & Nascimbene, Y. (2019). *Crouching Tiger*. Candlewick Press.

This contemporary story introduces readers to several Chinese traditions such as Chinese New Year and the parade and the practice of martial arts. Vinson, a young Chinese American boy, is excited that his grandfather from China is visiting. He sees his grandfather practicing Tai Chi in the yard and wants to learn it too. Tai Chi is too slow for Vinson; he wants Kung Fu, and he does not understand why he has to participate in some of the Chinese traditions. This book is about a growing friendship and respect between grandson and grandfather. Grade level recommended: Grades 1–4.

Jorisch, S., & Uegaki, C. (2003). *Suki's Kimono*. Kids Can Press.

The character in this story models cultural pride in the face of ridicule. It also shows that when we take the time to learn about another culture we can develop an appreciation and acceptance of others and show respect for diversity. On the first day of school, Suki wants to wear the beloved Kimono her grandmother had given her. Although warned by her sisters that it wasn't a good choice, she proudly walks to school with the breeze blowing her Kimono sleeves like butterflies. Upon arriving, she quickly notices the other children laughing at her. The teasing continues in the classroom until the teacher arrives and asks Suki what she did this summer. She tells the class about the Japanese festival that her grandmother took her to and shows them how they danced in their Kimonos. When finished, the class is silent until the teacher compliments her and begins to clap. The class joins in and Suki heads home happy that she wore her Kimono. Grade level recommended: K–2. Awards: 2005—Chocolate Lily Award, Short-listed; 2004—Mr. Christie Book Award, Runner-up; 2004—Amelia Frances Howard-Gibbon Illustrator's Award, Runner-up; 2004—Christie Harris Illustrated Children's Literature Prize, Short-listed; 2004—Ruth Schwartz Children's Book Award,

Short-listed; 2004—Children's Book Award Notable Book, International Reading Association, Winner; and 2004—Book of the Year—Bronze Medal, ForeWord Magazine

Lazo Gilmore, D. K. (2014). *Cora Cooks Pancit.* Shen's Books.

This text goes into detail about the ingredients and steps needed to cook an authentic Filipino dish. It shows young readers there is so much to learn about self and family right inside their own home. The text also captures the warmth between mother and daughter as they share a special moment in the kitchen. Cora loves helping in the kitchen, but she is tired of getting the "kid jobs" like licking the spoon. One day, while her older siblings are out of the house, Cora gets to be her mother's assistant chef. Mama and Cora decide to make Cora's favorite Filipino dish, Pancit. Cora gets to do all of the grownup jobs that go into preparing the dish. Grade level recommended: K–5; Awards: 2010 Asian/Pacific American Award for Literature.

Lê, M. (2018). *Drawn Together.* Little, Brown Books for Young Readers.

The author, Minh Le, based this book off of his own relationship with his grandfather and the many "awkward silences" that the two experienced. The major theme that this text hits is the notion of acceptance and tolerance. It provides readers with the ability to find connections and learn to communicate with those who are different from them without always having to use words. A young boy and his Thai grandfather struggle to find similarities between the two of them. From television shows to foods and most importantly their language, the two cannot find a way to communicate and fall into silence. When the grandfather notices that his grandson loves to draw, he grabs his own sketchbook and the two begin to draw and create an adventure together. It is then that they discover how their love for art connects them where their language barrier separated them. Grade level recommended: Preschool–Kindergarten. Awards: Asian/Pacific American Award for Literature Picturebook Winner (2019), Charlotte Huck Award (2019), and CHHIBBER Medal for Best Picturebook (2019).

Lee, M., & Choi, Y. (2006). *Landed.* Farrar Straus Giroux.

The book provides an authentic portrayal of Chinese immigrants and shows readers the difficulties and injustices they faced during the 1800s. Students gain insight into the challenges immigrants face and how harmful discrimination can be. Sun Chor is finally allowed to join his brothers and immigrate to the United States. However, he must first stay at Angel Island in San Francisco due to the Chinese Exclusion Act. Sun must pass his interrogation and is challenged with learning the culture of a new land, while still maintaining his own. Grade level recommended: Grades 3–5.

Lin, G. (2007). *The Red Thread: An Adoption Fairy Tale.* Albert Whitman.

This book introduces readers to another diverse way that families can be formed, and Chinese values and beliefs. A young adopted Chinese girl listens to the story of a King and Queen who begin a family through adoption. The story is a modern-day fairytale that weaves in the Chinese belief that all people who belong together are connected by a red thread. Grade level recommended: K–grade 3.

Lin, G. (2014). *Dim Sum for Everyone!: Board Book.* Alfred A. Knopf.

Students will be introduced to a special Chinese food tradition and the customs that surround it. In this brightly colored picturebook, a young Asian American family enjoys dim sum together. Many foods are highlighted in this story. The author also includes background information about dim sum. Grade level recommended: Kindergarten–grade 2.

Lord, M. (2008). *A Song for Cambodia.* Lee & Low.

This book is the inspirational true story of Arn Chorn-Pond. His heartfelt music created beauty in a time of darkness and turned tragedy into healing. Arn was a boy who was separated from his family and sent to a work camp because of the Pol Pot regime. When Vietnam invaded Cambodia, the Khmer Rouge forced children in the camp to fight against Vietnam. Then, Arn ran away to the jungle but saved himself. After that, he was adopted by Reverend Peter Pond, a volunteer worker from the United States, and he brought Arn to the United States. However, Arn still could not forget about his lost family and his country. So, he decided to return to Cambodia in order to restore and rebuild the devastated culture and tradition. Grade level recommended: grades 1–2.

Park, L. S., & Downing, J. (2004). *The Firekeeper's Son.* HMH Books for Young Readers.

The book provides a historical and accurate look into Korean culture and heritage. Readers are encouraged to embrace their heritage and to work hard to overcome challenges. In Korea in the early 1800s, news from the countryside reached the king by means of signal fires. When the village firekeeper is unable to light the fire one night, his son, young Sang-hee, must help take his place. Sang-hee knows how important it is for the fire to be lit, but he wishes that he could see soldiers. Through the struggle, Sang-hee learns about his Korean heritage and overcomes challenges with his strong will and determination. Grade level recommended: Preschool–grade 3. Awards: 2004 Parents' Choice Recommended Winner, 2004 AISLE Read-Aloud Books Too Good to Miss, 2004 New York Public Library 100 Titles for Reading and Sharing, 2005 CCBC Choices, 2005 IRA Teachers' Choice Reading List, 2005 Kansas State Reading Circle Recommendation, 2005 Bank Street Best Children's Books of the Year, 2006 Asian/Pacific American Award for Literature, 2006 Young Hoosier Book Award (IN) Nominee, 2006 Kentucky Bluegrass Award Nominee, 2004 Bank Street College of Education Irma Simonton and James H. Black Award for Excellence in Children's Literature Honor Book, 2007 Volunteer State (TN) Book Award Master Reading List, 2007 Georgia's Children's Book Award Nominee, and 2008 Monarch Award Nominee (IL).

Phi, B., & Bui, T. (2017). *A Different Pond*. Capstone Young Readers.

This thoughtful story offers the reader insight into the difficult life of a Vietnamese refugee family living in poverty in America. The characters are represented as kind and hard working. It presents opportunities to discuss equality, issues of immigration, and the value of diversity in America. A young boy is woken up early to go fishing with his father, not for pleasure, but for food. As they make their way to the pond, he questions his dad why they still need to fish for food when dad now has a second job. His dad tells him that everything in America costs a lot of money. As they fish, the father shares stories about fishing in another pond in Vietnam and the Vietnam war. After catching two fish they head home to find mom getting ready to go to work as well. The boy is left in the care of his older siblings and when mom and dad return from work the family has a joyful meal of fish for dinner. Grade level recommended: K–4. Awards: Caldecott Honor Book 2018, Charlotte Zolotow Award Winner 2018, Asian/Pacific American Award for Literature Winner 2018, Ezra Jack Keats New Writer Honor 2018, Ezra Jack Keats New Illustrator Honor 2018, *Boston Globe*-Horn Book Honor Book 2018, Notable Social Studies Trade Books for Young People 2018, The

Cooperative Children's Book Center (CCBC) Choices 2018, Bank Street Best Children's Books of the Year 2018, Minnesota Book Award 2018, Huffington Post Best Picture Books of the Year 2017, *Washington Post* Best Children's Books of the Year 2017, *The Boston Globe* Best Children's and YA Books of the Year 2017, *Publishers Weekly* Best Books of the Year 2017, *Kirkus Reviews* Best Picture Books of the Year 2017, *School Library Journal* Best Books of the Year 2017, *Booklist* Editor's Choice 2017, Horn Book Fanfare 2017, and New York Public Library Best Books for Kids 2017.

Reibstein, M., & Young, E. (2008). *Wabi Sabi* (Library Binding ed.). Little, Brown Books for Young Readers.

This book contains strong cultural relevance to the Japanese tradition of Wabi Sabi. Children will learn about Japanese poetry, Haiku, and the meanings of names. Symbolism can be taught through a critical examination of text and interpretations of metaphorical meanings. Wabi Sabi is a poetic story translated from Japanese Haiku into English. When a beautiful cat hears his owner discussing with guests that his name has a significant meaning, he journeys out on a quest to discover what it is. After speaking to another cat, a dog, a bird, and eventually a monkey, he learns the exact message that his name holds. Wabi Sabi is a book of beautiful simplicity. Grade level recommended: Preschool–Grade 3. Awards: 2009 Asian/Pacific American Award for Literature, 2009 Notable Books for a Global Society, 2009 NCTE/CLA Notable Children's Book in the English Language Arts, and 2008 New York Times Best Illustrated Children's Book.

Saeed, A., & Syed, A. (2019). *Bilal Cooks Daal*. Salaam Reads/Simon & Schuster Books for Young Readers.

This book focuses on Pakistani Americans and traditional Pakistani foods. Readers get to learn about the importance of food and how it can help connect people from different backgrounds. Readers also learn to be patient and to be open-minded and accepting when it comes to learning about different cultures. Bilal is having friends come over for dinner. She and her father decide to cook Daal for them. Her friends are very unfamiliar with Daal and begin to learn about the ingredients and help gather them. While the Daal cooks, the children learn about patience more about Daal food. They play games and eventually taste and enjoy the Daal meal. Grade level recommended:

Preschool–Grade 3. Awards: A *Kirkus Reviews* Best Picture Book of 2019, and an Asian/Pacific American Award for Literature Honor Book 2019.

Surat, M. M. (1989). *Angel Child, Dragon Child*. Scholastic Paperbacks.

This story unveils the difficulties associated with adjusting to a new environment and culture. A girl named Ut moved to the United States from Vietnam with her father and siblings, and misses her mother, who had to stay behind. At school, Ut is laughed at because of the clothes she wears and the way she speaks and has trouble adjusting to her new life. One day, she and a classmate enter into a physical altercation and must spend time getting to know one another as a consequence. This new and unexpected friendship enables others to learn about Ut's life and leads to her feeling accepted. This story promotes acceptance and encourages readers to embrace the things that make us different from one another. Grade level recommended: Preschool–Grade 3. Awards: Shalom Readers Club Book List (Preschool–Grade 2).

Tran, T. (2012). *Going Home, Coming Home/Ve Nha, Tham Que Huong*. Lee & Low Books Inc.

This picturebook serves to educate children on Vietnamese culture, as well as exposes them to themes of cultural identity and "home" being in two countries for families who have migrated to the United States from their native land. Ami Chi visits her grandmother in Vietnam where her parents were born. While there, she goes through different experiences and learns that she can call both Vietnam and the United States home. Grade level recommended: Grades 1–3.

Uegaki, C. (2005). *Suki's Kimono*. Kids Can Press.

This book will give students authentic information and background on Japanese American culture, traditions, values, and customs, while teaching them the importance of cultural identity and being true to yourself no matter what. Suki's kimono is her favorite gift from her grandmother, her obachan. She gave it to Suki when she visited her last summer, and Suki wore it on the first day of school, regardless of what anyone thought or had to say. Suki delighted her classmates though, who thought it odd to wear a Kimono to school at first, with a dance and story of how she and her obachan attended and danced in a street festival over the summer. Grade level recommended:

Preschool–Grade 3. Awards: 2005 Chocolate Lily Award Short-listed, 2004 Mr. Christie Book Award Runner-up, 2004 Amelia Frances Howard-Gibbon Illustrator's Award Runner-up, 2004 Christie Harris Illustrated Children's Literature Prize Short-listed, 2004 Ruth Schwartz Children's Book Award Short-listed, 2004 Winner of International Reading Association Children's Book Award Notable Book, and 2004 ForeWord Magazine Book of the Year Bronze Medal.

Wong, J. S., & Chodos-Irvine, M. (2006). *Apple Pie 4th of July.* Harcourt.

Readers will be given a glimpse into the contemporary Asian American experience and the conflict that can occur when living between two cultures. A young Chinese American girl wrestles with celebrating American culture and Chinese culture. Her family cooks chow mein on the Fourth of July, while her American neighbor bakes an apple pie. As she tries to explain American life to her parents, she learns a surprising lesson about embracing her culture. Grade level recommended: Kindergarten–grade 3.

Yamasaki, K. (2019). *Fish for Jimmy: Inspired by One Family's Experience in a Japanese American Internment Camp.* Holiday House.

This picturebook gives students detailed insight into internment camps through the eyes of a child and is an adaptation of the author's true family story of being Japanese American. It is a story of love, courage, and strength, and will give students a historical background on the bombing of Pearl Harbor, and the war between Japan and the United States. A Japanese American family is forced to leave their home for an internment camp during the bombing of Pearl Harbor. The family's eldest son, Taro, sneaks out of the camp each night to get fish for his younger brother, Jimmy, so that he will be able to eat and be strong. Grade level recommended: Grades 1–4.

Yin, & Soentpiet, C. K. (2003). *Coolies.* Puffin Books.

This historical fiction story will teach readers about the immigration of Chinese men in the mid-1800s who were fleeing famine and rebellion in their country to come and build the transcontinental railroad. Prejudice against and mistreatment of these immigrants was prevalent. Two brothers from China come to America as part of the railroad labor force in the hopes of making money to send for their parents and siblings, so that they can join them. The boys endure unexpected hardships along the way. Grade level recommended: Grades 2–5.

RESOURCES ON ASIAN AMERICAN CULTURE AND LITERATURE FOR CHILDREN

Asan Society. (n.d.). *Asian Society kids booklists.* https://asiasociety.org/education/asia-society-kids-booklists.
This website provides rich resources to understand Asian American culture and literature for young students.

Colorín Colorado. (n.d.). *Celebrating Asian Pacific American heritage.* https://www.colorincolorado.org/books-authors/literacy-calendar/celebrating-asian-pacific-american-heritage.
This bilingual site for educators and families of English language learners includes a great resource page of family traditions and the rich diversity of Asian and Pacific Americans with books, activities, and a variety of resources and ideas for ELL educators.

Gienapp, R. (2021, April 28). *12 children's books to celebrate Asian American Pacific Islander heritage.* Public Media Group of Southern California. https://www.pbssocal.org/education/families/12-childrens-books-to-celebrate-asian-american-pacific-islaner-heritage.
Twelve books for preschool and elementary-age children that offer positive, diverse representations of Asian American Pacific Islander history and culture that can help deepen knowledge of the AAPI community.

Kiang, P. (n.d.). *Understanding our perceptions of Asian Americans.* Asia Society: Center for Global Education. http://asiasociety.org/education/understanding-our-perceptions-asian-americans.
An overview of Asian American identity, demographics, perceptions and misperceptions, use of terminology, and the extreme diversity contained within the term.

Lim. S. G. (2000). Asian American literature: Leavening the mosaic. *U.S. Society & Values*, February, 18–22. https://usa.usembassy.de/etexts/soc/ijse0200pp18-25.pdf.
This article reviews Asian American literature history and themes present in Asian American narratives.

Penguin Random House. (n.d.). *Books to understand the Asian American experience.* https://www.penguinrandomhouse.com/the-read-down/understand-the-asian-american-experience.

While there is no singular Asian American experience, these books scratch the surface of the varied stories of Americans across the country.

Reading Rockets. (n.d.). *Celebrating Asian Pacific American history and culture.* https://www.readingrockets.org/booklists/celebrating-asian-pacific-american-history-and-culture.

This collection of picturebooks for kids three to twelve years old, from family stories (*Grandfather's Journey*) to folktales (*Yeh-Shen: A Cinderella Story*) to feeling connected to a new culture (*The Name Jar*) discover the rich culture, humor, and traditions of Japan, Korea, China, the Philippines, Vietnam, and Hawaii.

Say, C. (2021, March 25). *13 kids books that celebrate Asian American and Pacific Islander (AAPI) culture and heritage.* Reading Partners. https://readingpartners.org/blog/13-kids-books-aapi-culture/.

A list of thirteen books celebrates diverse AAPI cultures, communities, and people.

Social Justice Books: A Teaching for Change Project. (n.d.). *Asian Americans: Early childhood.* https://socialjusticebooks.org/booklists/asian-americans/#early.

Teaching for Change carefully selects the best multicultural and social justice books for children, young adults, and educators.

Brada-Williams, N. (2014, September 29). *Asian American literature: Resources for research.* http://www.sjsu.edu/faculty/awilliams/AsianAmResources.html.

This is an annotated list of online research resources for students of Asian American Literature conceived and composed by Dr. Noelle Brada-Williams of San José State University.

REFERENCES

Abrams, Kerry (2005, April). Polygamy, prostitution, and the federalization of immigration law. *Columbia Law Review*, 105 (3), 641.

Asian American Journalists Association. (1991). *Project Zinger: The good, the bad and the ugly: A critical look at news media coverage of Asian Pacific Americans.* Asian American Journalists Association.

Bernard-Jacobs. (2021, March 18). *On "Eyes That Kiss in the Corners" & talking to our kids about anti-Asian racism.* Romper: Making Change. https://www

.romper.com/parenting/joanna-ho-eyes-that-kiss-in-the-corner-anti-asian-racism-children.

Bishop, R. S. (2003). Reframing the debate about cultural authenticity. In D. L. Fox & K. G. Short (Eds.), *Stories matter: The complexity of cultural authenticity in children's literature* (pp. 25–37). National Council of Teachers of English.

Borah, E. G. (1995). Filipinos in Unamuno's California Expedition of 1587. *Amerasia Journal*, 21(3), 175–83. http://dx.doi.org/10.17953/amer.21.3.q050756h25525n72.

Budiman, A., & Ruiz, N. (2021, April 29). *Key facts about Asian Americans, a diverse and growing population*. Pew Research Center. https://www.pewresearch.org/fact-tank/2021/04/29/key-facts-about-asian-americans/.

Cai, M. (1995). Can we fly across cultural gaps on the wings of imagination?: Ethnicity, experience, and cultural authenticity. *The New Advocate*, 8, 1–16.

Cai, M. (1994). Images of Chinese and Chinese Americans mirrored in picture books. *Children's Literature in Education*, 25(3), 169–91.

Casas, J. M., & Mann, D. (1996). MCT theory and implications for research. In D. W. Sue, A. E. Ivey, & P. B. Pedersen (Eds.), *A theory of multicultural counseling and therapy* (pp. 139–54). Brooks/Cole.

Council on Interracial Books for Children. (1976). Criteria for analyzing books on Asian Americans. *Interracial Books for Children Bulletin: Asian Americans in Children's Books*, 7(2–3), 4–5.

Kang, K. (2002, September 7). *Yuji Ichioka, 66; Led way in studying lives of Asian Americans*. Los Angeles Times. http://articles.latimes.com/2002/sep/07/local/me-yuji7.

Keely, C. (1971). Effects of the Immigration Act of 1965 on selected population characteristics of immigrants to the United States. *Demography*, 8(2), 157–69. http://www.jstor.org/stable/2060606.

Kiang, P. (n.d.). *Understanding our perceptions of Asian Americans*. Asia Society. http://asiasociety.org/education/understanding-our-perceptions-asian-americans.

Kim, B. S., Atkinson, D. R., & Umemoto, D. (2001). Asian cultural values and the counseling process: Current knowledge and directions for future research. *The Counseling Psychologist*, 29(4), 570–603.

Kim, B. S. K., Atkinson, D. R., & Yang, P. H. (1999). The Asian Values Scale: Development, factor analysis, validation, and reliability. *Journal of Counseling Psychology*, 46, 342–52.

Kim, B. S., & Omizo, M. M. (2005). Asian and European American cultural values, collective self-esteem, acculturative stress, cognitive flexibility, and general self-efficacy among Asian American college students. *Journal of Counseling Psychology*, 52(3), 412–19.

Kwoh, S. (2021, December 15). *Asian American history IS American history: But why is it often ignored in U.S. classrooms?* Asia Society. https://asiasociety.org/magazine/article/asian-american-history-american-history.

Le, C. N. (2021a, August 1). *The First Asian Americans.* Asian-Nation: The Landscape of Asian America. http://www.asian-nation.org/first.shtml.

Le, C. N. (2021b, August 1). *The 1965 Immigration Act.* Asian-Nation: The Landscape of Asian America. http://www.asian-nation.org/1965-immigration-act.shtml.

Le, C. N. (2021c, August 1). *Welcome to Asian-Nation.* Asian-Nation: Asian American History, Demographics, & Issues. http://www.asian-nation.org/.

Mo, W., & Shen, W. (2003). Accuracy is not enough: The role of cultural values in the authenticity of picture books. In D. L. Fox & K. G. Short (Eds.), *Stories matter: The complexity of cultural authenticity in children's literature* (pp. 198–212). National Council of Teachers of English.

Moreillon, J. (1999). The candle and the mirror: One author's journey as an outsider. *The New Advocate*, 12, 127–39.

Norton, D. (2013). *Multicultural children's literature: Through the eyes of many children* (4th ed.). Pearson.

Short, K., & Fox, D. (2004). The complexity of cultural authenticity in children's literature: A critical review. In J. Worthy, B. Maloch, J. Hoffman, D. Schallert, & C. Fairbanks (Eds.), *53rd yearbook of the national reading conference* (pp. 373–83). National Reading Conference.

Sue, D. W., & Sue, D. (2003). *Counseling the culturally different: Theory and practice* (4th ed.). Wiley.

U.S. Census Bureau, Population Estimates Program (PEP). (n.d.). *Asian.* https://www.census.gov/quickfacts/fact/note/US/RHI625219.

Yokota, J. (2009). Asian Americans in literature for children and young adults. *Teacher Librarian*, 36(3), 15–19.

Yoo-Lee, E., Fowler, L., Adkins, D., Kim, K. S., & Davis, H. N. (2014). Evaluating cultural authenticity in multicultural picture books: A collaborative analysis for diversity education. *The Library Quarterly*, 84(3), 324–47.

Zhao, X. (2009). *Asian American chronology.* Greenwood Press.

CHILDREN'S BOOKS CITED

Handforth, T. (1938). *Mei Li.* Doubleday.

Ho, J., & Ho, D. (2021). *Eyes that Kiss in the Corners.* HarperCollins.

Mosel, A. (1968). *Tikki Tikki Tembo* (B. Lent, Illus.). Henry Holt.

Chapter 5

Jewish Children's Literature

Melanie D. Koss and Deborah Greenblatt

UNDERSTANDING JEWISH CULTURE

Shalom is a Jewish greeting that means hello, goodbye, and peace in Hebrew, the historical and modern-day language of the Jewish people and official language of the state/country of Israel. Other languages associated with Judaism are Yiddish and Ladino, but since Jews are found all over the world, they speak many different languages. So what, exactly, is Judaism? Who are people who identify as Jews? Judaism is complex and multifaceted.

Judaism is not solely a religion, although many people are only familiar with this aspect. However, this is only one possible definition/description. Judaism is also an identity or heritage passed down for generations. It is a combination of "cultural, social, and religious behavior" (Dimont, 1978/2001, p. xiii). It is not a race, ethnicity, or nationality, but a group of people descended from Abraham, a historical figure in the Torah or Old Testament (Dimont, 2004). Not all Jews are religious, and many live secular lives yet retain elements of their Jewish identities. (See Pew Research Center, 2013, for additional background on Jewish identity constructs.) Jews live worldwide and can be connected by common holidays, artifacts, foods, languages, and traditions. Jewish tradition also follows the solar-lunar calendar rather than the Gregorian calendar, similar to the Chinese calendar.

Culture is a social construct, so sometimes one's identity is determined by how others see us (Payne, 2020). Stereotypes are perpetuated and throughout history being identified as a Jew led to antisemitism and Jewish people being banned from owning property or businesses, forced to live in ghettos,[1] and, most egregiously, persecution (Levy et al., 2005). During the Holocaust, the Nazis considered Jews an inferior race and sought to eliminate them. In this instance, Jews were considered a race, although this is not accurate. Calling Judaism a racial or ethnic identity erases Jews of color. After World War II, the perception became that all Jews are White (Levine-Rasky, 2020), and many Jews in America are White; however, not all. There are many Jews of color. White nationalists and antisemites do not consider Jews White but view Jews as Others (Maizels, 2011). Some people are visibly religious Jews, based on clothing, hairstyles, and outward presentations. Other Jews blend in with no set external trappings and may identify as nonreligious or one of the many denominations, including Reform, Conservative, and Orthodox (My Jewish Learning, n.d.).

Judaism is over 4,000 years old (Davies, 2016; Segal, 2009). The Jewish people originally lived in the Middle East, but due to years of persecution, there have been a series of Jewish diasporas spreading the Jewish people around the world (Levine, 2003; Schwartz, 2015). This led to the creation of two distinct Jewish cultural groups: Ashkenazi Jews who landed in Eastern Europe and who are speakers of Yiddish; and Sephardic Jews who landed in North Africa, Spain, and Portugal and who are speakers of Ladino (Mays, 2020). Many Sephardic Jews were persecuted during the Spanish Inquisition in the late 1400s. The first Jews to come to America were Sephardic Jews in Colonial times (Dimont, 1978/2001); however, the majority of American Jews came from Europe. The first wave of European Jews to the United States was in the early to mid-1800s and were primarily from Germany (Dimont, 1978/2001). The second wave, resulting from a series of attacks against the Jews, called pogroms, in Eastern Europe, was in the late 1800s to early 1900s (Birmingham, 1984). Descendants of these two waves make up a significant portion of today's American Jews and are the immigrants who passed through Ellis Island (Dimont, 1978/2001). European attacks against the Jews intensified during World War II in the Holocaust. This led to the creation of the State of Israel. We recognize that Israel is controversial and has a conflicted history; however, its constitution is called *The State of Israel as a Jewish State* (Knesset, n.d.) and all those who are ethnically Jewish have a right to citizenship (*Apply for Israeli Citizenship According to Section 4A of the Law*

---

[1] Ghetto—refers to a neighborhood where Jews were segregated and forced to live.

of Return, n.d.). Not all people who live in Israel are Jewish. Not all Jews in the diaspora have the desire to live in or feel connected to Israel. The Jewish American identity is a separate, although connected, entity.

Persecution of the Jewish people continues today, and many Jews face antisemitism, which is on the rise in contemporary America (Schuba, 2022). Antisemitism is the hatred of and blaming of society's ills on the Jewish people. The white Supremacy movement and the KKK are rooted in antisemitism (SPLC, n.d.). We recognize this is a challenging topic for grades PK–3; however, we include it as we feel it is critical to be aware of this at developmentally appropriate levels, as many people may be unaware of Judaism and the Jewish people, and others may be one of few Jews in an environment.

EVALUATING AND SELECTING JEWISH CHILDREN'S BOOKS

All books should be evaluated for bias, but when analyzing Jewish children's literature look for things that aren't stereotypical but that represent Jewish culture authentically. Whose stories are being told? Whose are missing? Books need to go beyond holidays or major historical events. Contemporary titles showing the diversity of Jews, especially within America, are needed to situate the Jewish people in the present day. It is recommended that authors and illustrators are Jewish or that there is an author's note about the authenticity of the research and depiction of the characters in the story.

In picture books, analyze the illustrations for stereotypes to ensure books are mirrors or windows (Bishop, 1990) for readers. Many times, visual depictions of Jewish people are physically stereotypical (e.g., wearing a kippah; having a large nose or dark, curly hair; or being presented as white or of Eastern European descent). Look for cultural cues in illustrations such as cultural objects (e.g., mezuzahs or menorahs). (See table 5.1 for a list of common Jewish apparel, objects, places, holidays, and food.)

Cues are also provided in the text. Words are often common identifiers of Jewish culture. Jewish characters will often use Hebrew, Yiddish, or Ladino words such as *mazel tov, kvetch, shelp, chutzpah, haberes buenos*, and so on. Also, a common way books denote Jewish content is by the mention of a holiday.

Table 5.1 Common Jewish Apparel, Objects, Places, Holidays, and Foods

Category (Hebrew/Yiddish/Ladino)	Definition	Image
Apparel		
Kippah/Yamulke	A small hat or head covering.	
Tallit/Tallis/Tallet	Prayer shawl with long fringes on the corners called tzitzit.	
Objects		
Mezuzah	A decorative case placed upon the doorposts of Jewish homes containing a prayer.	
Torah	Scroll contains the five books of the Old Testament or the Jewish Bible.	
Star of David (Magen David/Magon David)	Two overlaid equilateral triangles that form a six-pointed star: a symbol of Judaism.	
Hamsa	The symbol of an eye embedded in an open palm; symbol of protection in Jewish, Muslim, and Christian beliefs.	

(continued)

Table 5.1 (Continued)

Category (Hebrew/ Yiddish/Ladino)	Definition
Menorah/ Hanukkiah	The word menorah is Hebrew for "lamp" and is a seven-branched candelabra. The Hanukkiah has nine branches and is used during Hanukkah.
Dreidel	A four-sided spinning top. There are four Hebrew letters on the dreidel which stand for "A Great Miracle Happened Here," referring to the miracle of the oil on Hanukkah.
Kiddush Cup	A Kiddush Cup is a designated cup used for the blessing over the wine on Shabbat and holidays.
Candlesticks	The act of lighting a pair of candles marks the beginning of Shabbat and many holidays.

Places

Synagogue/Shul	Jewish house of worship.

(continued)

Table 5.1 (Continued)

Category (Hebrew/ Yiddish/Ladino)	Definition	Image
Major Holidays[a]		
Shabbat	The Jewish sabbath. It begins on Friday night at sundown and ends one hour after sundown on Saturday night.	
Rosh Hashanah	The Jewish New Year.	
Yom Kippur	The Day of Atonement; holiest day of the Jewish year.	
Passover/Pesach	Celebration of the liberation of the Jewish people from slavery in Egypt. Celebrated with a seder meal telling the Passover story.	
Hanukkah	Holiday commemorating the rededication of the Temple in Jerusalem after it was destroyed by the Greeks. A Hanukiah is lit for eight nights representing the miracle oil that lasted for eight days. (Note: Hanukkah is not an important Jewish holiday. It is celebrated due to its proximity to Christmas.)	
Common Foods (*denotes from the Ashkenazi tradition)		
Bagels and lox*	Originating in Eastern Europe, boiled bread rings are schmeared (Yiddish word for spread) with cream cheese and covered in smoked salmon. A common brunch food.	
Latkes*	Potato pancakes fried in oil. Typically served on Hanukkah, a day people eat food fried in oil to commemorate the miracle.	
Chicken Matzoh ball soup*	Often called "Jewish penicillin," matzoh ball soup is chicken soup with large dumplings made from matzoh meal, eggs, and fat.	
Gefilte fish*	Oblong fish balls traditionally made from carp or other white fish. Often served on Passover or other holiday meals with horseradish.	
Matzoh	Unleavened bread eaten on Passover. Ashkenazi matzoh is often in the shape of a square while Sephardic matzoh is round.	

(continued)

Table 5.1 (Continued)

Category (Hebrew/Yiddish/Ladino)	Definition	Image
Challah*	Often served on Shabbat, a braided egg bread.	

^aFor a complete list of Jewish holidays see https://www.chabad.org/holidays/default_cdo/jewish/holidays.htm and children's book Newman, L (2014) *Here is the world: A year of Jewish holidays*. (S. Gal, Ilus.) Harry N. Abrams.

Table 5.2 Jewish Values

Jewish/Hebrew Value (Transliterated from the Hebrew. Note that the "ch" sound is not pronounced as a ch like in chance but as a gutteral hard H.)	English Translation
Chesed	Caring; Kindness among people
T'shuvah	Repentance
Kehillah	Community
Ba'al Tashchit	Do not destroy; Reuse and recycle
Chaverut	Friendship
Tikkun Olam	Social justice/Repair the world/Activism
Bikkur Cholim	Visit the sick
Kavod	Respect
L'dor Vador	Connect generations
Tzedakah	Charity in the form of justice
S'lichah	Forgive
Zachor	Remember

Judaism contains a set of values that provide guidance on how Jewish people should live (see table 5.2). These are not distinct to Jewish people but are emphasized and promote social justice, being kind, and activism. We recognize that these values are not specific just to Judaism but are solid values across many cultures and populations. Diversity is not just differences among groups but also connections among them.

We know that in early childhood, a typical unit is the study of folktales from around the world. Representation of Jewish culture is often not present. Some examples of Jewish versions of common folktales include *The*

Cholent Brigade (Herman, 2017), a variant of *Stone Soup*, *The Way Meat Loves Salt* (Jaffe, 1998), and *Raisel's Riddle* (Silverman, 1999), Jewish versions of *Cinderella*. There are many additional Jewish folktales that stem from Jewish, often Eastern European, tradition. *It Could Always Be Worse* (Zemach, 1990) is a traditional tale in which a father complains that his house is too crowded and noisy, and the rabbi's advice is to bring different animals into the house. Once they all leave, he realizes his house wasn't as bad as he thought. Two contemporary versions are *No Room for a Pup* (Suneby, 2019) and *Such a Library: A Yiddish Folktale Re-imagined* (Nadler, 2020). Other folktales of note are *Something From Nothing* (Gilman, 2012), *Joseph Has a Little Overcoat* (Simms Taback, 1999), and *Golem* (Wisniewski, 1996).

USING AUTHENTIC JEWISH LITERATURE IN THE CLASSROOM WITH YOUNG CHILDREN

Included within each of the following titles are resources for further lesson plan ideas and materials. Resources are designated here by PJ Library (PJ) and Book Connections (BC).

The Ninth Night of Hanukkah by Erica Perl (PJ)
Grades: PK–2
Genre: Realistic fiction
Summary: Max and Rachel move into a new apartment on the first night of Hanukkah, but their family cannot find the box with the items for the holiday. Every night they get help from their new neighbors to try to celebrate, although it continues to "not feel quite like Hanukkah." Max and Rachel plan an additional night of Hanukkah—a "shamash night" in honor of their new friends—because the shamash helps light all the other candles. As a miracle of Hanukkah, their box arrives in time for the party.
Vocabulary to preview: menorah, latkes, shamash, dreidel, gelt
Context to preview:
- Explain what an apartment is for students who may be unfamiliar
- Show a video on how to play dreidel
- Significance of jelly donuts for Hanukkah

Reading comprehension strategies: infer, predict, make connections
- "He followed his nose downstairs." What does that mean? (literal vs. figurative language)
- What was on the "steaming platter?" How are they like latkes?
- What is the toy that the Watson twins brought that spins? Have you ever used a hula hoop?
- Based on the text, what is "gelt?"
- Why does it say "It turned out they were *almost* right?" What instrument is that? (ukulele)
- What is "mmuht it mmushsn't feel quite like Hummukkah?" Why do Rachel and Max sound like that? Look at the picture. (Have students talk as if they had a mouth full of peanut butter.)

Post-reading connection to Jewish values prompts:
- *Kehillah* (community), *Chesed* (kindness)
- Text-to-text connection: community with *A Chair for my Mother* by Vera Williams
- Text-to-self: When have you helped someone in your community? Are there problems in your community your neighbors might work together to solve?
- *Ba'al Tashchit* (reuse): use newspaper to wrap presents

Interdisciplinary connections:
- Math: counting the days, nominal vs. ordinal numbers, playing dreidel with gelt (counting money, halves, doubles)

Related texts:
- *Mrs. Katz and Tush* by Patricia Polacco
- *All-of-a-Kind Family Hanukkah* by Emily Jenkins

Big Dreams, Small Fish **by Paula Cohen**
Grades: PK–3
Genre: Historical fiction
Summary: Shirley and her family move to America and open a grocery store featuring homemade food. The neighbors try some items but not the gefilte fish. Shirley has ideas on how to help the store, but her family doesn't want her help. When Aunt Ida goes into labor, the whole family rushes to the hospital, and Shirley and Mrs. Gottlieb watch the store while they are gone. Shirley puts her ideas into practice and gives out samples of gefilte fish with

every order. When the customers go home, they taste what they were so hesitant to try and come back the next day for more!

Vocabulary to preview: See Glossary, noodle kugel

Context to preview:
- Hebrew lettering on the gefilte fish, yarmulkes on the boys.
- This book is set in an urban area.
- This book is set in 1930s/1940s. (Notice cars, clothing, and egg delivery truck).
- Her father said, "We didn't come to this country for you to solve problems." Connect to any of the students who might be immigrants.

Reading comprehension strategies: Prediction, making connections, inferring
- From the first to the second picture (title page), what do we learn about Shirley?
- Recap the ways Shirley was trying to solve the problem. Do you have any advice?
- Has anyone ever told you that you were too little to help even though you had an idea to solve a problem? How do you think Shirley feels?
- Why do you think Mama says: "The neighbors don't know from good gefilte fish"?
- Shirley is left in charge of the store: What do you think Shirley will do next?
- Look at the picture: Make an inference. What do they think of the gefilte fish?
- If everyone is in line for the gefilte fish, what do you think "delicacy" might mean?

Post-reading connection to Jewish value:
S'lichah (forgiveness)
- In trying to solve a problem, Shirley did something she wasn't supposed to do. Why do you think they forgave her? What if Shirley's idea didn't work? Would they/should they still forgive her?
- Connection to *Little Critter* series

Word Study:
- The first illustration has all the letters of the title mixed up. Choose vocabulary to do the "making words" activity.

Writing:
- Make a shopping list: Glue or draw the amount of each item (PK); list with pictures and write the first sound of each word or invented spelling for the items (K–1); make your own advertisement for food items (2–3).

Interdisciplinary Connections:
- Social Studies: immigration in the 1930s (links to archival photos from the time).
- STEM: building structures (stacking the cans).
- Math grade PK–1: Create a matching game with the cans in the store.
- Math grades 1–3: Use the items in the store, make a budget, "shop," and make change with play money; use the recipe to measure out some ingredients.

Related Texts:
- *The Carp in the Bathtub* by Barbara Cohen
- *Five Little Gefiltes* by David Horowitz

Tía Fortuna's New Home: A Jewish Cuban Journey by Ruth Behar

Grades: 1–3

Genre: Realistic fiction

Summary: Estrella loves to visit her Tía at her Miami casita by the sea and hear her Tía's stories about her childhood in Cuba. Tía Fortuna must move again, and Estrella struggles with losing the place she loves until she learns that memories are what matter and that home is where the heart is. Sprinkled with authentic elements of Sephardic Jewish and Cuban traditions, this book shows that hope and resilience exist across many cultures and families.

Vocabulary to preview: See Glossary. Many of the words will need to be defined in context since there are so many words. We suggest previewing the following words, which are used frequently in the story:
- Tía: aunt
- Que Dios le bendiga: May G-d bless you[2]
- Amor Eterno: Eternal Love
- Duerme amor mío: sleep my love
- La Casa de los Viejitos: The house of the elderly
- See chart for mezuzah, hamsa, Shabbat (Shabbos) candlesticks, Star of David

---

[2] Typically, Jewish people write out god as a proper noun and spell it with a hyphen to not "take the name in vain."

Context to preview:
- Many languages are in this story and not all of them are in italics. A teacher unfamiliar with Yiddish/Ladino and/or Spanish should preview the book for these words.
- Use the inside of the cover of the book to find images of the vocabulary above.
- The quote, "We come from a people who found hope wherever they went," refers to the historical persecution of the Jewish people. See the section above on "Understanding Jewish Culture."

Reading comprehension strategies: Prediction, making connections, inferring
- The banyan tree nods its head at Tía and says: hola, hola, hola (example of personification).
- Symbolism of the key and passing it on to Esperanza. (Look at the author's note.) Connect to the Jewish diaspora.

Post-reading connection to Jewish value:
L'dor Vador (connect generations)
- Text-to-text connection with *Wilfred Gordon McDonald Partridge* by Mem Fox
- Do you have any special people in your life who have traditions/keepsakes? What is their significance?
- Have students bring in items or photos of the items
- Grades 2–3: Interview someone who moved or immigrated and share their story. Students could also go on a field trip and visit a senior-living facility

Interdisciplinary connections:
Social studies:
- Map the journey from Spain to Turkey to Cuba to Miami.
- What sea are they talking about? What bodies of water are near Miami?
- Map areas where Sephardic Jews live.
- What are other ways to say "thank you?"

Related texts:
- *Lola Levine is Not Mean!* by Monica Brown
- *The Key from Spain: Flory Jagoda and Her Music* by Debbie Levy

***Dear Mr. Dickens* by Nancy Churnin (BC)**
Grade: 2–3
Genre: Biography
Summary: Based on a true story, Eliza Davis is a fan of the famous author Charles Dickens, but she notices that Dickens's portrayal of Jewish people is degrading. Despite being a woman, Eliza dares to write a letter to Dickens to explain why his descriptions of Jewish people are hurtful and to ask him to revise them. Dickens is defensive and not easily convinced; however, Eliza is persistent and unintimidated by the famous author. She answers his rebuttal and leaves Dickens with much to contemplate.
Vocabulary to preview: atone
Context to preview:
- Can heroes be flawed? Can people undo their mistakes of the past?
- Preview and discuss "England was a difficult place for Jewish people in the 1860s. Many jobs were closed to them. They didn't have the right to vote or study or work in universities."
- Give background on societal expectations for women at the time.
- Give background on Charles Dickens and remind students of Ebenezer Scrooge from "A Christmas Story."

Reading comprehension strategies: inferring, predicting, connecting
- How would you feel if you were Eliza?
- Explain the simile: "Like a hammer in Eliza's heart."
- In Dickens's letter back to Eliza, he writes, "Any Jewish people who thought him unfair and unkind—and that included Eliza—were not 'sensible' or 'just' or 'good-tempered.'" What do you think of Dickens's reply?
- Why do you think Eliza said, 'He might as well have said, '*Bah! Humbug!*'?
- What would you have done if you were Eliza? What would you have said?
- Discuss how Eliza uses the strategy of Dickens's own writing with the ghosts visiting him.
- Eliza let her young son mail it. Why do you think she did that?

Post-reading connection to Jewish values:
Tikkun Olam (activism)
- Eliza stands up for her people and writes to Dickens and continues to do so until there is change.

S'lichah (forgiveness)
- Eliza rushes to buy copies of his new publications. Why do you think she does?
- Although Eliza is a woman and Dickens is a famous writer, she speaks up for the portrayal of Jewish people.

T'shuvah (repentance)
- At first, Dickens is defensive of Eliza and then he changes his mind. Although Dickens rejects Eliza's critique, she is persistent and is able to convince him.
- Read and discuss the last two paragraphs of the "Author's Note."

Writing:
- Have students write a persuasive letter to someone. Brainstorm real issues and situations affecting them and who they might write to about making change.

Interdisciplinary connections:
Social studies:
- Civil rights and activism

Awards:
- National Jewish Children's Book Award Winner
- Sydney Taylor Book Award Honor
- A Junior Library Guild Selection

Related texts:
- *Brave Girl: Clara and the Shirtwaist Makers' Strike of 1908* by Michelle Markel
- *A Poem for Peter: The Story of Ezra Jack Keats and The Snowy Day* by Andrea Davis Pinkney

Jewish Children's Books to Start With

Contemporary

And a Cat from Carmel Market
Capucilli, A. S. (2021) *And a cat from Carmel Market.* (R. Teplow, Illus.) Kar-Ben.
Grade: PK–2
Jewish Value: *Kehillah* (community), *Ba'al Tashchit* (reuse)
Rationale: This book introduces the traditions of Shabbat and many Jewish items gathered from a market in Israel. Bubbe uses a reusable bag as she gathers her necessities.
Summary: Bubbe goes shopping for a Shabbat dinner in Carmel Market in Tel Aviv, Israel. She buys challah, candles, a tablecloth, a chicken, and other items, and is followed home by multiple cats. Everything is going as planned until the cats disrupt Shabbat dinner! When Bubbe lights the Shabbat candles they all settle down and the meal goes on as planned.
Additional book on Israeli culture:
- *Ella's Trip to Israel* by Vivan Bonnie Newman

Chicken Soup, Chicken Soup
Mayer, P. (2016) *Chicken soup, chicken soup.* (D. Melmon, Illus.) Kar-Ben.
Grade: PK–2
Jewish Value: *L'dor Vador* (connect generations), *Kavod* (respect)
Rationale: This book shows similarities and differences among cultures through food. The Jewish Chinese main character brings together her two grandmothers to celebrate having a blended family.
Summary: Sophie loves her Bubbe's Jewish chicken soup with kreplach and her Nai Nai's Chinese chicken soup with wontons. Chicken soup with dumplings is delicious! When each grandmother complains that Sophie doesn't know Jewish from Chinese food, Sophie has an idea. She brings the grandmothers and their soup recipes together, so the soups can be blended, just like her.
Awards:
- Sydney Taylor Book Award Notable Book

Additional books that blend food across cultures:
- *Sweet Tamales for Purim* by Barbara Bietz
- *Queen of the Hanukkah Dosas* by Pamela Ehrenberg
- *Jalapeño Bagels* by Natasha Wing

Mitzvah Pizza
Scheerger, S. L. (2019). *Mitzvah pizza*. (D. Melmon, Illus.) Kar-Ben.
Grade: K–4
Jewish Value: *Chesed* (caring), *Tzedakah* (charity)
Rationale: Doing a *mitzvah*, a good deed, is an essential concept in Judaism. The illustrations show Missy as a non-stereotypical Jewish-looking child.
Summary: On Saturday's daughter-dad day, Missy saved up her allowance to treat her dad. While waiting in line at a pizza shop, Missy becomes friends with a girl. The girl grabs two sticky notes from the wall to pay for her pizza, and Missy is confused. She learns each sticky note represents a slice of pizza for someone in need. Missy uses her allowance to not only buy her dad a slice but to buy sticky notes for future customers. Inspired by a real restaurant in Philadelphia.
Additional books on mitzvahs:
- *The Christmas Mitzvah* by Jeff Gottesfeld
- *A Hat for Mrs. Goldman: A Story About Knitting and Love* by Michelle Edwards

Historical Events

Gittel's Journey: An Ellis Island Story
Newman, L. (2019). *Gittel's journey: An Ellis Island story* (A. J. Bates, Illus.) Abrams.
Grade: K–3
Jewish Value: *Zachor* (remember), *Kehillah* (community)
Rationale: Immigration through Ellis Island is a traditional story for many Jewish Americans.
Summary: *Gittel's Journey* is based on the author's family history of immigrating through Ellis Island and its accompanying excitement, confusion, and fear. When Gittel arrives, she is separated from her mother at the health inspection and realizes ink has smudged her cousin's address on the paper her mom gave her.
Awards:
- National Jewish Book Award
- Sydney Taylor Book Award Honor
- Christopher Award for Young People

Additional books about Jewish immigration:
- *When Jessie Came Across the Sea* by Amy Hest
- *The Memory Coat* by Elvira Woodriff and Michael Dooling
- *Oskar and the Eight Blessings* by Richard Simon and Tanya Simon

Raquela's Seder
Stein, J. E. (2022). *Raquela's seder* (S. Ugolotti, Illus.) Kar-Ben.
Grade: K–3
Jewish Value: *Zachor* (remember)
Rationale: This picture book tells of a time in Jewish history many are not familiar with, the Marrano Jews of Spain during the time of the Inquisition who hide their religion in order to avoid persecution.
Summary: Raquela's family were hidden Jews and celebrated Shabbat weekly in their basement. Raquela had heard of the holiday of Passover but had never celebrated and had always wanted to participate in a seder. Thanks to her father's ingenuity, Raquela and her family found a way to hold a secret seder.
An additional book about Marrano Jews:
- *Always an Olivia: A Remarkable Family History* by Carolivia Herron

Biographies

The People's Painter: How Ben Shahn Fought for Justice with Art
Levinson, C. (2021). *The people's painter: How Ben Shahn fought for justice with art* (S. Tan, Illus.). Abrams.
Grade: 1–3
Jewish Value: *Tikkun Olam* (activism)
Rationale: Activism and social justice are essential Jewish values. Ben Shahn exemplified *tikkun olam* by seeing the truth in the world and exposing the world's ills through art.
Summary: Growing up in Lithuania, Ben Shahn saw injustice and internalized the need to be an advocate. As a new emigrant to America, Ben was the victim of bullying and took refuge in art, his passion. Although his artistic style belied the norm, Ben told the true stories of the American people and the injustices they undertook. The US government hired him to paint the American people's experiences during the Great Depression, shocking many and helping to promote change. He spent his life painting stories and advocating for justice.

Awards:
- Robert F. Sibert Informational Book Medal
- Sydney Taylor Book Award Notable Book

Additional books on Jewish activists:
- *Goldie Takes a Stand* by Barbara Krasner
- *Hannah G. Solomon Dated to Make a Difference* by Bonnie Lindauer

Nicky & Vera: A Quiet Hero of the Holocaust and the Children He Rescued

Sís, P. (2021). *Nicky & Vera: A quiet hero of the Holocaust and the children he rescued.* Norton.

Grade: 1–3

Jewish Value: *Zachor* (remember), *Tikkun Olam* (activism)

Rationale: The Holocaust is not often taught in an age-appropriate way for young children, yet it cannot be forgotten. This picture book provides an entry point into the Holocaust through an activist's lens.

Summary: In 1938, Englishman Nicholas Winton went to Prague at the bequest of a friend. While there, he saw a way to save refugee children. He took pictures, kept records, paid for visas, and found foster families in England for almost 700 children. He then hid his records and never spoke of it again. Vera was one of those saved children. When Nicky's wife found the hidden records, she shared them with the news and a famous television appearance brought Nicky back in contact with the children he saved.

Awards:
- Jane Addams Children's Book Award Finalist
- *Kirkus Reviews* Best Children's Book
- *Horn Book* Fanfare Best Book
- Sydney Taylor Book Award Honor

Additional books on the Holocaust:
- *I Will Come Back for You: A Family in Hiding During World War II* by Marisabina Russo
- *Stone Angel* by Jane Yolen
- *The Butterfly* by Patricia Polacco

Holidays

Red and Green and Blue and White
Wind, L. (2021). *Red and green and blue and white* (P. O. Zelinsky, Illus.). Levine Querido.
Grade: PK–2
Jewish Value: *Tikkun Olam* (activism), *Kehillah* (community)
Rationale: A community bands together against antisemitism, promoting Jewish values of community and fighting injustice.
Summary: One night, the window Issac's family displayed their menorah was smashed. In the face of antisemitism, Issac's family continued to display their menorah, and his Christian friend, Teresa, drew a menorah and put it in her window in solitary. Friends, neighbors, and local businesses were inspired by Teresa's actions and the community banded together and became UPstanders instead of BYstanders. Inspired by a true story.
Awards:
- Sydney Taylor Award Notable Book
- Association of Jewish Libraries Best of the Year

An additional book on blending holidays:
- *A Moon for Moe and Mo* by Jane Breskin Zalben (Ramadaan and Rosh Hashanah)

Chik Chak Shabbat
Rockliff, M. (2016). *Chik chak Shabbat* (K. Brooker, Illus.). Candlewick.
Grade: PK–3
Jewish Value: *Kehillah* (community), *Bikkur Cholim* (visit the sick)
Rationale: This book celebrates a diverse community and how people become a family by choice. It emphasizes helping the sick and keeping traditions even if they don't look exactly the same. It also provides context for the weekly observance of Shabbat.
Summary: Every Friday Goldie makes *cholent*, a slow-cooking stew typical for a Saturday Shabbat meal. Every Friday her diverse neighbors smell the cooking stew and look forward to their group dinner. One Saturday they don't smell the cholent and everyone gets worried. When they learn that Goldie was sick and wasn't able to make the cholent, they all bring what they have to

continue their tradition of a Saturday meal. Even though it wasn't traditional, Goldie loves it and says it smells like Shabbat.

Awards:
- Cooperative Children's Book Center
- Junior Library Guild Selection

An additional book on Shabbat:
- *Bubbe and Bart's Matzoh Ball Mayhem* by Bonnie Grubman

Welcoming Elijah: A Passover Tale with a Tail
Newman, L. (2019). *Welcoming Elijah: A Passover tale with a tail* (S. Gal, Illus.). Charlesbridge.
Grade: K–3
Jewish Value: *Chesed* (caring)
Rationale: Kindness and opening your home to those in need is a significant Jewish value, which includes people and animals in need.
Summary: Told in alternating perspectives in patterned text, inside a boy celebrates Passover and goes through seder traditions, and outside a stray kitten roams, alone and hungry. Both are waiting for something. They discover what it is when the boy opens the door for the Prophet Elijah and the kitten finds a new home.
Awards:
- Sydney Taylor Book Award
- National Jewish Book Award
- Charlotte Zolotow Award Honor

Additional books on Passover:
- *The Passover Guest* by Susan Kusel
- *Meet the Matzah: A Passover Story* by Alan Silberberg

RESOURCES ON JEWISH CULTURE AND LITERATURE FOR CHILDREN

(Resources—websites, articles, books, and so on—to help classroom teachers further understand the culture, evaluate and select more children's books on the culture or group.)

Association of Jewish Libraries
www.jewishlibraries.org
An international professional organization that supports Jewish literacy and librarianship. Their website contains numerous resources, including the blog Sydney Taylor Shmooze which reviews Jewish-themed books.

Sydney Taylor Book Award
https://jewishlibraries.org/sydney_taylor_book_award/
Given by the Association of Jewish Libraries, this award honors outstanding books for children and young adults that represent the Jewish experience. There are Winner, Honor, and Notable books.

For an analysis of the Sydney Taylor Book Award Winners for Children, see: Leket-Mor, R., & Isaac, F. (2020). The Sydney Taylor Book award at fifty: Trends in canonized Jewish children's literature (1968–2020). *Judaica Librarianship, 21*, 58–94. https://documentcloud.adobe.com/link/review?uri=urn:aaid:scds:US:6e1df4c6-5a35-4849-b246-32d09faf6946.

Jewish Book Council
https://www.jewishbookcouncil.org/
The Jewish Book Council's website contains a wealth of resources on books as well as a literary journal, book clubs, and author and commemorative events.

National Jewish Book Award for Children
https://www.jewishbookcouncil.org/awards/national-jewish-book-awards
Given by the Jewish Book Council, this award recognizes authors of English books on Jewish interest.

Kalaniot Books
http://kalaniotbooks.com/
This publishing company publishes diverse books on the Jewish people and their history and culture. Their website features resources about books for booksellers, educators, and librarians. They also have reviews related to Multicultural Children's Book Day.

Kar-Ben Publishing

https://www.karben.com/

A publishing company that focuses on books that celebrate and represent today's diverse Jewish families. They offer a seasonal book box subscription. Their website is full of resources and book reviews divided into accessible categories.

PJ Library

https://pjlibrary.org/home

PJ Library is an organization that sends free books to Jewish children of any background every month for ages zero to eight and nine to twelve. Their goal is to provide books that help families talk about Jewish culture and values. Their website contains music, recipes, activities, and podcasts for the whole family. There is also a companion blog https://www.pjourway.org/ with children and parent views that allows for comments and reviews of the books.

Be'Chol Lason/Global Jews.org

https://globaljews.org/resources/childrens-books/

A website that celebrates the diversity of the Jewish people that contains a variety of resources including a page devoted to books for children. https://globaljews.org/resources/childrens-books/

Anti-Defamation League (ADL)

https://www.adl.org/

The Anti-Defamation League is an anti-hate organization that fights against antisemitism, bigotry, and discrimination. Their website is full of information and programming, including a resource page for educators and families, featured books of the month with companion discussion guides, and an early childhood educator FAQ page with information on books, activities, and strategies to fight hate and bullying, including gender bias, examining prejudice, and fostering respect.

REFERENCES

Birmingham, S. (1984). *The rest of us: The rise of America's Eastern European Jews.* Little Brown.

Davies, P. R. (2016). *On the origins of Judaism.* Routledge.

Dimont, M. I. (1978/2001). *The Jews in America: The roots, history, and destiny of American Jews*. Olmstead Press.

Knesset. (n.d.). *The state of Israel as a Jewish state*. https://knesset.gov.il/constitution/ConstMJewishState.htm.

Levine, A. (2003). *Scattered among the peoples: The Jewish diaspora in twelve portraits*. Overlook.

Levine-Rasky, C. (2020). Jewish whiteness and its others. *Journal of Modern Jewish Studies*, *19*(3), 362–81.

Maizels, L. (2011). On whiteness and the Jews. *Journal for the Study of Antisemitism*, *3*(2), 463–89.

Mays, D. (2020). *Forging ties, forging passports: Migration and the modern Sephardi diaspora*. Stanford University Press.

My Jewish Learning. (n.d.). *The Jewish denominations*. https://www.myjewishlearning.com/article/the-jewish-denominations/.

Segal, E. (2009). *Introducing judaism*. Routledge.

Schuba, T. (2022, April 26). *Cases of antisemitic hate reach historic levels across U.S., Illinois, new report finds*. Chicago Sun Times.

Schwartz, B. (2015). *Scattered among the nations*. Weldon Owen.

Southern Poverty Law Center. (n.d.). *Antisemitism*. https://www.splcenter.org/fighting-hate/extremist-files/ideology/antisemitism.

CHILDREN'S BOOKS CITED IN THE CHAPTER

Behar, R. (2022). *Tía Fortuna's new home: A Jewish Cuban journey* (D. Holzwarth, Illus.). Knopf.

Bietz, B. (2020). *Sweet tamales for Purim* (J. Kanzler, Illus). August House.

Brown, M. (2015) *Lola Levine is not Mean!* (A. Dominquez, Illus.). Little, Brown Books for Young Readers.

Cohen, B, (1987) *The carp in the bathtub* (J. Halpern, Illus.). Kar-Ben Pub.

Cohen, P. (2022). *Big dreams, small fish*. Levine Querido.

Churnin, N. (2021). *Dear Mr. Dickens* (B. Standcliffe Illus.). Albert Witman & Company.

Edwards, M. (2016). *A Hat for Mrs. Goldman: A story about knitting and kindness* (G. B. Karas, Illus.). Schwartz & Wade.

Ehrenberg, P. (2017). *Queen of the Hanukkah Dosas* (A. Sarkar, Illus.). Farrar, Straus and Giroux.

Fox, M. (1989). *Wilfred Gordon McDonald Partridge* (J. Vivas, Illus.). Kane Miller.

Gottesfeld, J. (2021). *The Christmas mitzvah* (M. L. Agatha, Illus.). Creston.

Herron, C. (2012). *Always an Olivia: A remarkable family history* (J. Tugeau, Illus.). Kar-Ben.

Horowitz, D. (2007). *Five little gefiltes*. G. P. Putnam's Sons Books for Young Readers.

Jenkins, E. (2018) *All-of-a-kind family Hanukkah* (P. Zelinsky, Illus.). Schwartz & Wade.

Krasner, B. (2014). *Goldie takes a stand: Golda Meir's first crusade* (K. Garrity-Riley, Illus.). Kar-Ben.

Kusel, S. (2021). *The Passover guest* (S. Rubin, Illus.). Neal Porter.

Levinson, C. (2021). *The people's painter: How Ben Shahn fought for justice with art* (S. Tan, Illus.). Abrams.

Levy, D. (2019). *The key from Spain: Flory Jagoda and her music* (S. Wimmer, Illus.). Kar-Ben.

Lindauer, B. (2021). *Hannah G. Solomon dared to make a difference* (S. Moore, Illus.). Kar-Ben.

Mayer, P. (2016) *Chicken soup, chicken soup* (D. Melmon, Illus.). Kar-Ben.

Markel, M. (2016). *Brave girl: Clara and the shirtwaist makers' strike of 1908* (M. Sweet, Illus.). Balzer + Bray.

Nadler, J. R. (2020) *Such a library: A Yiddish folktale re-imagined* (E. van den Berg, Illus.). Intergalactic Afikoman.

Newman, L. (2019). *Gittel's journey: An Ellis Island story* (A. J. Bates, Illus.). Abrams.

Newman, L. (2019). *Welcoming Elijah: A passover tale with a tail* (S. Gal, Illus.). Charlesbridge.

Newman, V. N. (2014) *Ella's trip to Israel* (A. Guiterrez, Illus.). Kar-Ben.

Perl, E. S. (2020) The ninth night of Hanukkah (S.Kober, Illus.). Union Square Kids.

Pinky, A. D. (2016) *A poem for Peter: The story of Ezra Jack Keats and The Snowy Day* (S. Johnson & L. Fancher, Illus.). Viking Books for Young Readers.

Polacco, P. (1994). *Mrs. Katz and Tush*. Dell.

Polacco, P. (2005) *The Butterfly*. Puffin Books.

Rockliff, M. (2016) *Chik chak Shabbat* (K. Brooker, Illus.). Candlewick.

Russo, M. (2011) *I will come back for you: A family in hiding during World War II*. Schwartz and Wade.

Suneby E. (2019). *No room for a pup*. Kids Can Press.

Scheerger, S. L. (2019). *Mitzvah pizza* (D. Melmon, Illus.). Kar-Ben.

Stein, J. E. (2022). *Raquela's seder* (S. Ugolotti, Illus.). Kar-Ben.

Wind, L. (2021). *Red and green and blue and white* (P. O. Zelinsky, Illus.). Levine Querido.

Wing, N. (1996). *Jalapeño bagels* (R. Casilla, Illus). Atheneum.

Williams, V. (2007). *A chair for my mother*. Greenwillow Books.
Wisniewski, D. (1996). *Golem*. Clarion.
Yolen, J. (2015). *Stone angel* (K. M. Greene, Illus.). Philomel Books.
Zalben, J. B. (2018). *A Moon for Moe and Mo* (M. Amini, Illus.). Charlesbrigdge.
Zemach, M. (1990). *It could always be worse: A Yiddish folktale*. Square Fish.

Chapter 6

Latinx Children's Literature
Why Latinx Children's Literature Is Essential for All Classrooms

Julia López-Robertson

Marisela: ¿De dónde eres? Yo soy de Guatemala./Where are you from? I am from Guatemala.
Julia: Yo nací aquí en los Estados Unidos pero mi papá era cubano y mi mamá era colombiana. Soy Latina./I was born here in the United States, but my father was Cuban, and my mother was Colombian. I am Latina.
Marisela: Ah, yo sabía que eras como yo. Mis Papi's nacieron allá y yo aquí. Pero yo soy de Guatemala y soy Latina, igual que tú./Ah, I knew you were like me. My parents were born over there (Guatemala), and I was born here. But I am from Guatemala, and I am Latina, like you.
Jorge: Yo soy de Puerto Rico y Latino lo mismo que el libro que leímos./I am from Puerto Rico, the same as in the book we just read.
Griselda: Yo soy dominicana y Latina./I am Dominican and Latina.

The excerpt is from a conversation that I had with a group of first graders (all names are pseudonyms) during one of our weekly meetings. I spend time weekly in their classroom where I do a whole class read aloud and then small group work in reading and writing with Spanish-speaking children who might need extra support with English. After the whole class read aloud, the children join me at a table in the back of the classroom. As we settled into our seats, Marisela jumped right in and began the query of my origin; she was curious to know my background and share hers while Jorge shared his origin and made a connection between himself and the story we read, and Griselda shared her Latina origin. Like many Latinx children in our schools, they are seeking connections and to see their language, culture, and images in their classroom.

Latinx, Hispanic, Latino?

This classroom, like many in the United States, has a growing number of Latinx children; the National Center for Education Statistics reported that of the 50.7 million students enrolled in public elementary and secondary schools, in fall 2018, 13.8 million were Hispanic. Before we proceed, an explanation of terms is necessary; I will use the gender-neutral term Latinx when referring to people with roots in Spanish-speaking countries who live in the United States and who may or may not speak Spanish. When I use the term Latino, Latina, or the country of origin, it is because the person to whom I refer has self-identified as such. Similarly, I will use Hispanic when the research cited uses that term. The discussion on terminology is serious and beyond the scope of this chapter, the brief explanation is not meant as disrespect.

As seen in the opening excerpt, the children noted that they were Latinxs from Guatemala, Puerto Rico, and the Dominican Republic supporting the fact that the Latinx community is made up of people from many places. Nevertheless, there is a widespread misconception that all Latinx people are Mexican; this stems from the fact that people of Mexican origin accounted for nearly 62 percent of the Latinx population in the United States in 2019 (Krogstad & Noe-Bustamante, 2021). In addition to the countries listed above, the US population of Latinx peoples also represent El Salvador, Honduras, and Peru, to name a few. Therefore, to say that there is one Latinx community and that we are all the same would be inaccurate; each of these groups practices different traditions and customs, language variations, and have "different histories in relation to their presence in the United States" (González, 2009, p. 171). Furthermore, considering all Latinx peoples as one group runs the risk of perpetuating a stereotype and promoting a single narrative of Latinx communities.

So, what is Latinx children's literature? Does it have to be written in Spanish? Who is Latinx children's literature for? In the sections that follow, we will explore those questions, as well as discuss book selection and authenticity. Integrated throughout the sections will be Latinx children's literature, some ideas on how to use Latinx children's literature in the classroom, and resources on locating Latinx children's literature.

What Is Latinx Children's Literature?

Rudine Sims Bishop's (1990) seminal work introduced the concept of books as windows, sliding glass doors, and mirrors. Engaging children with literature can open their minds to people and places near and far (windows), allow them to step into and out of ways of living with which they may not be familiar (doors), and hopefully to seeing people who look and sound just like them (mirrors). Diverse children's literature provides an avenue for understanding the world in which we live and "helps children understand that everyone has a story to tell and that those stories are to be valued and appreciated" (López-Robertson, 2021, p. 34).

Latinx children's literature represents a varied diaspora; it is rooted in the oral tradition and is a culturally particular way of conveying family values, traditions, cultural beliefs, and customs. While the literature needs to communicate the "distinctiveness of Latino cultural experiences and the universality of human experience" (Smith et al., 2016, p. 35), it does not have to be written in Spanish.

The linguistic choices made by authors are reflective of the linguistic diversity within the Latinx community; Latinx children's literature can be all English, all Spanish, bilingual with some Spanish and English, or with Spanish words interspersed throughout the text written mainly in English. Importantly, Latinx children's literature "needs to be seen as reflective of a tradition that has survived and has undergone cultural adaptation within the scope of the social cultural context of the U.S. and all places where Latinos reside" (Clark & Flores, 2016, p. 7) as Latinx communities have a long and varied history in the United States.

Who Is Latinx Children's Literature For?

Classrooms in the United States continue to reflect the growth of the Latinx population, and it stands to reason that Latinx children's literature needs to be present in all schools—not simply those with Latinx students. Latinx children's literature provides benefits for all students. For Latinx children, the literature helps provide a positive sense of self, helps them feel valued, and it can also improve their academic performance (Clark & Flores, 2016). Latinx literature also benefits non-Latinx children by exposing them to cultures, languages, and ways of being that they are unfamiliar with, and it "helps them develop a consciousness and familiarity with an important part of the U.S. population" (López-Robertson, 2021, p. 43). When sharing Latinx children's literature, we want to include books and stories representing the diversity within the community as shown by the examples below.

Felíz New Year, Ava Gabriela! Alexandra Alessandri (2021). Ava Gabriela is spending the holidays with her extended family in Colombia. Even though she is excited to take part in her family's New Year's traditions such as making buñuelos, being around so many relatives and in an unfamiliar place makes Ava quiet and shy.

Tía Fortunas new home: A Jewish Cuban story by Ruth Behar (2022) tells the story of Tía Fortuna's move from her apartment building where she lived for a very long time to an assisted living community. While packing her belongings, Estrella learns about her family heritage as Tía Fortuna explains the significance of her dearest possessions from her Cuban and Jewish culture.

Dinner on Domingos by Alexandra Katona (2021). Alejandra and her family have dinner at Abuelita's house every domingo (Sunday). Dinner at Abuelita's means dancing, hugging, playing games with aunts, uncles, and cousins, and having delicious Ecuadorian home cooking. Alejandra decides to be brave one domingo and tries to speak Spanish with Abuelita.

Three pockets full: A story of love, family, and tradition by Rodriguez (2022). Beto's mami is getting married, and there is no way he is going to wear a guayabera, a traditional Mexican wedding shirt. He is not giving in, no matter what. Mami has lost her patience and insists that Beto wear the special guayabera that she bought for him, it is after all a part of his heritage.

Coquí in the city by Nomar Pérez (2021). Miguel lives in Puerto Rico with his parents and loves spending time with his grandparents and his pet frog, Coquí. Miguel learns that he and his parents are moving to the US mainland, which means leaving behind his home, his grandparents, and even Coquí.

AUTHENTICITY

The National Council of Teachers of English Position Statement on Indigenous Peoples and People of Color in English and Language Arts

Materials notes that "school materials should foster the development of attitudes grounded in respect for and understanding of the diverse cultures of American society" (NCTE, 2020). Presenting students with books containing inaccurate, stereotypical views of others is harmful and works against these goals and hurts both Latinx and non-Latinx students. But how can educators make informed decisions about book selection, particularly when they are not familiar with Latinx cultures? With the variety found within Latinx communities, how does one know what is authentic? The most comprehensive explanation of authentic literature comes from Nieto (1997):

> The search for authentic literature is not the search for an upbeat, consistently positive, sentimental, romanticized, or idealized reality. Rather, it is the search for a more balanced, complete, accurate, and realistic literature that asks even young readers to grapple with sometimes thorny issues . . . literature that attempts to reflect the range of issues and possibility with the community's experience. (p. 62)

Rather than combining selected aspects from different Latinx cultures into one, authentic literature maintains the uniqueness of the Latinx culture (s) being discussed and does so in a respectful and accurate manner. It is also critical to consider the author's cultural background: Are they from the Latinx community? Can they write from an insider's perspective? Having a Spanish surname is not an indication of authenticity, and at the same time, not having a Spanish surname does not automatically mean inauthenticity. Clark et al. (2016) suggest that "these books need to be written by authors who can portray those realities authentically, from their own lived experiences, their own intimate association with a particular culture, and their own continued learning" (p. x). The list below provides questions to consider when selecting books (López-Robertson, 2021, pp. 59–60).

Questions to Consider When Analyzing Texts for Cultural Authenticity

Literary Merit

- Is the book written with realistic characters, engaging in believable activities?
- How well does the author tell the story? Is it engaging?

Origin of Book

- Who was the original publisher and in what country?
- Who is the author? Illustrator? What are their backgrounds?

Authorship

- How do the author's experiences connect to the setting and characters in this book?
- What are the experiences and/or research on which the book is based?

Believability

- Is this story believable? Could it happen?
- Are the characters larger than stereotypes but less than "perfect" heroes?

Accuracy of Details and Authenticity of Values

- How do these values connect to the actual lives of people within the culture?
- Does this book reflect a specific cultural experience, or could it happen anywhere?

Perspectives

- Whose perspectives and experiences are portrayed?
- Who tells the story?

Power Relationships

- Which characters are in roles of power or significance within the book?
- Where does the story go and how does it get there? Who takes it there? Why?

Audience

- Who is the intended audience?
- Is the book written for children from that country or to inform children in other parts of the world about that country or culture?

Relationship to Other Books

- How does this book connect with other books about this cultural experience?
- Do the available books about this culture reflect a range of perspectives and experiences within that culture?

Response by Insiders

- How have insiders responded to this book?

BOOK SELECTION

Selecting Latinx children's literature takes care of and must be done in a purposeful manner.

Carefully read each book and be aware of the following: pay attention to storylines, the use of the Spanish language, the character's knowledge of English, the relationships between the characters, the educational levels of adults, and the power relations that exist in the book. Are the storylines limited to immigration? Are the characters escaping? Considering Spanish language use in the text, does the book respectfully use Spanish or is it mocked? For example, is the letter "o" simply added to English words as in "my pencil-o," "the book-o"? Do the characters struggle to speak English and are they helped or mocked by other characters? Are the characters portrayed as uneducated and simple-minded? Are the Latinx characters in subservient roles?

Selection Criteria-Text

Representation of Culture

- Does the book depict just one image of all Latinx people?

Use of Spanish Language

- Is there an overall respect for the Spanish language?
- Is the Spanish language used as a prop to sell a book? Are there words inserted in the text that are meaningless?

Characters That Are Multidimensional

- Are the Latinx characters unnecessarily loud or boisterous?
- Are they working only in stereotypical roles, such as housekeepers, construction workers, or wait staff?

Knowledge of English

- Do the characters not know English?

- When a character is learning English, are the people around him or her helpful and kind, or do they mock his or her attempts at English?

Educational Level of Adults

- Are the adult characters portrayed as simple-minded or ignorant?

Storyline

- Are the books with Latino characters only about immigration?
- Are the characters fleeing something? Are they running away? Being chased?

In addition to reading the words, one must also carefully read the illustrations as images are central to meaning-making in picturebooks (Johnson et al., 2019) and can reinforce stereotypical views. Examine the illustrations and look for: How the characters are depicted; how the neighborhood is portrayed, and the make-up of the family. Below is a list of questions to consider in book selection, a complete list can be found in López-Robertson (2021).

Selection Criteria—Illustrations

Character Traits

- Are the Latinx characters afraid because they are being chased, or followed?
- Are the characters depicted as troubled, dishonest, or deceitful?

Physical Appearance

- Are the Latinx characters dark and sinister?
- Are they similar in appearance to one another or do they each have a unique look?
- Are they portrayed as criminals (e.g., as bandits or members of a gang)?

Depiction of Family

- Is the family always financially strapped?
- Always led by a single parent, usually a mother.

Depiction of Home

- Is the home messy, dirty, and poorly maintained because of lack of income?
- Is the home overcrowded with extended family members?

Depiction of Neighborhood

- Are the Latinx characters always living in the barrio?
- In subsidized housing or housing projects?

These lists can be used as starting points for discussions with your students, their families, and your colleagues. Talk with your students about the criteria and ask them to help you analyze books using them. Exposing children to Latinx children's literature is wonderful, better still is engaging them in careful examination of texts, and discussions about the issues they come across. Talking about the books and deeply engaging in dialogue helps them see that they can question things, form opinions, and have a right to share their thoughts.

LATINX CHILDREN'S LITERATURE IN THE CLASSROOM

Latinx children's literature needs to be a part of the curriculum, not simply an add-on during Hispanic Heritage Month. Latinx people have made and continue to make valuable contributions to our society, be intentional in including Latinx literature throughout the school year. Inclusion in the curriculum demonstrates to Latinx children that their culture has value and that it is something to be proud of all the time. Below are some ideas for how to infuse Latinx children in the classroom and curriculum.

Text Sets

Text sets are a wonderful way to include a broad range of materials in any unit of study. A text set is a group of resources focused on a theme or unit of study; these include magazines, websites, maps, charts, music, songs, videos, brochures, and of course books! Because the text set is focused on one topic/theme, it provides students the opportunity to deeply dive into the research of that theme while also exploring their own wonderings.

Text Set Día de los Muertos

One tradition that I was unfamiliar with prior to moving to Tucson, Arizona, was the Día de Los Muertos/Day of the Dead. Teaching in a predominantly Mexican, Mexican American elementary school and neighborhood, my students and their families taught me its significance. Día de Los Muertos is a celebration of the lives of loved ones that have passed and is rooted in the Aztec belief of an afterlife and takes place on November 1 (All Soul's Day) and November 2 (All Saints Day). Due to its growing awareness throughout the world, Día de Los Muertos has been recognized as a part of UNESCO's list of Intangible Cultural Heritage of Humanity since 2008. Years ago, while teaching first grade, I read aloud *Pablo recuerda la fiesta del Día de los Muertos* by George Ancona (1993). This book contains beautiful photographs that follow Pablo and his family as they prepare to honor the memory of Pablo's grandmother. The book was released in English as well, *Pablo remembers the fiesta of the Day of the Dead* (1993). During the discussion following the read aloud, one of my students asked if they could create an altar for their Abuelita who had recently passed away. Other children asked if they could do the same for family members who had passed and together with their families, they created altars made from shoe boxes and displayed them in our classroom. For children who did not wish to create an altar or whose families chose not to do so, we created artifacts related to Día de los Muertos and decorated our classroom.

There are several picturebooks about Día de los Muertos; *I Remember Abuelito: A Day of the Dead Story/Yo Recuerdo a Abuelito: Un Cuento del Día de los Muertos* (Levy, 2007); a story about a little girl who misses her grandfather and is excited as she prepares for his visit. *A Gift for Abuelita/ Un regalo para Abuelita: Celebrating the Day of the Dead/En celebración del Día de los Muertos* (Luenn, 2004); Rosita misses her Abuelita and makes a special gift for her, a braid just like the one Abuelita taught Rosita how to make. *Calavera Abecedario: A Day of the Dead Alphabet Book* (Winter, 2006) tells the story of Don Pedro and his family's preparation for the Day of the Dead fiesta; each alphabet letter corresponds with a specific artifact of Día de Los Muertos. While not specifically about Día de Los Muertos, Yuyi Morales' books, *Just a Minute: A Trickster Tale and Counting Book* (2016) *and Just in Case: A Trickster Tale and Spanish Alphabet Book* (2018), follow Señor Calavera as he counts his way to Grandma Beetle's birthday and finds toys that correspond to the alphabet as he searches for birthday gifts.

Other types of texts: National Geographic and National Geographic Kids have short videos and photos appropriate for young children; there is a short film, *CGI 3D Animated Short Film: "Día De Los Muertos"* winner of the 2013 Student Academy Award Gold Medal, and the Disney movie *Coco* (2017).

Text Set Fairy Tales and Nursery Rhymes

Fairy Tales and Nursery Rhymes play a prominent role in schooling and are part of Language Arts standards beginning in Pre-K. Through them, we can teach a variety of standards and strategies such as story structure as they usually contain a well-defined setting, problem, and solution, sequencing, and cause and effect. Additionally, because there are several fairy tales and nursery rhymes representing a variety of cultures, they also help increase cultural awareness and can become part of the Social Studies curriculum. As discussed above, when selecting fairy tales and nursery rhymes, it is important to carefully read the text and illustrations when making book selection. Below is a text set of fairy tales and nursery rhymes followed by ideas for classroom use.

La princesa and the pea by Susan Middleton Elya (2017). This bilingual retelling of the Princess and the Pea gets a fresh twist accompanied by colorful art inspired by the culture of Perú. The book was awarded the Pura Belpré Medal for Illustration.

Federico and the wolf by Rebecca J. Gomez (2020). Red hoodie on and a bicycle with a basket full of food, Federico is on his way to visit Abuelo when he comes upon el lobo-a hungry wolf! El lobo has a plan, but Federico outsmarts him. Abuelo and Federico celebrate with special salsa, a recipe included in the book.

María had a little llama/María tenía una llamita Angela Domínguez (2013). Beautiful Peruvian-inspired illustrations, this fresh new twist on the classic rhyme is captivating.

The runaway piggy/El cochinito fugitivo James Luna (2010). In this retelling of *The gingerbread man*, Martha's panaderia is full of fresh hot Mexican pastries, conchas, orejas, cuernitos, empanadas, and cochinitos all waiting for customers except for the piggy/cochinito cookie. He leaps off the bakery tray and runs away through the barrio avoiding being caught until he meets a clever little girl named Rosa.

Once upon a time/Había una vez: Traditional Latin American tales/ cuentos tradicionales latinoamericanos by Rueben Martínez (2010). This bilingual collection of short stories introduces readers to some of Latin America and Spain's most beloved tales retold and accompanied by beautiful illustrations.

The tooth fairy meets/El Ratón Pérez by René Colato Laínez (2010). The Tooth Fairy has some competition. El Ratón Pérez is an adventurous mouse who collects children's teeth in Spain and Latin America. Miguelito loses his tooth and both the Tooth Fairy and El Ratón Pérez arrive to claim it. Who does it belong to? El Ratón Pérez has collected Miguelito's parent's and his grandparent's teeth. Who will rightfully claim Miguelito's tooth?

Text Set Cumulative Stories

A Cumulative Story is a story that builds on a pattern. It starts with one person, place, thing, or event. Each time a new person, place, thing, or event is shown, all the previous ones are repeated. A popular example is *The old lady who swallowed a fly* story.

The Empanadas that abuela made/Las empanadas que hacía la abuela by Diane Gonzales Bertrand (2003). A playful look at the making of empanadas as the story follows Abuela, Abuelo, the cousins, aunts, uncles, and even the family dog join in the fun. An empanada recipe is included.

The cazuela that the farm Maiden Stirred by Samantha R. Vamos (2013). The maiden and the farm animals help make the rice pudding that will be served at the fiesta. Beautifully illustrated, the book skillfully includes Spanish words making learning the language fun and easy. Back matter includes a glossary of Spanish words and a recipe for arroz con leche!

The piñata that the farm maiden hung by Samantha Vamos (2019). The farm maiden and the animals are at it again, this time preparing a piñata from scratch for a birthday party. Back matter includes a glossary, definitions, and directions for making a piñata at home.

CLASSROOM ACTIVITIES

Beyond reading the books aloud with your students, below you will find a few ideas on classroom activities. The fairy tale and nursery rhyme text set is particularly suited for Venn Diagrams, T-charts, and other activities asking students to compare and contrast versions of the same story.

Somebody Wanted But So Then Finally (SWBTF)

SWBTF is a great way to guide students to give a summary. Students often struggle to summarize as they are usually eager to share everything they know about a story. While a retelling is a detailed "play by play" of all the events in a story, told in sequence, a summary is a brief overview of the story.

- *Somebody* Who is the main character?
- *Wanted* What did the character want?
- *But* What was the problem?
- *So* How is the problem solved?
- *Then* What was the resolution to the story?
- *Finally* How did the story end?

Five W's and One H

Five W's and One H helps students identify the main idea, important details, and main character in books they read.

- Who is the story about?
- What did they do?
- When did the action take place?
- Where did the story happen?
- Why did the main character do what s/he did?
- How did the main character do what s/he did?

Triple Entry Journal

Triple entry journal is effective with fairy tales. To do this strategy, students must be familiar with multiple versions of the same fairy tale. Working with one partner or small groups, students work together to fill out the chart. They must discuss the stories they are comparing and decide which events from the stories they will choose; in the first column, they select one event in the fairy tale and follow it through as they fill out the rest of the chart. I have filled out the chart based on *Federico and the Wolf* in table 6.1.

Table 6.1 Triple Entry Journal

Event in the original fairy tale	Changes the author made in the new version	How these changes affected the meaning of the story
Red Riding Hood walks to grandma's house.	Federico rides his bike to his abuelo's shop.	Federico appears more independent as he is allowed to ride his bike through town.

Pláticas literarias/Literature Discussions

Pláticas literarias/Literature discussions are literature circles (Short, 1997) where small groups of students gather to discuss a book that they read or had read to them. The goal of these pláticas is to have children think deeply about what they have read, make connections to their life experiences, and begin to make sense of issues, concepts, and ideas raised in the books. The pláticas open a space for students to engage critically with the text and "examine their own understandings of the issues raised in the text and share these with their classmates while participating in a 'two-way reciprocal relation' (Rosenblatt, 1978, p. 27) with the text to develop a more complex interpretation of it" (López-Robertson, 2012, p. 32).

Prior to joining the small group plática, each of the students is given a small piece of construction paper, about 5 × 7. On one side of the paper, they will draw their response to the text and on the other side, they will write about it. Drawing on one side allows students to express themselves through art while the written response is more standardized. The following questions guide the students' written and illustrated responses and the small group plática:

- Does the story remind you of anyone?
- Have you experienced anything similar?
- What connections are you making to your own life?
- What are your questions or wonderings?

Author and/or Illustrator Studies

Author and/or illustrator (A/I) studies provide students the opportunity to dig deeply into a particular A/I's craft. Engaging children in a focused study of an illustrator allows them to see that art is also a form of communication; it helps them learn how to appreciate art, and creating art like the illustrator's immerses them in the creative process. By focusing their research on one, A/I students can:

- Think deeply about the A/I's craft
- Become an expert on A/I which may lead to more confidence as a reader
- Make connections between the A/I's life and work
- Make personal connections between their own experiences and those of the A/I and their characters.

A/I studies typically culminate in a final project where students share what they learned about the A/I. Projects can take the form of a timeline of the A/I's life and books, a reader's theater of their favorite book, recreating the illustrator's artwork from a favorite book, or taking a picturebook and turning it into a comic strip or a graphic novel. Many picturebooks have notes explaining the process or medium used by the illustrator and sometimes the author and/or illustrator's webpage is also listed. Below is a list of some favorite Latinx authors and/or illustrators:

- Monica Brown http://www.monicabrown.net/
- Margarita Engle http://margaritaengle.com/
- Rene Colato Laínez http://www.renecolatolainez.net/
- Yuyi Morales http://yuyimorales.com/
- Juana Martínez Neal https://juanamartinezneal.com/
- Matt de la Peña https://mattdelapena.com/
- Duncan Tonatiuh https://duncantonatiuh.com/

Locating Latinx Children's Literature

It can be difficult to locate Latinx children's literature and with a limited budget, how do you know where to start and what to choose? The following book awards provide a wonderful starting point. The websites include annual winners as well as several resources for educators.

Américas Award for Children's and Young Adult Literature

Consortium of Latin American Studies Program founded the Américas Award in 1993 to encourage and commend authors, illustrators, and publishers who produce quality children's and young adult books that portray Latin

America, the Caribbean, or Latinx in the United States, and to provide teachers with recommendations for classroom use.

Pura Belpré Award

Established in 1996, the award is named after Pura Belpré, the first Latina librarian at the New York Public Library. The award is presented annually to a Latina/Latino writer and illustrator whose work best portrays, affirms, and celebrates the Latino cultural experience in an outstanding work of literature for children and youth.

Tomás Rivera Award

Texas State University College of Education created The Tomás Rivera Mexican American Children's Book Award in 1995 to honor authors and illustrators who create literature that depicts the Mexican American experience. It is named in honor of Texas State University distinguished alumnus Dr. Tomás Rivera.

CLOSING THOUGHTS

While reading aloud *La princesa and the pea* (2017) by Susan Middleton Elya, a Peruvian version of the *Princess and the Pea,* Orlando eagerly held his hand up and said, "Se parece a mi abuelita/she looks like my grandmother"—we were reading the fourth page in the book depicting the prince's mother. He then proudly shared that he knew how to speak her (his Abuelita's) language, "Yo hablo con mi abuelita así/I speak to my grandmother like this," and he proceeded to tell the class how to say "I love my Abuelita" in Quechua (an indigenous language of Perú), Spanish, and English. Like all children, Orlando is seeking connections to the books we share in school.

Children have a right to see themselves, their languages, and their cultures respectfully represented in books and school curricula. Similarly, they also need to widen their worldview by engaging with books that present people, places, languages, and cultures with which they may not be familiar. It is our responsibility as educators to do this for all our students through the books we share. It is important to remember that Latinx children's literature belongs in all classrooms and is for all children, so that like Orlando, they can make connections between the books and their lives. Our goal as educators is to foster a sense of curiosity in our students. We want them to share a sense of wonder and respect for not just diverse cultures, but essentially for their own culture.

REFERENCES

Appleton, S. (n.d.) *What is the day of the dead?* National Geographic. https://www.nationalgeographic.org/video/what-day-dead/.

Bishop, R. S. (1990). Mirrors, windows, and sliding glass doors. *Perspectives*, 6(3), ix–xi.

Clark, E. R., & Flores, B. B. (2016). Preface: Derrumbando fronteras/breaking boundaries. In E. R. Clark, B. B. Flores, H. L. Smith, & D. A. González (Eds.), *Multicultural literature for latino bilingual children: Their words, their worlds*. Rowman & Littlefield.

González, T. (2009). Art, activism and community: An introduction to Latina/o literature. In M. P. Steward & Y. Atkinson (Eds.), *Ethnic literary traditions in American children's literature* (pp. 171–89). Palgrave McMillan.

Graham, A., Reynolds, K., & St. Pierre, L. (2013). *Día De Los Muertos*. Ringling College of Art and Design. https://www.youtube.com/watch?v=jCQnUuq-TEE.

Johnson, H., Mathis, J., & Short, K. G. (2019). *Critical content analysis of visual images in books for young people: Reading images*. Routledge.

Krogstad, J. M., & Noe-Bustamante, L. (2021). *Key facts about U.S. Latinos for National Hispanic heritage month*. Pew Research Center. https://www.pewresearch.org/fact-tank/2021/09/09/key-facts-about-u-s-latinos-for-national-hispanic-heritage-month/.

López-Robertson, J. (2012). "Oigan, tengo un cuento": Crossing la frontera of life and books. *Language Arts,* 90(1), 30–43.

López-Robertson, J. (2021). *Celebrating our cuentos: Choosing and using Latinx literature in elementary classrooms*. Scholastic.

National Center for Education Statistics. (2021). Racial/ethnic enrollment in public schools. *Condition of Education*. U.S. Department of Education, Institute of Education Sciences. https://nces.ed.gov/programs/coe/indicator/cge.

National Council of Teachers of English. (2020). *Position statement on indigenous peoples and people of color (IPOC) in English and language arts materials*. https://ncte.org/statement/ipoc/.

National Geographic Kids. (n.d.). *Day of the dead*. National Geographic Kids. Retrieved April 15, 2022, from https://kids.nationalgeographic.com/celebrations/article/day-of-the-dead.

Nieto, S. (1997). We have stories to tell: Puerto Ricans in children's books. In V. J. Harris (Ed.), *Using multiethnic literature in the K-8 classroom* (pp. 59–93).

Rosenblatt, L. (1978). *The reader, the text, the poem: The transactional theory of the literary work*. Southern Illinois University Press.

Sánchez, M. T., & García, O. (2022). *Transformative translanguaging espacios: Latinx students and their teachers Rompiendo fronteras sin miedo*. Multilingual Matters.

Short, K. G. (1997). *Literature as a way of knowing*. Stenhouse Publishers.

Smith, H. L., Flores, B. B., & González, D. A. (2016). Exploring the traditions of Latino children's literature: Beyond tokenism to transformation. In E. R. Clark, B. B. Flores, H. L. Smith, & D. A. González (Eds.), *Multicultural literature for Latino bilingual children: Their words, their worlds* (pp. 25–48). Rowman & Littlefield.

UNESCO's list of Intangible Cultural Heritage of Humanity. https://ich.unesco.org/en/RL/indigenous-festivity-dedicated-to-the-dead-00054.

Unkrich, L. (Director). (2017). *Coco*. [Film]. Walt Disney Pictures and Pixar Animation Studios.

CHILDREN'S LITERATURE

Alexandra Alessandri, A. (2020). *Felíz New Year, Ava Gabriela!* (A. R. Sonda, Illus.). Albert Whitman & Company.

Ancona, G. (1993a). *Pablo recuerda la fiesta del Día de los Muertos* (G. Ancona, Illus.). HarperCollins Español.

Ancona, G. (1993b). *Pablo remembers the fiesta of the Day of the Dead* (G. Ancona, Illus.). HarperCollins.

Behar, R. (2022). *Tía Fortuna's new home: A Jewish Cuban journey* (D. Holzwarth, Illus.). Knopf Books for Young Readers.

Bertrand, D. G. (2003). *The Empanadas that abuela made/Las empanadas que hacia la abuela* (D. G. Bertrand, Illus.). Arte Público Press.

Domínguez, A. (2013). *María had a little llama/María Tenía Una Llamita* (A. Domínguez, Illus.). Henry Holt.

Elya, S. M. (2017). *La princesa and the pea* (J. Martinez-Neal, Illus.). G. P. Putnam's Sons.

Gómez, R. J. (2020). *Federico and the wolf* (E. Chavarri, Illus.). Clarion Books.

Katona, A. (2021). *Dinner on domingos* (C. Navarro, Illus.). Barefoot Books.

Laínez, R. C. (2010). *The Tooth Fairy meets El Ratón Pérez* (T. Lintern, Illus.). Tricycle Press.

Levy, J. (2007). *I remember abuelito: A Day of the Dead Story/Yo Recuerdo a Abuelito: Un Cuento del Día de los Muertos* (L. López, Illus.) (M. Arisa, Translator).

Luenn, N. (2004). *A gift for abuelita/Un regalo para abuelita: Celebrating the Day of the Dead/En celebración del Día de los Muertos* (R. Chapman, Illus.). Cooper Square Publishing LLC.

Luna, J. (2010). *The runaway piggy/El cochinito fugitivo* (L. Lacamara, Illus.). Piñata Books.

Martinez, R. (2010). *Once upon a time/Había una vez: Traditional Latin American Tales/Cuentos tradicionales latinoamericanos* (R. Colón, Illus.). HarperCollins español.

Morales, Y. (2018a). *Just a minute: A trickster tale and counting book* (Y. Morales, Illus.). Chronicle Books.

Morales, Y. (2018b). *Just in case: A trickster tale and Spanish alphabet book* (Y. Morales, Illus.). Chronicle Books.

Perez, N. (2021). *Coqui in the city* (N. Perez, Illus.). Dial Books.

Rodriguez, C. L. (2022). *Three pockets: A story of love, family, and tradition* (B. F. Corbalán, Illus.). Cardinal Rule Press.

Vamos, S. R. (2019a). *The Cazuela that the farm maiden stirred* (R. López, Illus.). Charlesbridge.

Vamos, S. R. (2019b). *The piñata that the farm maiden hung* (S. Serra, Illus.). Charlesbridge.

Winter, J. (2021). *Calavera Abecedario: A day of the dead alphabet book* (J. Winter, Illus.). HMH Books for Young Readers.

Chapter 7

Middle Eastern–North African (MENA) Children's Literature

Zeynep Isik-Ercan

UNDERSTANDING MENA CULTURES

Middle East and North Africa (MENA) is a vast geographical area that has been a home to many ancient civilizations with rich political histories and dynamic cultures. After being ruled by a variety of kingdoms and later empires, this area today is divided into smaller countries that are created in the last century during the fall of the Ottoman State and through French and British colonialism. These countries include Iraq, Iran, Egypt, Israel, Jordan, Syria, Kurdistan, Lebanon, Palestinian Territories, Algeria, Bahrain, Kuwait, Libya, Morocco, Oman, Qatar, Saudi Arabia, Tunisia, United Arab Emirates, and Yemen. Some include Turkey in the Middle Eastern region in terms of its closeness and location in both Asia and Europe, as well as similarities in some cultural aspects (Pew Research Center, 2005). Prominent languages spoken in this are mainly concentrated in the countries/regions listed in parentheses: Arabic, Farsi (Iran), Kurdish (Southern Turkey, Northern Iraq, and Iran), Turkish (Turkey), Hebrew (Israel and Palestine Territories), Russian (Syria and Iraq), English (throughout the region as a second language), French (Morocco, Algeria, Tunisia, and Lebanon), neo-Aramaic (Iraq and Syria), and Tamazight languages (North African region) (Horesh, 2019). These languages lend themselves to great literacy explorations in P–3 classrooms, since many of their ancient and current alphabets include aesthetically pleasing and vibrant shapes representing letters, words, ideas, and concepts that are starkly different from the Latin alphabet.

In terms of faith diversity, the area is famously known as the birthplace of all Abrahamic religions: Judaism, dating around 4,000 years (Egypt, Israel, and Palestine Territories), Christianity, dating almost 2,000 years (Syria, Israel, and Palestine Territories), and Islam, dating over 1,400 years (Saudi Arabia). Today, the main faith traditions that people in MENA region identify with include Islam (over 90 percent), Christianity (close to 4 percent), Judaism (close to 2 percent), Hinduism (0.5 percent), folk religions (0.3 percent), and Buddhism (0.1 percent), among others (Pew Research Center, 2005). While non-Muslim minorities include Jews, Copts, Maronites, Greek Orthodox, Greek Catholic, Latins, and Protestants, Muslim minorities include the Alawites, Druze, Babism the Baha'is, Ismailis, and Ahmadis (Cavanaugh, 2016).

The MENA region has been home to several historical civilizations that are rich in material for children's literature, if underused. One of these inspiring civilizations is the Egypt civilization, which lasted 7,000 years. Egypt's history began around 5,000 BC with initial Neolithic farmer communities forming around the Nile River and delta and emerged as two kingdoms (Red Lands and White Lands) at around 3,100 BC. Perhaps, Egypt's richest period was around 2,700–2,200 BC when the great pyramids were built; this is regarded as the golden age of prosperity and scientific and spiritual invention (History, 2022).

Another intriguing ancient civilization is Mesopotamia, known as the cradle of all civilization. This region constitutes a fertile area between Tigris and Euphrates rivers in today's Turkey, Syria, and Iraq. Archeological finds reveal that communities that first emerged in this area date back 16,000 years, when domestication of animals and early agriculture appeared. These developments gave rise to vibrant cities, concentrated in urban areas of organized homes, food, art, and learning spaces, with advanced technology in agriculture, city planning, food, and trade. The region was dominated by different communities and dynasties over the ages including Sumers, Sargon and the Akkadians, Gutians, Ur-Namma, the Babylonians, the Hittites, the Assyrians, and the Persian and Roman Empire, each appearing and disappearing because of natural disasters, migration, and military conquests (History, 2022).

After the emergence of Christianity in today's Israel and Palestinian territories, MENA region was ruled by the Roman and Byzantine Empires. With the rise of Islam in the seventh century various Arab, Farsi, and Kurdish states, followed by the Ottoman rule, became a prominent presence until several smaller states were created in the aftermath of World War I. The remnants of these multicultural states, coupled with the ancient civilizations they were built upon, create an enchanting open-air museum in every town throughout the region with numerous sites of historical, religious, and cultural importance. There are constant archeological excavations in the region; it is typical to find a new city formation under another one through several layers of centuries or discover intricate ancient mosaics and artwork in common houses during renovations.

Despite the vast diversity in the region, there may arguably be some typical characteristics of Middle East culture. One of the apparent characteristics is the sense of community, and the importance of family structure, with parents associated with love, leadership, and close coordination of children's lives, built upon the concept of respect for parents, family, and elders in the community. MENA cultures focus on providing a space of acceptance and respect for each member as part of the family hierarchy, with relatives of each mother and father having unique salutations before their names based on gender and age.

Another typical characteristic of Middle Eastern culture is the understanding of offering food and help to strangers and friends (albeit often unsolicited) as part of generosity, love, and hospitality. Food and feast are important symbols of religious, national, and local holidays, with certain food offered or restricted in times of importance. Wasting food is not appreciated in the region; food and those preparing food are revered. This is not surprising, as the region was the birthplace of farming and had ancient gods associated with harvest and other important agricultural concepts.

In terms of significant days, Muslim tradition prioritizes Friday as a special prayer day, Christian tradition values Sunday as a day of reflection and prayer, and Jewish tradition honors Shabbat, Saturdays as a day of contemplation. Common holidays for the region include all holidays of Judaism, Christianity, and Islam, as well as important national days, and holidays for religious sects and ethnic minorities. There are historical sites where interfaith

Figure 7.1 Two Girls Reading Stories. *Source*: Photo Credit: Ben White—Unsplash.

activities were common in history with each tradition performing their rituals in nearby or the same places.

Judaic, Asian, and Islamic calendars are based on the lunar month. Since lunar months follow a full cycle of moon phases, each lunar month equals to about twenty-nine or thirty days. This is a concrete, visually observable calculation, as it is easy to mark the beginning of a new lunar month with the new crescent appearing in the night sky, with the full moon being in the middle of the month, and the waning moon through the end. Observing the skies and stories about the moon, sun, and stars are very common traditions in MENA cultures and can be integrated into STEM learning through children's literature (see figure 7.1).

EVALUATING AND SELECTING CHILDREN'S BOOKS ON MENA CULTURES

When it comes to deciding appropriate books for young children to learn about MENA cultures, educators may do well to have a critical perspective that avoids stereotypes and totalistic labeling of this diverse geography and its people. There are some stereotypes about Middle East culture stemming from centuries of imperialism and colonization of Middle Eastern indigenous lands by Western European forces (Gregg, 2005) as well as media portrayals about Muslims in the aftermath of 9/11; therefore, educators may benefit from clarifying some myths and understanding culture in the larger ecology of relationship, times, and interactions and in the local context. MENA cultures should not be represented by current social and political issues in the region

Educators may benefit from carrying an active sense of curiosity to find authentic and meaningful literature that represents interesting cultural aspects or characteristics of the MENA cultures while still focusing on the human experience. Particularly, literature covering current events or immigration experience should make strong ties with common human emotions, activities, and values such as family and hospitality, expressed in diverse contexts and events so that all learners can make connections to the topic and some learners are not singled out as involuntary representatives due to their appearance. Similarly, current MENA cultural practices in the region should not be expected to be replicated by immigrants to the United States who have hyphenated identities (Sirin & Fine, 2008) because of many years of living and raising generations in their new country. When thinking about multicultural events that use literature featuring MENA cultures, it may be important to take an approach that honors the culture but avoids a tourist approach by featuring a particular country, which the students who are asked to represent it may have never seen or lived in.

Another criterion for the selection of children's books depicting MENA cultures in the context of immigrant experience is that educators would do well to represent ideals of social justice and equity in addressing cultural diversity and resist expressions and representations that may advertently marginalize "other" communities as exotic, distant, different, or inferior.

For example, one prominent stereotype about Middle Eastern culture is the sense that women are oppressed in Middle East cultures. Several popular literature pieces, such as Breadwinner and Malala Yousifzadeh, may be taken to generalize a view toward women in the Pakistan/Afghanistan region or to be associated with a religion, while they actually depict a particular period, regional culture, geography, and the influence of specific marginal groups, and intend to focus on the fierce spirit of humans, especially girls, who still share the general mainstream cultural perspective, while resisting the attempts to silence women voices. It is important to note that women have a highly regarded value in traditional Middle Eastern cultures and in all the Abrahamic religions, especially as conceived in the role of mothers and in family as the protector, a compassionate guide, and the symbol of holiness. Girls are treasured and doted on, despite contemporary fundamental groups' efforts to narrow women's rights. Wearing head scarves or *hijab*, for instance, is a shared tradition in the Abrahamic religions and is often considered a symbol of independence and socialization by many women who practice it today, despite the stereotypical media portrayal. Educators may benefit from reviewing the texts to pay attention to these nuances, while avoiding a stereotypical depiction of diverse cultural groups in the region. For instance, when sexism or the issue of child marriage is mentioned in classroom discussions, similar examples from policies of other countries including the United States can be brought up to create awareness for this universal women's rights matter.

Similarly, educators would benefit from focusing on particularities and nuances within the diverse MENA cultures in terms of the idea of economic prosperity. MENA region is economically diverse, with each country having its own social and economic context in terms of income and varying degrees of urban, suburban, and rural living, with economic inequalities persisting just as in the United States. Current issues of political conflict, high unemployment rates, and economic struggle in poorer countries in the MENA region are coupled with extreme wealth and prosperity visible in other countries that have oil and other natural resources or countries with prospering democracies. Accordingly, the recent increase in the number of books treating the topic of recent immigration from the MENA region due to the political turmoil and civil wars should be taken with a critical eye to assess how it honors human experience and common human struggles. For instance, a well-chosen children's book may depict the process of political asylum which is escaping from persecution through noble ideals of freedom, equality, and human rights, and reflect the diversity of a large community fleeing for safety, including doctors, engineers, educators, and scholars who once had a happy and content life before their lives were shattered by war. Conversely, another book may simplify the main idea of asylum or immigration by depicting immigrants as just people trying to move into a prosperous life from a low-income country because of economic reasons, creating a biased or limited perspective. As the books focusing on immigration and refugee experiences increase in numbers in recent years, it is very important to develop a critical perspective and resist depictions and storylines insinuating White supremacist ideas.

Thinking about the representation of voices, educators benefit from assessing the quality of children's books portraying MENA region cultures through the lens of authentic ownership and authentic experience. Instead of merely accepting the ideas in a book with a tourist approach featuring the exotic representation of a cultural community at face value, educators may see if the author or the illustrator has firsthand experience understanding the culture and is able to represent complexity and nuances through text and/or the illustrations. These suggestions may help break cultural biases educators may have toward the literature focusing on the cultural heritage of the Middle East region.

Several new lines of work in children's literature in the MENA region explore ancient literature including myths, folktales, and biographical stories from history. This strand of creative work is rich and remains under-explored. Another growing theme in books inspired by MENA culture is the idea of acculturation and integration into American mainstream culture while carrying one's traditions, especially modeling these practices for young children to support positive cultural identities in the first- and second-generation immigrant families. While these books do not directly represent MENA cultures and traditions, many authors are still inspired by a desire to transform authentic traditions into the new culture and context.

USING AUTHENTIC MIDDLE EASTERN AND NORTH AFRICAN LITERATURE IN THE CLASSROOM WITH YOUNG CHILDREN

Educators may use authentic MENA literature in the classroom in many creative ways with many interdisciplinary connections. Below are some brief examples that may help practitioners guide young readers:

Nowruz: The New Year

Nowruz is the name of the new year in Iranian and Kurdish traditions, which occurs in the Spring equinox each year around March 23. There are so many celebrations around fire pits, rituals with symbols like goldfish, flowers, and certain dishes akin to contemporary Spring holidays. Educators may engage children in discussions on why the new year begins at the time of Spring equinox versus January 1st in this cultural tradition. Setting the stage with Solmaz Parveen and Tata Bobokhidze's The New Year's Goldfish: A Nowruz Story (2016), P–3 educators may open up children's explorations into the different times of the year when we celebrate the new year around the globe. New interdisciplinary connections such as writing poems for the new year with inspiration from the awakening earth and working with simple hands-on or virtual models of the earth and the sun to understand the concept of the seasons, light, and temperature are some examples of play-based inquires with young learners.

Hebrew, Arabic, Hieroglyphics, and Farsi Writing Experiences

Educators may benefit from exploring different alphabets of the MENA region, with many similarities and some differences in sounds and alphabet symbols shared across all scripts. They may be able to find, print, and laminate simple writing samples from these alphabets for young learners to trace, copy, and use in writing challenges. For example, young learners can be invited to make art connections in collaboration with the art teachers; they may make bookmarks, small patchwork napkins, and other art with letters from these scripts, such as floral and symbolic decorations existing in MENA region traditions. Two sample books to use for this approach include the Patchwork Torah by Allison Maile Ofanansky and Elsa Oriol (2014) and the Arabic Quilt: An Immigrant Story by Aya Khalil and Anait Semirdzhyan (2020).

Caring for Animals and Nature

Instead of planning for a generalist lesson about caring for animals and nature, educators may choose to include environmentalist and historical stories that focus on protecting valuable natural resources and helping animals in the backdrop of MENA cultures. Educators may help children discuss the similarities and differences between the current issues of the environment, such as the scarcity of clean water, animal welfare, or climate change in the historical context of the story. Children may be encouraged to take action to address a minor issue in their local community as a result of their reading and inspiration, such as making a visit, fundraising, or writing a letter to a leader. Some valuable reads for this line of learning experiences include The Cat Man of Aleppo by Irene Latham, Karim Shamsi-Basha, and Yuko Shimizu (2020), Suzanne Del Rizzo's My Beautiful Birds (2017), Evan Turk's The Storyteller (2016), and Tami Lehman-Wilzig and Tami Shuttlewood's Stork's Landing (2014).

Holidays, Feast, and Food

Educators may have much success exploring the theme of holidays, feasts and food with very young learners as it is a simple and easy concept to relate to MENA cultures through common human connections. Ramadan, Orthodox Noel, Rosh Hashanah, Passover, and Nowruz are examples of holidays where a reflection of community, family, unity, and diversity are encouraged. Therefore, this topic allows children to draw parallels among these faith traditions and go past beyond seeing them as incompatible or strange. Lesson plan ideas include but are not limited to following simple dessert recipes synonymous with holidays, such as macaroons, simple rice puddings, and pastry sheets filled with cream and fruit as small group experiences, and comparing and contrasting recipes from one country to another.

Self-Acceptance and Identity-Building

Educators may focus on the theme of overcoming challenges as another common human connection, especially as it relates to self-acceptance and cultural pride. Using children's literature examples such as Sigal Samuel and Vali Mintzi's Osnat and Her Dove (2021), and Malala Yousafzai and Kerascoët's Malala's Magic Pencil (2017), educators explore what it means to be able to pursue a dream and find one's way even though one may feel lonely and less liked at the time. Children may be encouraged to create mini-drama experiences where they enact some important scenes from these books and others with similar themes to develop empathy and strength in their imagination and reflect on their own cultural identities.

CHILDREN'S BOOKS ON MIDDLE EASTERN CULTURES TO START WITH

Samuel, S., & Mintzi, V. (2021). *Osnat and Her Dove: The True Story of the World's First Female Rabbi*. Levine Querido.

Jewish history and heritage are an important part of MENA cultures, and this book will add to the cultural diversity of the region. This book depicts the legendary life of the first-known female Rabbi, Osnat, who was born as a Kurdish woman in today's Iraq. Osnat lived a life of scholarship of Jewish scripture and defied gender norms when she took over her father's yeshiva, an orthodox Jewish school and temple. While telling Osnat's story, the book also introduces child-friendly Hebrew vocabulary and depicts beautifully illustrated Hebrew letters and scripture writings. This book is recommended for P–3 levels as a great introduction to Jewish history and legacy in the MENA region. Osnat and Her Dove received many accolades including the Canadian Jewish Literary Award and National Jewish Book Award Finalist and was listed among Evanston Public Library's 101 Great Books for Kids, School Library Journal Best of the Year, and Tablet Best of the Year.

Kimmel, E. A., & Rayyan, O. (2013). *Joha Makes A Wish: A Middle Eastern Tale*. Two Lions.

Eric Kimmel specializes in retelling folktales of diverse cultures to an American audience. This book is a good attempt to depict some stories of Nasraddin Hodja, a character much beloved by people in Turkey, Iran, and Central Asia. Besides the hiccup with the name, the author does justice to the lively spirit and humor that "Joha" possesses. The story is told against the historical backdrop of rural West Asia and has elements of magic, adventures, and twists. This book is recommended for P–3 levels.

Latham, I., Shamsi-Basha, K., & Shimizu, Y. (2020). *The Cat Man of Aleppo*. G. P. Putnam's Sons Books for Young Readers.

The Cat Man of Aleppo tells the story of young Alaa, who found himself in the middle of the Syrian War, later deciding to become an ambulance driver to help the people who are wounded. Street cats of Aleppo become a passion for Alaa when he discovered they too suffered from the war, often staying hungry. He challenges himself to find solutions with the help of others. This book is one of the best examples of addressing current political issues in MENA region, while focusing on the common themes of humanity, human vulnerabilities, resilience, and love in the worst circumstances, and still carrying the main elements of a great story such as connecting to our feelings and creating suspense and curiosity for the storyline and great resolve. The book is recommended for P–3 levels. Cat Man of Aleppo has received many accolades including the Caldecott Honor, the 2020 Middle East Book Award, the 2021 Bank Street Best Children's Book of the Year, the 2021 ALA Notable Children's Book, and the 2020 BCCB Blue Ribbon Book, as well as some important mentions such as the 2022 Texas Topaz Reading List Pick, the 2022 ALSC Notable Children's Recording, the 2021–2022 New York Three Apple Book Award Nominee, Ohio Buckeye Children's and Teen Book Award Nominee, and Missouri Dogwood Book Award Nominee.

Yousafzai, M., & Kerascoët (2017). *Malala's Magic Pencil*. Little, Brown Books for Young Readers.

This book depicts Malala Yousafzai's story in the context of a metaphor, a magic pencil. Inspired by a TV show with a boy who has a magic pencil, Malala uses this metaphor to talk about her resistance to oppression which is gently covered in an age-appropriate manner. The book is recommended for P–3 levels and received many recognitions including Jane Addams Children's Book Awards (2018), Rise: A Feminist Book Project Top Ten Commended for 2018, Junior Library Guild Selections (2018), and Notable Social Studies Trade Books for Young People (Women's History Selections, 2018).

Da Costa, D., Hu, Y-H., & Wright, C. V. (2008). *Snow in Jerusalem*. Albert Whitman & Company.

This story depicts life in today's Jerusalem and encourages a multicultural perspective on human experience in the city. Through the story of Avi and Hamudi, love for families, animals, and cultural practices are introduced as patterns of the same humanistic traditions. It may be intriguing for the young learners to know through the map depicting Jerusalem that the city indeed has four quarters: Armenian, Christian, Jewish, and Muslim. The story is recommended for P–3 levels. This book is included in CCBC Choices.

Parveen, S., & Bobokhidze, T. (2016). *The New Year's Goldfish: A Nowruz Story*. CreateSpace Independent Publishing Platform.

This picturebook with rich illustrations depicts the story of Keyan, who loses the goldfish the family is keeping for the Nowruz celebrations and chases it down the river. Goldfish is an important symbol and artifact for Persian and Kurdish celebrations of Nowruz, the Spring equinox. It is a tradition to watch the movements of the goldfish at the exact time of the equinox. Through Keyan's story, the book introduces the young readers to Iranian traditions. This book is suitable for P–3 levels.

Pellicioli, A., & Atilgan, M. (2020). *Song of the Old City.* G. P. Putnam's Sons Books for Young Readers.

With Merve Atilgan's vibrant illustrations, this book takes us to the heart of Turkey, the most famous and historical city, Istanbul. Istanbul sits on a bridge between Asia and Europe and has a rich historic landscape created by several civilizations, most notably the Roman Empire and the Ottomans. This book takes young readers on a tour of important landmarks in the city, while integrating a story of giving and kindness. The book is recommended for children at P–3 levels.

Behrangi, S., Mesghali, F., & Rassi, A. (2019). *The Little Black Fish.* Tiny Owl Publishing.

The Little Black Fish is an allegorical story that represents the struggle for freedom, free speech, and asserting one's identity. Behrangi was a literacy teacher and activist participating in the resistance toward the politics of the authoritarian Iranian government in the 1960s. The story elements are symbolic, but in the eyes of a young child, it is still a beautiful story of courage, strength, and curiosity that the Little Black Fish carried in exploring and learning about the outside world. The book is recommended for children at P–3 levels.

Lumbard, R. Y., & Horton, L. K. (2019). *The Gift of Ramadan.* Albert Whitman & Company.

The Gift of Ramadan by Rabiah York Lumbard is an interesting read about Ramadan that includes diverse perspectives and, through humor, tells about the challenges children experience as they begin practicing fasting. The book is recommended for children at P–5 levels.

Rechter, S., & Gerard, K. (2000). *The Girl From Over There: The Hopeful Story of a Young Jewish Immigrant.* Sky Pony Press.

While this chapter book is lengthy and appears to target an older audience, this new addition to Middle East literature is another story building on the immigration theme. The Israeli author Sharon Rechter wrote this story when she was eleven. The story focuses on a young girl, Miriam, who just immigrated from Poland after facing the horrors of Holocaust, the cold reception she got from her classmates, the animosity and jealousy one peer had toward her, and her struggle to build new friendships. This book is recommended for grades 2–7.

Del Rizzo, S. (2017). *My Beautiful Birds*. Pajama Press.

This book follows Sami's stories of the loss he endured when he left everything behind to flee the Syrian civil war with his family, especially his pigeons. In the refugee camp, Sami begins to see the light again, with the help of new friends, a canary, a dove, and a rose finch. The awards and recognitions for this book include but are not limited to Marilyn Baillie Picture Book Award Finalist (2018), Notable Books for a Global Society (2018), Middle East Book Award—Honor (2017), Junior Library Guild Selections—Multicultural (2017), the 2017 New York Times Notable Children's Books selection, Malka Penn Award for Human Rights in Children's Literature (2017), and the 2018 SCBWI Crystal Kite Award for Canada Winner. UNICEF USA Voice "The Perfect Gift for the Holidays: Books That Inspire" (2017) is recommended for K–5 levels.

Turk, E. (2016). *The Storyteller*. Atheneum Books for Young Readers.

This book tells the story of the ancient Kingdom of Morocco, which attracted people, storytellers, and merchants. At the core of the theme is the water, as a metaphor for quenching people's thirst, and stories as a metaphor for quenching people's thirst for words. With the magic of the words, a young boy and a storyteller came to the rescue of the city's people by first filling a bowl, then replenishing the city wells with water. The book is very rich in possible interdisciplinary connections with science, art, history, and the environment. The accolades for the book include the Children's Africana Book Awards (2017), ALSC Notable Children's Books (2017), Notable Children's Books in the Language Arts Award (2017), and Junior Library Guild Selection (2016). This book is recommended for P–5 grade levels.

Yuksel, M. O., & Aly, H. (2021). *In My Mosque*. Harper Collins.

M.O. Yuksel takes us to the colorful pages of a child's experience with mosques, which are broadly used as community centers for prayer, youth events, friendship gatherings, and celebrations. The text and illustrations show the diversity of traditions and people who can get together in mosques across their backgrounds, as well as inform the young readers about common practices in Islam. This book received many accolades including ALSC Notable Children's Books—commended (2022), CCBS Choices (2022), Recent Book Award Winners and Honorees—Honor (2022), Anna Dewdney

Read Together Award (2022), and School Library Journal Best Books of the Year (2021).

Lehman-Wilzig, T., & Shuttlewood, A. (2014). *Stork's Landing*. Kar-Ben Publishing.

Stork's Landing is an Israeli story that focuses on Jewish values of protecting nature and teaches young learners about the environment. Maya lives in a kibbutz (a special collective community) and observes a stork getting injured on its migration way from Africa to Europe which passes by the kibbutz. Maya and her father strive to find ways to help the stork get healed and even find foster babies to raise. This book is recommended for the P–3 levels.

Shamsi, S., & Mirza, M. (2022). *Zahra's Blessing: A Ramadan Story*. Barefoot Books.

In the tradition of growing Muslim American identities, Zahra's Blessing by Shirin Shamsi (illustrated by Manal Mirza) includes a bit more complexity and may be a good choice. Zahra's story of losing her favorite toy, then connecting with a refugee friend, is engaging and happens in the backdrop of Ramadan, adding to its meaning. This story is suitable for children at P–5 levels.

Shami, W., & Farouki, S. (2019). *Olive Harvest in Palestine: A Story of Childhood Memories*. Bowker.

The main theme of the story is helping young readers understand olive farming and how olive is grown and harvested and processed to be ready for the table through the memories of two young girls by also illustrating the landscape of Palestinian territories. Since olive farming is a significant part of the MENA region and Mediterranean cultures, this book makes connections to humor, joy, and community during this hard work, which makes it suitable for learning about trees and fruits at young ages.

Vafaeian, M., & Rassi, A. (translator) (2019). *The Parrot and the Merchant* (A Tale by Rumi). Tiny Owl Publishing.

Covering MENA cultures in children's books, I would be remiss if I did not mention Rumi, the highest-selling poet in the United States and a beloved figure for the MENA cultures. Rumi was a Sufi scholar, philosopher, and poet who lived in thirteenth-century Iran and Turkey and carried universal messages of spirituality, love, and self-growth. With bright colors and vibrant drawings, author and illustrator Marjan Vafaeian retells the famous story of Rumi, Mah Jahan, a rich merchant, who keeps her exotic birds in cages and is willing to grant a wish her talking parrot made, which will teach her much about life. This book was identified as USBBY Outstanding International Books (2020) and Read for Empathy Collection (2018). This book is recommended for P–3 levels.

Rumford, J. (2004). *Traveling Man: The Journey of Ibn Battuta 1325–1354*. Clarion Books.

The author James Rumford, who is also a world traveler, added so many interesting details to this book such as maps of the different regions of the world where Ibni Batuta, who is akin to Marco Polo for the MENA cultures, traveled in the fourteenth century. Young readers are encouraged to interact with Ibni Batuta's thinking and his journey through beautiful illustrations and intriguing ideas in the text. This book earned a few accolades, including the ALSC Notable Children's Books—commended (2002), CCBC Choices (2002), and the Middle East Book Award (2002).

CHILDREN'S BOOKS CITED IN THE CHAPTER

Khalil, A., & Semirdzhyan, A. (2020). *The Arabic Quilt: An Immigrant Story*. Tilbury House Publishers.

Ofanansky, A. M., & Oriol, E. (2014). *The Patchwork Torah*. Kar-Ben Publishing.

RESOURCES ON MENA CULTURES AND LITERATURE FOR CHILDREN

Some articles and websites to help educators further understand the culture, evaluate and select more children's books on the culture or group are listed below:

- Al-Hazza, T. C. (2006). *Arab children's literature: An update*. https://www.ala.org/ala/booklinksbucket/ArabChildrensLit.pdf.
- Samples and suggestions for using Israeli children's literature https://theicenter.org/icenter_resources/israeli-childrens-literature/.
- ThGhaeni, Zohreh. (2006). Children's literature in Iran from tradition to modernism. *Barnboken, 29*. DOI: 10.14811/clr.v29i1.95. Retrieved from https://www.researchgate.net/publication/314811528_Children's_Literature_in_Iran_From_Tradition_to_Modernism on June 1, 2022.

- Children's Picture Books: Stories About Characters Of Iraqi Ethnicity https://diversebookfinder.org/ethnicity/iraqi/.
- A blog post by Children's Library Lady https://childrenslibrarylady.com/books-for-ramadan-eid/.
- A critical discussion on Teaching for Justice geared toward educators teaching older children https://www.learningforjustice.org/magazine/teaching-about-ramadan-and-eid.
- A quick dive into the holidays dilemma by Anne O'Brien https://www.edutopia.org/blog/december-dilemma-religious-holidays-anne-obrien.
- Teaching While Muslim website has lesson plans about Ramadan across different grade levels https://www.teachingwhilemuslim.org.
- And this practical article by Louise Derman-Sparks and Julie Olsen Edwards at National Association for Education of Young Children's blog on anti-bias approaches to holidays https://www.naeyc.org/resources/blog/anti-bias-and-holidays.

REFERENCES

Cavanaugh, K. (2016). *The Politics of Identity: Minority Discourse in the MENA Region.* Retrieved from https://www.iemed.org/publication/the-politics-of-identity-minority-discourse-in-the-mena-region/ on June 12, 2022.

Gregg, G. S. (2005). *The Middle East: A Cultural Psychology.* Oxford University Press.

History. (2022). *Ancient Egypt.* Retrieved from https://www.history.com/topics/ancient-history/ancient-egypt on June 1, 2022.

Horesh, Uri. (2019). Languages of the Middle East and North Africa. In J. S. Damico & M. J. Ball (Eds.), *The SAGE Encyclopedia of Human Communication Sciences and Disorders* (pp. 1058–61). DOI: 10.4135/9781483380810.n349.

PBS. (2022). *Culture: A Rich Mosaic.* Retrieved from http://www.pbs.org/wgbh/globalconnections/mideast/themes/culture/ on June 20, 2022.

Pew Research Center. (2005). *Population Growth Projections 2010–2050.* Retrieved from https://www.pewresearch.org/religion/2015/04/02/middle-east-north-africa/ on June 15, 2022.

Sirin, S. R., & Fine, M. (2008). *Muslim American youth: Understanding hyphenated identities through multiple methods.* New York University Press.

Chapter 8

Caribbean Children's Literature
Melissa García Vega

•

UNDERSTANDING CARIBBEAN CULTURE

Through approaching the Caribbean region from a geographical perspective, picturebooks of and about this part of the world forge an inclusive context. The guiding questions, what does it mean to be from the Caribbean or to exist within the Caribbean, are embedded in the work of several luminary literary voices. A theoretical hermeneutics reflecting a Caribbean literary aesthetic invokes the following foundational Caribbean thinkers: Antonio Benítez-Rojo, Kamau Brathwaite, Edouard Glissant, Wilson Harris, and Sylvia Wynter. Much of their work largely stems from that of Frantz Fanon, the mid-twentieth-century psychiatrist and political philosopher, from the French colony of Martinique. Pairing their theoretical approaches elucidates how current children's literature advances a global understanding of the human experience while stories remain rooted in an island-specific awareness.

The geographical region has historically been described as: the Antilles distinguishing the Greater Antilles from the Lesser Antilles, the Leeward Islands, Leeward Antilles, and the Windward Islands. Other terms used to locate the region include the Caribbean Basin, Caribbean Lowlands, Caribbean Plate, Caribbean Sea, Caribbean South America, Latin America and the Caribbean, Southern Caribbean, Western Caribbean zone, and finally the West Indies. The access to water routes is a common feature when looking at a map of what constitutes the Caribbean region. The fluidity of water and culture is significant and reflects the dynamic influence the Caribbean region continues to have in our current world. The geographical region alongside the political and historical pathways specific to what comprises the Caribbean aid in understanding the common cultural features while also preserving the distinct identity of each place.

Specific to geographical proximity there are also several locations, as noted in table 8.1, within South American and Central American countries that reflect a Caribbean culture. There are also historical Caribbean ties within the coastal cities in the following US states: Florida, Louisiana, and Texas, which reflect a Caribbean aesthetic. I make a distinction between the historical relevance of these US states to Caribbean culture in the growing and current Caribbean diaspora presence in several other states.

Table 8.1 presents languages associated within the Caribbean region and provides an overview of the language used alongside the current political classification for each Caribbean space. There are sixteen sovereign countries within the Caribbean. I include Costa Rica and Panama as sovereign Caribbean spaces because of their proximity to the Caribbean, the historical relationship each has to the Caribbean community, as well as an overall cultural connection. There are sixteen islands identified as either dependencies or territories with historical and political ties to Western cultural powers, that is, Canada, France, Netherlands, the United Kingdom, and the United States.

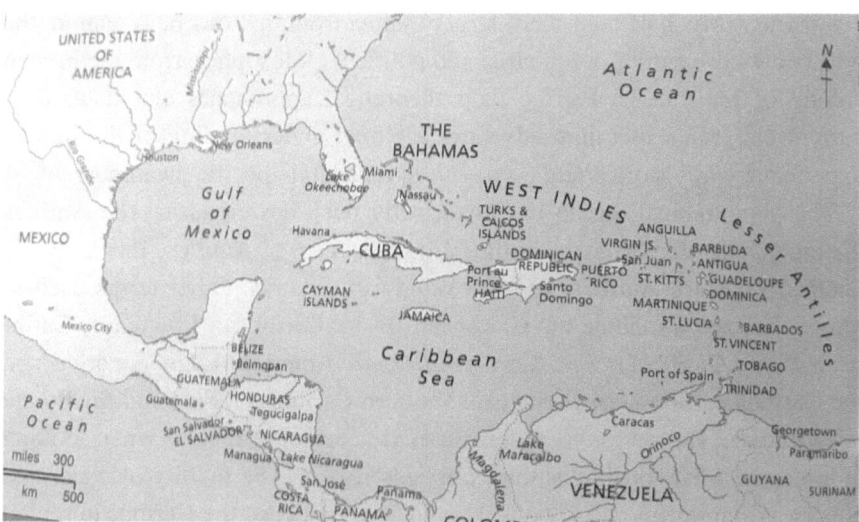

Figure 8.1 Map of the Caribbean. (Morgan, 1997).

Table 8.1 Languages Associated with the Caribbean Region

Spanish	French and Haitian Creole	English	Dutch and/or Papiamento
*Archipelago of San Andrés, Providencia & Santa Catalina - Colombia	Haiti (Creole & French)	Antigua and Barbuda	Aruba Papiamento
*Bay Islands - Honduras	French Guiana	Anguilla	Suriname
*Coastal Mainland States & Insular Region of Venezuela	Guadeloupe	Bahamas	Bonaire—Papiamento, Sint Eustatius & Saba—Dutch (BES islands)
Costa Rica	Martinique	Barbados	Curaçao Dutch, Papiamento & English
Cuba	Saint Barthelemy	Belize * several other languages such as Spanish spoken	Sint Maarten
Dominican Republic	Saint Martin	British Virgin Islands/BVI (Tortola, Virgin Gorda, Anegada and Jost Van Dyke)	
*Guatemala		Cayman Islands	
*Nicaragua Atlantic coast, Caribbean side		Dominica	
Panama		Grenada	
Puerto Rico		Guyana	
*Quintana Roo-Mexico		Jamaica	
		Saint Kitts & Nevis	
		St. Lucia	
		Montserrat	
		Saint Vincent & the Grenadines	
		Trinidad & Tobago	
		Turks & Caicos Islands	
		US Virgin Islands/UVI (St. Croix, Saint John, and Saint Thomas)	

Note: Sovereign countries listed within each language column are presented in red for contrast. The (*) identifies coastal areas within a country.

Apparent to the expansive space that reflects a Caribbean aesthetic is the diversity within the region in terms of language use, cultural influences, and status as either independent, dependent, or existing in relation to a European country. Inherent to centering a Caribbean epistemology is the coalescence of how the current Caribbean region may be understood through a cultural arts lens. The Caribbean as a region is an early example of multiculturalism, therefore, familiarity with literary Caribbeanists serves as a guide for classroom teachers.

In *Black Skin, White Mask* (1967) Frantz Fanon discusses how "Beside phylogeny and ontogeny stands sociogeny" (p. 11). Sylvia Wynter builds on Fanon's extension of how phylogeny pertains to a group of organisms evolving, with ontogeny presenting the developmental history of an organism within its own lifetime, to sociogeny, which looks at the origin or development of a person or thing as a result of social factors to distinguish a "sociogenetic principle" (2001, p. 31). Wynter's thoughts on how poetics serve to enact individuals to envision a new existence outline what it means to be human where a poetics of life reflects a literacy of the imagination.

Calling upon the imagination aligns Wynter's theory with the Guyanese writer, Wilson Harris, who explored how individuals counter an illiteracy of the imagination that requires an ability to read that goes beyond, what he calls, "a uniform kind of way, a uniform kind of narrative, a uniform kind of frame" (Harris & Bundy, 1999, p. 77). What and how current children's literature about and largely through Caribbean voices challenges or illustrates a break from a uniform way of understanding story illustrates the role children's literature serves to expand what it means to live in the twenty-first century.

Engaging young readers in Caribbean stories enacts Sylvia Wynter's advancement of Fanon's theory. Wynter guides an understanding of Caribbean culture through her labeling the "three intellectual revolutions that define our 'modern' world: the Copernican, the Darwinian, and the Fanonian" (Eudell & Allen, 2001, p. 7). Her proposal of the "After Man" formed by biology and mythology negates and ends the existence of a so-called "man" defined in Western terms. Children's literature centering on the Caribbean and its children is sowing the seeds for a deeper engagement with this third phase of understanding humanity.

Antonio Benítez-Rojo, the Cuban novelist and essayist, also explored the Caribbean in terms of a "big bang theory" (p. 55) where fragments of culture land in different directions. This cultural explosion resonates with what the French writer, from Martinique, Édouard Glissant, addressed as "the relationship between the center and the periphery [and how it] will be completely different" ("The Cultural 'Creolization' of the World" 2000). Benítez-Rojo (1996) speaks to this relationship in terms of cosmic explosion (p. 55). In discussing people(s) who fall under the heading of the Other, Glissant (2000) describes an archipelago that extends to the diaspora, therefore changing who is the Self and the Other. Glissant's proclamation of who forms the center and the periphery is in dialogue with Benítez-Rojo's description of creolization (2006, p. 55). The artistic creation that Benítez-Rojo outlines is present in the production of Caribbean children's literature.

The connection is also highlighted by Kamau Brathwaite, the Barbadian poet, academic, and recognized voice in the Caribbean literary canon who identified decades ago the need for "content curriculum research and its relationship to the embodying culture" (p. 6) in "Caribbean Man in Space and Time" (1975). Regardless of place and time, teachers in the classroom inhabit a space where personal beliefs from home meet public and national policy as Brathwaite depicts the intersection between the inner and outer realms of past and present society.

Postcolonial—Transnational

The Caribbean regional history has patterns of sustaining life that correlate with how successful learners build on their prior knowledge. Wynter's elucidation of how humanity and philosophy, over the ages, have evolved guide our understanding of where current societies reside within a rupture of a collective identity. Many books for children embody the fragments that have evolved from the collision of cultures throughout the Caribbean. Wilson Harris approached time and consciousness outside of a linear chronology, often within the natural environment which illuminates the role of setting/location within the story. Teague's (2021) recent discussion of "Narratives of African diaspora border crossings [that] disrupt stories of linear migration" (p. 35) also addresses a nonlinear use of time.

Upon the arrival of people and the sorting out of establishing homes throughout the Caribbean, Harris argues there was an interruption to the genesis of imagination. He addresses the idea of rupture from the perspective of how the human imagination grappled with the Middle Passage to the Americas. Wynter's call for how poetics enact individuals to bring something new into existence is an effort toward healing the rupture of what Teague (2021) outlines as "forced migration" (p. 35) to the current transnationalism, a dominant theme within Caribbean children's literature. Caribbean stories and storytelling foster a fulfillment of the genesis of imagination.

Using Wynter's theory for a human praxis in relation to children's literature enacts what Brathwaite calls "the inner metropole, with the ancestors" (p. 11). His conclusion that "The unit is submarine" (p. 11) calls on an educational grassroots movement where learning evolves between what the learner brings to a given pedagogical moment and what resources the teacher draws upon. Further exploration of what exists in the unit requires an understanding of the Caribbean region prior to the Middle Passage and colonial formation. Babacar M'Baye (2009) shows "Pan-African dimensions" (p. 19) across the Caribbean region related to the African folktale. Inherent to understanding Caribbean children's literature is the connection between enslaved people brought from African countries to the various island nations throughout the region. In the introduction to *African Diaspora: African Origins and New World Identities* (1999), the Nigerian scholar and novelist Isidore Okpewho traces the relationship between people from Africa and the Americas. Those who survived the Middle Passage to arrive in tropical and sub-tropical places such as the Caribbean region attempted to continue traditions in a new home with a somewhat familiar landscape. A Caribbean theoretical framework encompasses these diverse factors in understanding the relationship between a Caribbean aesthetic in children's books and how these books depict and address a variety of issues for young readers.

Voices such as Jan Carew (1977) and the fifteenth-century friar, Ramon Pane in *An Account of the Antiquities of the Indians: Chronicles of the New World Encounter*, edited by José Juan Arrom (1999) provide insight into how an Amerindian mythology pre-Western/Modern ethos existed. The experiential explanation of what occurred, how, and what was often lost, reflecting an Afro-Caribbean religiosity, is dominant in Caribbean literature for the adult reader and has a growing presence in picturebooks for young readers.

In discussing pedagogical instruction and curriculum within the Caribbean region, the oral tradition takes precedence and upon closer examination of the oral story, the role of spirituality is central. There is a wonderful presence in Caribbean children's literature of language rhythms, tone, and specific vocabulary that reflect a communal language use. Close textual analysis makes visible the permutations of Caribbean culture rooted in oral traditions. Veronica Chambers, Tami Charles, Lynette Comissiong, Nadia Hohn, Lynn Joseph, Tere Marichal, Valdene Mark, and Emma Otheguy are just some of the authors exploring and extending orality in their storytelling. Others such as Edwidge Danticat and Olive Senior author books for both adults and young readers.

What Are Authors Writing About?

Hutchinson and Snell in *Children and Cultural Memory in Texts of Childhood* (2014) present the relationship between collective experiences "and the operative structures, such as identity formation, patriotism, or political and moral values, through which cultural memory exists or operates" (p. 1). Much of Caribbean children's literature invites readers to interact with what Snell and Hutchinson call a "national past" (p. 8). Authors such as Michael Anthony, Petronella Breinburg, and Lynn Joseph translate to paper the oral stories passed from one generation to another in the Caribbean. For example, in *A Wave in Her Pocket* (1991), Lynn Joseph presents the manner and custom of a Tantie or elder woman, telling stories to children at gatherings. In her final story "The Bamboo Beads," the young narrator Amber learns how Tantie first met Papa Bois, described by Joseph as, "protector of the trees and animals in the woods . . . known to carry a cow's horn [to] blow it to warn animals of approaching hunters" (p. 47). Joseph's story shows how the family elder bears witness to the forest guardian Papa Bois. Joseph's story, *The Color of My Words* (2000), won an Américas Award for Children and Young Adult Literature and a Jane Addams Children's Book Award. Her stories reflect a Caribbean aesthetic through the oral use of language captured on the printed page.

Many stories present a complexity drawing on the oral tradition and local folk culture, while also speaking to the contemporary realistic features of growing up in the Caribbean today. Realistic fiction, biography, historical fiction, poetry, and folktales embody current themes to children. The presence of this growing collection of picturebooks centers on children growing up in the Caribbean or with Caribbean ancestry today and often in more than one language.

EVALUATING AND SELECTING CARIBBEAN CHILDREN'S BOOKS

Five guiding factors for evaluating and selecting Caribbean children's books are: (1) theme, (2) identity, (3) orality and language use, (4) history, and (5) setting. Determining what Caribbean children's literature books can best live in a P–3 classroom requires teachers to synthesize a historical understanding of the Caribbean region. This global history teacher knowledge aligns with various story themes and content. Universal experiences such as play, friendship, and family are often present and reflect the rich complexity of history and setting in relation to the natural environment. Equally significant to theme and setting is orality, a key lens through which evaluating Caribbean children's literature must be viewed. Finally, the status and/or role of identity in relation to nation, ethnicity, and/or race reflects the dynamic transnationalism inherent to the Caribbean experience at large.

Playing with Themes

Play is central to learning for young children and is present in the most engaging stories for children.

Several women throughout the Caribbean and/or currently living abroad born of Caribbean ancestry have authored books for young readers that reflect the distinct features of growing up within the region. For example, Lynette Comissiong through stories such as *The Parrots & Papa Bois* (2002) advances a greater awareness of the shared cultural links between the Caribbean islands across language traditions. Other authors such as Jamaican historian Suzanne Francis-Brown approaches traditions through a historical lens as in *The Mermaid Escapade* (2013).

Identity

The question of sovereignty and transnational identity is present in several stories that also address growing up, friendships, and deepening a sense of self and connection to others. The shared Caribbean culture for many children residing in the region or with Caribbean roots in the diverse diasporic communities reflects identity formations in progress. Many of the evaluation tools that support selecting a Caribbean children's text touch upon a colonial identity. Scholars, such as Clare Bradford, Greta Gaard, and Michaela Moura-Koçoğlu, address dominance and coloniality in discussing children's literature in ways that support the growing collection of Caribbean children's literature.

Orality and Language

Oral narrative plays an important role in Caribbean communities. Cynthia James in "From Orature to Literature in Jamaican and Trinidadian Children's Folk Traditions" (2005) shows how the West Indian children's folk tradition has evolved from a history of various peoples' arrival to the region (p. 165). Current children's book authors explore ways to combine oral and written stories as well as capture the diverse richness of language use. Children's literature, published within the last twenty years, builds upon the early phase of the oral tradition.

History

Enrique Perez Diaz acknowledges the impossible act of separating history from the culture with regard to children's literature in "Central and South America and the Caribbean" (*International Companion Encyclopedia of Children's Literature*, 1996). He cites the recent publishing presence after "five-centur[ies] of the New World being a meeting-place of cultures" (p. 883) invoking the interactions between Western countries and the societies they colonized. Although historically many colonies within the Caribbean region saw postwar independence, the decolonization process is still ongoing. Central to this decolonization are cultural identity formations.

The Natural Environment—Setting

Dobrin and Kidd, in their introduction to *Wild Things, Children's Culture and Ecocriticism* (2004), state, "children's texts . . . detect and combat cultural hegemony" (p. 9). Likewise, Greta Gaard (2008) suggests guiding questions for developing an ecopedagogy that addresses the natural world environment in stories for young readers. This perspective is important to the current global and regional ecology as well as relevant to the sustenance of the Caribbean as a whole.

See table 8.2 for guiding tools for P–3 classroom teachers to evaluate and select authentic children's books for examples of how story features engage readers in connecting to universal themes while specific to an island cultural experience. Furthermore, as teachers we can consider the patterns and commonalities across the themes in relation to key features of each school grade. Prominent themes are apparent across the sample collection of texts. For example, in pre-kindergarten classrooms, relationships; in kindergarten, growing up and body movement; in first grade, a transition to completing an activity independently; in second grade, an awareness of community leadership skills; and finally in third grade, a sense of community connection via multimodality.

Orality and language, history (both personal and public), the natural environment as setting, artifacts, and illustration are all indicators of the complexity of books about or created by Caribbean people for children. For children in the Caribbean or growing up within the Caribbean diaspora, these stories mirror realistic features of life today as well as of the past.

USING AUTHENTIC CARIBBEAN LITERATURE IN THE CLASSROOM WITH YOUNG CHILDREN

Caribbean children's books with an explicit relationship between orality and literacy offer an infinite number of opportunities for all young readers in a twenty-first-century world to see reflections of who they are as well as to explore their curiosity about the world outside their windows. Furthermore, within the context of centering a Black and/or Brown personhood story of and from the Caribbean presents how individuals feel connected, safe, and seen within communities that are familiar or new. Through these stories is an awareness of the commonalities among people, languages, and communities across the Caribbean region accessible to implement in lesson plan strategies and activities.

Most of the Caribbean children's literature presented here for use in the P–3 classroom bears a Caribbean diaspora experience and many of the writers/illustrators have connections within the diaspora as well as the island

Table 8.2 Guiding Tools for P–3 Classroom Teachers to Evaluate and Select Authentic Children's Books

Grade Level and Age	Themes What big questions does the text explore?	Identity Theme How does the child protagonist evolve?	Orality and Language How does the text sound and/or use sound to tell story?	History What facts does the text expand on or address?	The Natural Environment as Setting How does the context of place and time deepen meaning?	Artifacts What objects/tools connect readers to the characters and their stories?
Pre k Age 4	Friendship/Family/Ancestry Growing Up Fear	As a friend leaving/saying goodbye/new ways to communicate As the youngest in the family As a descendant of two cultures	Refrain rhyme; poetry	Present migration access to water, habits, and culture	Outside home Dominican landscape	Mango trees; carving in wood skin color
K Age 5	Family/Moving Transnationalism Crossing borders	As a child relocating with parents As a child growing up as a Black Cuban musician	Onomatopoeia: croac/coquí Boom, clap, shake rhythm of language; refrain: "Pitit, pitit, not just yet. Pitit, pitit, build your nest"; kompa music	Present migration PR/USA Cuba—Havana/NY/revolution, house, dad, and mom, community	Community PR/NYC Haiti house; town/marketplace	Bakery music songbird, sugar, Sonora Mantancera panye—basket; mouchwa—scarf

(continued)

Table 8.2 (Continued)

Grade Level and Age	Themes: What big questions does the text explore?	Identity Theme: How does the child protagonist evolve?	Orality and Language: How does the text sound and/or use sound to tell story?	History: What facts does the text expand on or address?	The Natural Environment as Setting: How does the context of place and time deepen meaning?	Artifacts: What objects/tools connect readers to the characters and their stories?
First Age 6	Growing Up/Independence Family Tradition Survival and Freedom History/Community Food	As a child learning to comb her hair As a child learning to cook As a child able to run errands alone	Positive adjectives *plena* music refrain cooking steps to *kompa* beat/ dancing/oral storytelling within the story	Change overtime with hairstyles grandmother/slavery/ revolution folklore figures/roots	Home community Haiti city; past scenes in plantation, revolution, battlefield on beach city block, town plaza in Puerto Rico	Hairbrushes, hairstyles, soup, dance, *kompa* music, *pilon; vejigante, pilon*; *vejigante*, mural, *plena* music, instruments
Second Age 7	Leadership, Taking Risks, Death	As a graceful child athlete as a creative poet/ performer as a community advocate	Verbs spoken language, eavesdropping name, cheers	Migration, school, key community figures accomplishments and in public service	Barbados, Brooklyn Jamaica, town bus, school, house Puerto Rico, baseball park	Postcards, trolley/ bus; balls, statistics, blessings

142   *Melissa García Vega*

	Growing Up Independence Family members Survival and Freedom History/Belonging	As a child dreamer-as an artist/poet/activist as a storyteller, Multilingual librarian and advocate within the community	Sounds in environment captured in poetry; *Ayiti* and talk back; proclamation, kids to come to library, spreads the word	Leading historical figures: pioneers within their cultural contexts—the first to do	New York, Haiti, community, home Harlem	Poetry, newspaper, history, brushes, pictures, and frames; *pilon*, library, candle
Third Age 8						

Figure 8.2 Under the Mango Tree. (Mark, V. et al., 2021).

culture. While discussing authenticity in literature involves a complex web of factors, this suggested list of stories to start with captures significant details in relation to the guiding tools for evaluation. Furthermore, the potential for building content knowledge alongside language development and establishing classroom community is present within each book.

Strategies for Classroom Teachers

Strategies to use Caribbean children's literature reflect a community-building project approach ethic. Teachers as facilitators of conversation set learning goals that exist alongside a school curriculum and standards specific to a grade. Particularly when working with multilingual learners as well as in an Early Childhood classroom is the role of language practice. With these two audiences in mind: young learners and/or learners thinking in more than one language learning goals/objectives for content knowledge and language practice allow for activities and strategies to be used in meaningful contexts. For example,

1. Cross-Language Strategies Teachers explicitly identify the similarities and differences between two languages side by side. There is an opportunity to transfer language skills from a home language to a target language successfully. Both oral language and printed text are accessible.

2. **Grouping for Peer Interactions** Student talk, where kids can ask specific questions and share answers with a larger group, enables authentic talk among children appropriate to their developmental age. Learning will mostly occur when kids are able to practice language use and build content knowledge with their classmates within a student-centered classroom. Constructing knowledge is a social activity.
3. **Multimodal Displays for Interaction** Teachers beginning a lesson will have materials prepared that support how they demonstrate a learning goal for kids. Thinking beyond the visual tools to engage all the senses as well as learning styles becomes possible in modal displays where kids are creating artifacts, hearing sounds while moving, exploring landscape environments to experience what feels different and/or the same, smelling and tasting fruits and vegetables specific to an environment, and finally having the opportunity to self-reflect as well as socially share their experiences.
4. **Sensorial Areas** in relation to multimodal displays identifying how senses engage with artifacts that are presented throughout a story. Inviting guests with direct experience and/or knowledge connected to the story. Listening to various voices on thematic topics expands a classroom learning community. Guests may be family members who reflect the roles present in stories as well as the larger community of leaders who facilitate an understanding of serving in public life.
5. **Question Types** Building on the rich oral and printed language opportunities throughout stories serves as conversation for learners and their teachers. Teachers using an interplay of open-ended and close-ended questions will generate talk about story themes and content. Teachers facilitate discussion in response to the diverse collection of stories. While some details will be familiar designing and using discussion questions can address how similarities and differences impact individuals and/or groups. Using a variety of question types lays the foundation for students later using a reader response approach as adult readers.

Activities with Caribbean Children's Literature

The following lesson plan examples, see table 8.3 lesson plans for implementing activities and strategies with children, showcase how Caribbean

Table 8.3 Lesson Plans for Implementing with Children: Activities and Strategies

Grade Level	Content Focus and Story Title	Grade Theme What are the big/essential questions?	Identity Theme How does the child connect using prior knowledge?	Objective What will the students be able to do? Students will be able to (SWBT)	Strategy What strategy will support students in meeting the objective?	Assessment How do I observe and measure student thinking and completing the lesson goal?
Pre k	Math/ELA Anna Carries Water	Relationships Where do we and/or objects we use fit in our lives?	As a member within a family and the age order as a person/living needs for water and various water uses	SWBT organize water collection containers by size. ELA speaking	Peer grouping will support students' problem solving how they order their containers and discuss how much water each containers holds	Students will present a size chart using containers
K	Physical Development/Science/ELA My Day with Panye	Movement How does balance work in my body in similar ways to objects around me?	As a child growing up and building body strength/ comparing objects for balance	SWBT walk and balance in various instances using objects as well as their bodies. ELA listening	Multimodal displays for interaction	Students will move in an interactive gallery walk showing how they balance objects using various scales or their own bodies

Grade	Subject / Book	Theme	Essential Question	Objective	Focus Area	Additional Objective
First	ELA/ELA *Sofi and the Magic, Musical Mural*	Growing Up Independent Tasks	What everyday activities/chores/tasks can I do on my own?	As a child learning to run errands alone such as buying something in the store, cooking, or daily hygiene self-care, i.e., brushing their hair	SWBT order, explain and <u>record</u> the steps for how to complete a task independently. ELA writing	Sensorial areas	Students will <u>compose</u> the procedural steps to complete a task
Second	S.S./ELA *Shirley Chisolm is a Verb!*	Leadership Models	When did you know you really enjoyed something? How did you begin practicing being your best at a skill?	As a child becoming good at something such as asking questions, forming opinions, playing a game reciting a poem, speaking up for a group such as friends, or community group	SWBT ask to <u>formulate and ask</u> interview questions. ELA reading	Question Types	Students will <u>use their interview questions</u> and <u>gather information</u> for a specific community member in their home or neighborhood

(continued)

Table 8.3 (Continued)

Grade Level	Content Focus and Story Title	Grade Theme What are the big/essential questions?	Leadership Tools Who inspires us to create? Where do we feel most happy to be? Why?	Identity Theme How does the child connect using prior knowledge?	Objective What will the students be able to do? Students will be able to (SWBT)	Strategy What strategy will support students in meeting the objective?	Assessment How do I observe and measure student thinking and completing the lesson goal?
Third	Art/Science/ELA Auntie Luce's talking paintings			As a child dreamer- as an artist/family member/ person connected to a community	SWBT <u>identify and create a profile</u> portrait of a person or place. ELA speaking	Cross language	Students will produce a profile <u>of a person or place</u> selecting from a variety of media: paint and brushes, collage, natural foliage specific to a place

148 Melissa García Vega

children's literature addresses essential questions specific to the age and grade level. For example, while Poet Louise Bennett Coverley is recognized for her oral performance skills throughout the Jamaican community, how she grew up and first began performing is wonderfully illustrated in *A Likkle Miss Lou: How Jamaican Poet Louise Bennett Coverley Found Her Voice* (2019) written by Nadia L. Hohn and illustrated by Eugenie Fernandes. Readers will learn and connect with how young Louise was curious about every sound around her. The narrator says, "words tickled Louise's ear, and like peanut drops they stuck . . . special words snuck into the margins of her notebook pages . . . and letters tasted like the crisp water crackers she loved to eat with Mummy's thick Saturday punkin soup." Later when she was in school, she would use her everyday experiences to tell stories and paint images with the words and sounds she loved so much. However, it is only after thinking, the support of her new schoolteacher, and her effort to practice that Louise finds the courage to perform poems she has composed herself.

Caribbean Children's Books to Start With in Grades P–3

As shown in table 8.2, guiding tools for P–3 classroom teachers to evaluate and select authentic children's books, the relationship between history and the story setting is central in stories that reflect the Caribbean experience. Authors and illustrates embed the complexity of a colonial past in ways that engage the nuance of the diverse roles within a colonial society where racial hierarchy informed practices, yet a fluidity of how people built their own meaning and formed individual identities despite colonial oppression is present for young readers to understand a recent past. For example, illustrations in *Freedom Soup* (2019) and *Martí's Song for Freedom/Martí y sus versos* (2017) present children engaging with slavery in direct ways. The young girl serving the soup to the three white people is in the background as Ti Gran tells Belle the story of how Freedom Soup came to exist in Haiti. The illustration serves as a mental image of how Belle composes the images in her mind. Likewise, we see the young José Martí witnesses people forced to labor in the sweltering Caribbean sugarcane fields. The narrator tells us how the image angers José Martí so as a child his commitment to social justice is formed.

P–3 classroom teachers evaluate and select authentic children's books with attention to how stories work together. A comprehensive collection of children's books continues to grow for use in all classrooms for all children.

While many of the stories have been awarded and recognized for how Black and Brown children are centered in stories, the overall Caribbean story for children presents themes significant to all readers.

Recio, S., & McCarthy, B. (2020). *If Dominican were a color*. Simon & Schuster Books for Young Readers.

Book Summary

A poetic description of how colors connect and help us describe our identity. Recio uses figurative language to connect with the landscape of the Dominican environment. References to the ancestral relationship between the Haitian and Dominican cultures are made. There is an author's date explaining how Recio was inspired to create this book.

Awards

2021 Américas Award Honorable Mention (Simon & Schuster Books for Young Readers, 2020)
Notable Social Studies Trade Books for Young People, 2015–2022 Geography, People, Places Selection, 2021
Recent Book Award Winners and Honorees Third Place Winner, 2021
Notable Children's Books in the Language Arts Award, 1997–2022
International Latino Book Awards, 2000–2021; Third Place Winner, 2021
Grade Level Recommended: Pre-kindergarten–Kindergarten; Ages four to eight

Senior, O., & James, L. (2018). *Anna Carries Water*. Jacana.

Book Summary

A fun story of growing up where Anna aspires to balance a water container on her head like her older siblings. Rich, rhythmic, and playful language is used to narrate Anna's feelings. Language repetition highlights the daily need for water "water for cooking . . . cleaning teeth and for washing dirty feet."

Awards

Winner of the Isabel Sissons Canadian Children's Story Award
Shortlisted for the Kirkus Prize 2014 (Young Reader's Literature)

Nominated for the 2014 Rainforest of Reading Award "100 Magnificent Children's Books 2014" (Picturebook for ages two to six), Schools Library Journal
Listed on New York Public Library's "100 Titles for Reading and Sharing"
Grade Level Recommended: Pre-kindergarten–Kindergarten; Ages four to seven years

Mark, V., & Cloud, S. (2021). *Under the mango tree.* Sugar Apple Books.

Book Summary

Readers see how two young girls become good friends. Their play space is in connection to the mango tree, and it becomes their third friend. The common refrain, "Under the mango tree we will always be," is used throughout even when one friend must say goodbye because her family is moving away. In the final scene, we see the two girls pictured in different locations speaking to each other via digital technology. Sugar Apple Books was started by Valdene Mark and gives special consideration to international authors from the Caribbean region and diaspora.

Grade Level Recommended: Pre-kindergarten–Kindergarten; Ages four to seven years

Brown, M., & López Rafael. (2017). *My name is Celia the life of Celia Cruz = me Llamo Celia: La Vida de Celia Cruz.* Luna Rising.

Book Summary

Several wonderful picturebooks tell the story of who was Celia Cruz. Here, Monica Brown uses rich language presented in playful fonts to communicate movement. There is a consistent use of onomatopoeia (boom, clap, shake) and rhythmic repetition of key phrases such as "all of the children of the Americas" that are natural invitations for a performance read alouds.

Awards

Pura Belpré Awards, 1996–2022 Illustrator Honor, 2006
Américas Award, 1993–2022 Winner, 2004
Grade Level Recommended: Kindergarten; Ages five to eight years

Charles, T., & Palacios, S. (2021). *My day with the Panye.* Walker Books Ltd.

Book Summary

Fallon, a young girl, gets her turn to accompany her mother to the town market. She watches and mimics her mother getting ready by trying to wear her *mouchwa* (scarf) in the same way and place the *panye* (basket) on her head. Fallon's mom tells her "Pitit, pitit, not just yet. Pitit, pitit build your nest" and describes how "we move gracefully." Rhythmic language and environmental sounds, such as "tap-tap bus chug-a-lugs by, carrying people with sun-beaten faces full of laughter louder than a rooster's crow" immerse readers in walking alongside Fallon. The Author's Note tells us how carrying a panye is ancient, familiar worldwide, and done by both female and male people of all ages.

Awards

Grade Level Recommended: Kindergarten; Ages five to nine years

Perez, N. (2021). *Coquí in the city*. Dial Books for Young Readers.

Book Summary

This realistic fiction story has one fantastical detail. The main character Miguel is a young boy who lives in San Juan and carries his *coqui*, pet, everywhere. Miguel finds out that he and his parents will move off the island and he must leave his beloved friend along with his grandparents. Two settings are developed through illustrations rich with detail and symmetry showing a street in San Juan and New York. While available in Spanish the English book version uses lots of descriptive Spanish vocabulary and sound language to support meaning supported by detailed illustrations.

Awards: Pura Belpre honors for both Author and Illustrator at the 2022 ALA Youth Media Awards
Grade Level Recommended: Kindergarten; Ages four to seven years

Ortiz, R. M. (2015). *Sofi and the magic, musical mural*. Arte Público Press.

Book Summary

Young Sophie is first seen bored, lying on her bed, and readers are told she is bored. While walking to the corner New York City store to buy milk, she pauses in front of a large mural of musicians, dancers, and a *vejigante*, a Puerto Rican folklore figure. Soon she becomes the *vejigante* dancing to *plena* music with rhythmic words sung in repetition plays and flying, as the *vejigante*, over different island landscapes such as El Yunque (the rainforest), waterfalls, and to the Southern coasts along the Caribbean Sea. Sophie's imagination is immersed in music, movement, and language.

Awards: International Latino Book Awards, 2000–2021 Second Place Winner, 2016
Grade Level Recommended: Kindergarten; Ages five to eight years

Charles, T., Alcántara Jacqueline, & Turpin, B. (2020). *Freedom soup*. Findaway World, LLC.

Book Summary

Readers first see how Belle gets to help her grandmother, Ti Gran, make Freedom Soup for New Year's Day in her apartment. Ti Gran dances and tells Belle the recipe steps while illustrations of sounds and language twirl around them in the kitchen. Sound words are present throughout and cooking tools sing, such as the pilon, "Click! Clack!" "to the kompa beat." Once the soup is set to boiling, begins her oral story saying, "Oh, Belle. Nothing in this world is free, not even freedom." Belle snuggles with her Ti Gran as they discuss how the tradition has been passed down through generations. Belle will continue and is complemented by her extended family who all come to share and have Freedom Soup.

Awards

We Are Kid Lit Collective Summer Reading Lists, 2015–2022 Selection, 2021
Junior Library Guild Selections, 2012–2022 Multicultural Selection, 2020
Notable Children's Books in the Language Arts Award, 1997–2022
Jane Addams Children's Book Awards, 1953–2022 Finalist, 2020
Américas Award, 1993–2022 Commended, 2020
Notable Social Studies Trade Books for Young People, 2015–2022
World History & Culture Selection, 2020
Grade Level Recommended: Grade 1; Ages five to nine years

Senior, O. (2019). *Boonoonoonous hair*. Tradewind Books.

Book Summary

When Jamilla's mother looks for the comb to plait her hair, Jamilla points to her stuffed animal elephant and shouts the animal is hiding the comb as did the camel, and other bedroom animals. Told in rhyme, we see Jamilla unhappy and hear her cries complaining its hurts to plait her hair. Her mother tells her in rich rhythmic descriptive language about how her hair can be different every day of the week. The word "boonoonoonous" is declared at the end of the week as Jamilla is ready for the first day of a new school year. Continuing in rhyme, Jamilla's mom tells her when she is busy to ask her big sister for help "electric, kinetic, Bombastic, fantastic, Twirly, whirly, curly, fuzzy, snappy, nappy, Wavy, crazy . . . boonoonoonous hair."

Chambers, V., & Baker, R. (2020). *Shirley Chisholm is a verb!* Dial Books for Young Readers, an imprint of Penguin Random House LLC.

Book Summary

Born in New York, Shirley Chisholm's mother was from Barbados, and her father was from Guyana. The biography begins with how "words become magical." The verb "CONNECT" is used within the text but is presented in capital letters and a contrasting color blue. Each page forward has verbs highlighted in the same manner throughout the text. Transitions from saying, "Verbs are words that move the world forward" to how Shirley and her family understood the idea of moving, the illustrator uses a postcard template to show the two Caribbean islands where Shirley's parents come from alongside New York City. Readers next see how Shirley and her sisters traveled on a ship back to Barbados to live with their grandmother while their parents could work more hours to save money and buy a home. Growing up in the Caribbean, Shirley is surrounded by extended family and attends school. There are thirty-one verbs highlighted across the pages that detail her accomplishments. In a personal note from the author, the legacy of Shirley Chisholm makes clear how she continues to impact the present.

Awards

Septima Clark Book Award, 2019–2022 Honor, 2021
Jane Addams Children's Book Awards, 1953–2022 Finalist, 2020

Grade Level Recommended: Grade 2; Ages four to eight years

Perdomo, W., & Collier, B. (2016). *Clemente!* Square Fish.

Book Summary

Clemente is a boy named after his father's hero Roberto Clemente, the Puerto Rican baseball legend. Using rhythmic poetry with a metered arrangement of descriptive language readers learn simultaneously how Clemente worships his namesake and why. In the end, we see mom hugging her son, saying, "And that, my love . . . is why we named you Clemente." A timeline of Roberto Clemente's life and notes from the author and illustrator are provided at the end of the book.

Awards

Américas Award, 1993–2022 Winner, 2011
Grade Level Recommended: Grade 2; Ages six to ten years

Hohn, N. L., & Fernandes, E. (2020). *A Likkle miss Lou: How Jamaican poet Louise Bennett Coverley found her voice.* CNIB.

Book Summary

How Louise Bennett finds her voice to become a national treasure in Jamaica is told in this poetic biography. From the first page and throughout the text and illustrations show how young Louise loved the word. Rich language captures the joy and curiosity the young girl had toward learning about her world. Phrases such as "words tickled Louise's ear, and like peanut drops they stuck," "special words snuck into the margins of her notebook pages," "words dance through the walls lively," and "The letters tasted like the crisp water crackers she loved to eat with Mummy's thick Saturday punkin soup" all describe in correlation with illustrations the passionate play that would later become the adult performer known as Miss Lou.

Book Summary

In this portrait of Pura Belpré readers learn about how she gathered all children to listen to stories in the library. Pura Belpré acted on her awareness of how public spaces such as the library should reflect the people living within a community. Her historical role as a Puerto Rican librarian in New York captures how orality and language use exist in relation to literacy. The author tells us, "But Pura knows that not all the stories worth telling are in books." Throughout the story, readers are asked questions such as, "Why aren't Abuela's stories on these shelves?" We also see how Pura prepares for storytelling by rehearsing sounds, gestures, and melodies. The emphasis on oral storytelling and composing is also contextualized in the environment and times of the Harlem Renaissance. Likewise, Belpré's training and efforts "to reshape library policy" are present so that her legacy as a community leader for all children resonates in our present world.

Awards

Orbis Pictus Award, 2000–2022 Commended, 2022
Recent Book Award Winners and Honorees Commended, 2022
Grade Level Recommended: Grade 3; Ages five to eight years

Otheguy, E., Domínguez Adriana, Vidal, B., Otheguy, E., Otheguy, E., Martí José, & Martí José. (2019). *Martí's song for freedom = martí y sus versos por la libertad*. Library Ideas, LLC.

Book Summary

This bilingual text with Spanish and English presented on each page tells the biography of José Martí.

Emphasis on how he formed his identity growing up in Cuba highlights the historical divisions between white and Black Cubans in the nineteenth century. Narration supports reader's understanding that Martí's empathy and respect for all life were born in him as a child. Likewise, his commitment and passion for social justice are narrated as part of his daily experiences and paired with excerpts from his published poetry.

Awards

CCBC Choices Selection, 2018
Américas Award, 1993–2022 Commended, 2018
Junior Library Guild Selections, 2012–2022 Spanish Selection, 2017

SLJ Best Books of the Year, 2010–2021 Selection, 2017
Grade Level Recommended: Grade 3; Ages seven to twelve years

Latour, F., & Daley, K. (2018). *Auntie luce's talking paintings*. Groundwood Books.

Book Summary

Ti Chou travels alone to Haiti to visit her aunt, her mother's sister, who paints and tells Ti Chou stories about Haiti. When Ti Chou asks, "When mom left for the States, why didn't you come?" Her Auntie Luce says how she and her sister are different. Perspective, within individuals, family members, and in general are present throughout this historical fiction story. Readers are invited to see the diverse angles and stories within the history of Haiti through Ti Chou's eyes. Ancestry and history engage the young girl in determining who she is, "In my face, I see colors I've never seen in a mirror—the caramel in my great-grandmother's skin and the deep berry in my grandfather's." Ti Chou explores her identity and private self as well as the public Haitian history.

Awards

Skipping Stones Honor Awards, 1994–2022 Multicultural and International Honor, 2019

CCBC Choices Selection, 2019
Outstanding International Books, 2006–2022 Grades K–2 Selection, 2019
Américas Award, 1993–2022 Honor, 2019
Grade Level Recommended: Grade 3; Ages four to eight years

RESOURCES ON CARIBBEAN CULTURE AND LITERATURE FOR CHILDREN

Articles

Caregiver guide Sofi and the Magic, musical mural . . . arte público press. (n.d.). Retrieved July 30, 2022, from https://artepublicopress.com/wp-content/uploads/2020/04/Sofi_CG_v3_2020.pdf.

Edward, S. (n.d.). *Cultural authenticity in the emerging Caribbean Picturebook aesthetic.* Cultural Authenticity in the Emerging Caribbean Picturebook Aesthetic |

Small Axe Project. Retrieved July 30, 2022, from http://www.smallaxe.net/sxsalon/discussions/cultural-authenticity-emerging-caribbean-picturebook-aesthetic.

Emma Otheguy. Teacher Guides and Lesson Plans | Martí's Song for Freedom. (n.d.). Retrieved July 26, 2022, from https://www.leeandlow.com/uploads/loaded_document/455/ MARTISSONGFORFREEDOM_ TeachersGuide.pdf.

Portnoy Brimmer, A. (2019). Let me write it first, and I'll tell you what it is later: An interview with Willie Perdomo. *CENTRO: Journal of the Center for Puerto Rican Studies, 31*(1), 87–102.

Tami Charles - Candlewick press. (n.d.). Retrieved July 25, 2022, from https://www.candlewick.com/book_files/0763697494.btg.1.pdf.

Zapata, A. (2022). (Re)animating children's aesthetic experiences with/through literature: Critically curating Picturebooks as sociopolitical art. *The Reading Teacher, 76*(1), 84–91. https://doi.org/10.1002/trtr.2128.

Books

Pura Belpré, & Sánchez-González Lisa. (2013). *The stories I read to the children: The life and writing of pura belpré, the legendary storyteller, children's author, and New York Public librarian.* Center for Puerto Rican Studies.

Websites

Anansesem. (2021, April 17). *The Caribbean Children's Literature Magazine.* Retrieved July, 2022, from http://www.anansesem.com/.

2022 International Latino Book Awards. (n.d.). Retrieved July 1, 2022, from https://www.latinobookawards.org/.

Academy of American Poets. (n.d.). Poets.org. Retrieved July 1, 2022, from https://poets.org/poet/willie-perdomo.

Admin, M. C. (n.d.). *Chla Home.* ChLA Home. Retrieved July 1, 2022, from https://www.childlitassn.org/.

Americas award. Americas Award @ CLASP, Consortium of Latin American Studies Programs. (n.d.). Retrieved July 17, 2022, from http://www.claspprograms.org/pages/detail/37/Americas-Award.

An engaging collection of resources that brings books to life. TeachingBooks. (n.d.). Retrieved July 12, 2022, from https://www.teachingbooks.net/.

Back to Main Site. (n.d.). *Home: Diverse bookfinder collection analysis tool (CAT).* Home|Diverse BookFinder Collection Analysis Tool (CAT). Retrieved July 25, 2022, from https://cat.diversebookfinder.org/.

Belpré, P., White, C. C., & New York Public Library (n.d.). *Guide to the Pura Belpré Papers 1897–1985 (bulk 1930s–1985) 1989–03.* Centro de Estudios Puertorriqueños.

Retrieved July 25, 2022, from https://centropr-archive.hunter.cuny.edu/sites/default/files/faids/belpref.html.

Black Hair in Children's Literature: Children's Books - Research guides: Home. Libraries. (n.d.). Retrieved July 20, 2022, from https://libguides.bc.edu/.

CentroPR. (2020, April 28). *SOFI and the Magic, musical mural - book reading.* YouTube. Retrieved July 19, 2022, from https://www.youtube.com/watch?v=PN2z5ZqTWck.

Change, T. for. (2022a, July 28). *Guide for selecting anti-bias children's books.* Social Justice Books. Retrieved July 28, 2022, from https://socialjusticebooks.org/guide-for-selecting-anti-bias-childrens-books/.

Change, T. for. (2022b, May 6). *Puerto Rican children's literature.* Social Justice Books. Retrieved July16, 2022, from https://socialjusticebooks.org/puerto-rican-childrens-literature-social-justice-bibliography/.

Children's Literature Center (Rare Book and Special Collections Division, library of Congress). (n.d.). Retrieved July 17, 2022, from https://www.loc.gov/rr/child/.

Clas Book Box K-12 Guide 1: Exploring Latin America in PictureBooks and poetry: Auntie luce's talking paintings. Research Guides. (n.d.). Retrieved July 14, 2022, from https://guides.osu.edu/c.php?g=1093627&p=7979161.

Colours of Us. (2022, June 16). *50 children's books set in the Caribbean.* Colours of Us. Retrieved July 17, 2022, from https://coloursofus.com/36-childrens-books-set-in-the-caribbean/.

Digital, S. (n.d.). *An academic study of the Universal Periodic Review (UPR) from the perspective of children's rights.* Save the Children's Resource Centre. Retrieved July 12, 2022, from https://resourcecentre.savethechildren.net/document/academic-study-universal-periodic-review-upr-perspective-childrens-rights/.

Hare, P. (n.d.). *Best spanish language picture book award.* Bank Street College of Education. Retrieved July 14, 2022, from https://www.bankstreet.edu/library/center-for-childrens-literature/best-spanish-language-picture-book-award/.

Home. Celeli Facultad de Educacion. (n.d.). Retrieved July 19, 2022, from https://educacion.uprrp.edu/celeli/.

Home Page. Cooperative Children's Book Center. (2022, July 25). Retrieved July 20, 2022, from https://ccbc.education.wisc.edu/.

Jacqueline Alcántara Illustration. (n.d.). Retrieved July 16, 2022, from http://jacquelinealcantara.com/.

Jdubin. (2022, May 22). *Pura Belpré Award.* Association for Library Service to Children (ALSC). Retrieved July 16, 2022, from https://www.ala.org/alsc/awardsgrants/bookmedia/belpre.

Journal 2019. Journal 2019 | Centro de Estudios Puertorriqueños. (n.d.). Retrieved July 16, 2022, from https://centropr-archive.hunter.cuny.edu/publications/journal-2019.

Kalyn. (2018, March 11). *¡mira, look!: Martí's song for Freedom / Martí y sus versos por la libertad*. Vamos a Leer. Retrieved July 21, 2022, from https://teachinglatinamericathroughliterature.wordpress.com/2018/04/30/mira-look-martis-song-for-freedom-marti-y-sus-versos-por-la-libertad/.

Latinxs in kid lit. Latinxs in Kid Lit. (n.d.). Retrieved July 23, 2022, from https://latinosinkidlit.com/.

Laura James. The Interior Beauty Salon. (n.d.). Retrieved July 23, 2022, from https://www.interiorbeautysalon.com/laura-james.

Luci soars. Lulu Delacre. (n.d.). Retrieved July 25, 2022, from https://www.luludelacre.com/lulu-delacre.

Nadia L. Hohn. (n.d.). Retrieved July 25, 2022, from https://www.nadialhohn.com/.

Notable Children's recordings. Notable Children's Recordings | Awards & Grants. (n.d.). Retrieved July 17, 2022, from https://www.ala.org/awardsgrants/notable-childrens-recordings.

Pura Belpré. (n.d.). Retrieved from https://vimeo.com/328854020.

Sugar apple books. Sugar Apple Books. (n.d.). Retrieved July 15, 2022, from https://sugarapplebooks.com/.

Teaching for change. Teaching for Change. (n.d.). Retrieved July 15, 2022, from https://www.teachingforchange.org/.

The best in Caribbean books from Caribbeanreads. CaribbeanReads. (2022, May 16). Retrieved July 20, 2022, from https://www.caribbeanreads.com/books/.

Welcome! The tiny activist. (2022, March 4). Retrieved July 16, 2022, from https://thetinyactivist.com/.

Welcome to book connections! Sign In. (n.d.). Retrieved July 16, 2022, from https://www.bookconnections.org/signin.cgi?op=signout.

Young Children - Books & Media. SNL IN HISD. (n.d.). Retrieved July 18, 2022, from https://www.studentsneedlibrariesinhisd.org/young-children---books--media.html.

YouTube. (n.d.). *Center for puerto rican studies-centro*. YouTube. Retrieved July 19, 2022, from https://www.youtube.com/user/CentroPR.

YouTube. (n.d.). *Sankofa read aloud*. YouTube. Retrieved July 18, 2022, from https://www.youtube.com/c/SankofaReadAloud/videos.

REFERENCES

Aggs, P., & Jenai, M. (2022). *Shirley Chisholm*. Sunbird Books.

Brathwaite, K. (1975). Caribbean man in space and time. *Savacou, 11–12*, 1–11.

Brown, M., & López Rafael. (2017). *My name is Celia the life of Celia Cruz = me Llamo Celia: La Vida de Celia Cruz*. Luna Rising.

Carew, J. (1977). The fusion of African and Amerindian folk myths. *Caribbean Quarterly*, 23(1), 7–21. https://doi.org/10.1080/00086495.1977.11671909.

Chambers, V., & Baker, R. (2020). *Shirley Chisholm is a verb!* Dial Books for Young Readers, an imprint of Penguin Random House LLC.

Chambers, V., & Maren, J. (2008). *Celia Cruz, queen of salsa*. Puffin Books.

Chanda, T. (2000). The Cultural 'Creolization' of the World: Interview with Edouard Glissant. Label France, 38.

Charles, T., Alcántara Jacqueline, & Turpin, B. (2020). *Freedom soup*. Findaway World, LLC.

Charles, T., & Palacios, S. (2021). *My day with the Panye*. Walker Books Ltd.

Comissiong, L. (2002). *The parrots and Papa Bois*. Macmillan Caribbean.

Denise, A., & Escobar, P. (2019). *Planting stories: The life of librarian and Storyteller Pura belpré*. Harper.

Fanon, Frantz. (1967). *Black skin, white mask*. New York: Grove.

González Lucía, M., & Delacre, L. (2017). *The Storyteller's candle = La velita de los cuentos*. Children's Book Press, an imprint of Lee & Low Books Inc.

Harris, W., & Bundy, A. J. M. (1999). *Selected essays of Wilson Harris: The unfinished genesis of the imagination*. Routledge.

Hohn, N. L., & Fernandes, E. (2020). *A Likkle miss Lou: How Jamaican poet Louise Bennett Coverley found her voice*. CNIB.

James, C. (2005). From orature to literature in Jamaican and Trinidadian children's folk traditions. *Children's Literature Association Quarterly*, 30(2), 164–78. https://doi.org/10.1353/chq.2005.0025.

Latour, F., & Daley, K. (2018). *Auntie luce's talking paintings*. Groundwood Books.

MacCann, D., & Smith, K. C. (2005). "This quest for ourselves": Essays on African and Caribbean children's literature: Introduction. *Children's Literature Association Quarterly*, 30(2), 137–139. https://doi.org/doi:10.1353/chq.2005.003.

Mark, V., & Cloud, S. (2021). *Under the mango tree*. Sugar Apple Books.

M'Baye, B. (2011). *Trickster comes west: Pan-African influence in early black diasporan narratives*. University Press of Mississippi.

McKittrick, K., O'Shaughnessy, F. H., & Witaszek, K. (2018). Rhythm, or on Sylvia Wynter's science of the word. *American Quarterly*, 70(4), 867–874. https://doi.org/10.1353/aq.2018.0069.

Okpewho, I. (2013). *African oral literature: Backgrounds, character, and continuity*. Indiana University Press.

Okpewho, I., Davies, C. B., & Mazrui, A. A. A. (2002). *The African Diaspora: African origins and new world identities*. Indiana University Press.

Olmos Margarite Fernández, & Paravisini-Gebert, L. (2011). *Creole religions of the Caribbean: An introduction from Vodou and santería to Obeah and Espiritismo.* New York University Press.

Ortiz, R. M. (2015). *Sofi and the magic, musical mural.* Arte Público Press.

Otheguy, E., Domínguez Adriana, Vidal, B., Otheguy, E., Otheguy, E., Martí José, & Martí José. (2019). *Martí's song for freedom = martí y sus versos por la libertad.* Library Ideas, LLC.

Pané Ramón, & Arrom José Juan. (1999). *An account of the antiquities of the Indians: Chronicles of the new world encounter.* Duke University Press.

Perdomo, W., & Collier, B. (2016). *Clemente!* Square Fish.

Perez Diaz, E., & G. Bannister Ray, S. (1996). Central and South America and the Caribbean. In P. Hunt (Ed.), *International companion encyclopedia of children's literature* (pp. 883–892). Routledge.

Perez, N. (2021). *Coquí in the city.* Dial Books for Young Readers.

Pimentel, A. B., & Morales, M. (2021). *Pura's cuentos: How pura belpré reshaped libraries with her stories.* Abrams Books for Young Readers.

Platt, K. I., Dobrin, S. B., & Kidd, K. (2004). Environmental justice children's literature: Depicting, defending and Celebrating Trees and Birds, colors and People. In *Wild things: Children's culture and ecocriticism* (pp. 183–97). Wayne State University Press.

Recio, S., & McCarthy, B. (2020). *If Dominican were a color.* Simon & Schuster Books for Young Readers.

Rojo Antonio Benítez. (2006). Part I society. In *The repeating island: The Caribbean and the Postmodern Perspective* (pp. 33–72). Duke University Press.

Russell-Brown, K., & Velasquez, E. (2020). *She was the first! The trailblazing life of shirley chisholm.* Lee & Low Books Inc.

Sciurba, K., & Rodriguez, E. (2007). *Oye, Celia! A song for Celia Cruz.* Holt.

Senior, O. (2022). *Boonoonoonous Hair.* Tradewind Books.

Senior, O., & James, L. (2018). *Anna carries water.* Jacana.

Teague, L. T. (2021). Not American enough: African diaspora, unfinished migrations, and transnational children's literature. *Journal of Children's Literature*, 47(2), 35–47. https://doi.org/ISSN 1521-7779.

Weikle-Mills, C. (2019). The obscure histories of Goosee Shoo-shoo and Black Cinderella: Seeking Afro-Caribbean children's literature in the nineteenth century. *Children's Literature*, 47(1), 57–78. https://doi.org/10.1353/chl.2019.0004.

Williams, A., & Harrison, A. (2021). *Shirley Chisholm dared: The story of the first black woman in Congress.* Anne Schwartz Books, an imprint of Random House Children's Books, a division of Penguin Random House LLC.

Wynter, S. (2013). Chapter 2: Towards the sociogenic principle: Fanon, identity, the puzzle of conscious experience, and what it is like to be "Black." In *National identities and sociopolitical changes in Latin America* (pp. 30–66). Routledge.

Wynter, S., & Corona-Gutiérrez, I. (1991). Tras el "hombre," su última palabra: Sobre el posmodernismo, Les Damnes y el Principio Sociogénico. *Nuevo Texto Crítico*, 4(7), 43–83. https://doi.org/10.1353/ntc.1991.0013.

Chapter 9

Books, Gender, and Sexuality in the Early Grades

Kate E. Kedley

UNDERSTANDING AND DEFINING LGBTQ+ IN EDUCATION: INDIVIDUALS, COMMUNITIES, AND THE LAW

For many, the idea of talking about gender and sexuality to children in the early grades (K–3) often leads to shock or reluctance (Hermann-Wilmarth & Ryan, 2019). Gender and sexuality (especially gender diversity and LGBTQ+ issues) are also topics that parents don't believe belong to classrooms. Teachers may believe the topic is too polarizing to include through texts or classroom discussions, even in older grades (Najarro, 2021; Rhoden, 2022).

However, informal and formal conversations about gender and sexuality ARE present in schools, even in elementary classrooms and as early as kindergarten! Students are grouped in boy-girl pairings, or divided into groups: boys on this side, girls on that side. Friendships are closely monitored (by children's peers and adults alike), especially as the children get older and if a boy spends "too much" time with only girls, or vice versa. And playground chants (like the one that suggests two children are sitting in a tree, K-I-S-S-I-N-G) are closely linked to (hetero)sexuality (Kedley, 2015). Bathrooms (and laws that are implemented to segregate bathrooms by sex, or women's and men's spaces) are separated to "protect" women and girls from the men and the public at large (Rhodan, 2016). Thus, these conversations (about sex and gender) are happening in schools in heteronormative ways that make some forms of gender and sexuality appear "normal" and "natural" but make gender fluidity and minoritized sexualities (like gay, lesbian, or bisexual) appear offensive, controversial, odd, and wrong.

The acronym LGBTQ+ (lesbian, gay, bisexual, transgender, queer, plus) is likely both familiar to and the source of confusion for many teachers and educators. Many may not understand the acronym itself (is the "Q" for questioning or queer? Why is there sometimes an "I" for intersex?). Newer teachers, especially, may have concerns about how to engage parents and students with topics surrounding the LGBTQ+ community, or how to work through conflict when the topic comes up. Others may be unclear about the responsibilities of teachers and the importance of including texts and critical conversations about gender and sexuality, even within the earlier elementary grades.

For the purposes of defining LGBTQ+ for this chapter, it is important to note that within the LGBTQ+ acronym, three of the letters stand for sexualities (lesbian, gay, bisexual), and one letter—the T—stands for gender identity (transgender). The Q (for queer) represents a flexible umbrella term that rejects stable identity categories (Weise, 2021). The "plus" sign acknowledges there are identities that are not binary and may sit outside the categories indicated. Thus, two distinct identities (sexuality and gender) have been grouped together in one acronym. Sexualities (lesbian, gay, bisexual) are ways of categorizing people into who they would be or desire to be romantically coupled with. Alternatively, gender identity (like transgender) is an individual's sense of who they are in terms of their gender; this could mean someone conceptualizes themselves as male, female, or a person who doesn't fit into either of those categories (or shifts between them). Gender identity is different than the sex one was assigned at birth (usually "girl" or "boy," based on genitals).

In terms of contemporary LGBTQ+ topics in education: just in 2022, Florida and other states in the United States implemented dangerous and dehumanizing bills that are nicknamed "Don't Say Gay" laws. These laws restrict the use of books with LGBTQ+ content and ban school conversation or instruction about sexual orientation or gender identity. Some teachers were even told to not use rainbow articles of clothing or have pictures of their same-sex spouses on their tests (Lavietes, 2022).

The reluctance of teachers to teach LGBT topics in K–12 classrooms is well-researched and documented (Hermann-Wilmarth & Ryan, 2019; Thein, 2013). And lawmakers and policymakers are restricting these topics from classrooms, which results in teachers being even more reluctant. However, teachers have an obligation to meet the needs of all students. No matter the opinion of a teacher on transgender students or gay marriage, it is still a teacher's responsibility to meet the needs of all students. And the reality is that some students will need to see positive representations of same-sex families and engage in conversations about gender diversity. Thus, it is a teacher's responsibility to look for ways to support the needs of these students.

EVALUATING AND SELECTING LGBTQ+ CHILDREN'S BOOKS

Literature that represents LGBTQ+ families, adults, and children in the early elementary classroom is integral to children learning about the diversity and depth of the human experience and possibility. Books can serve as "windows" into other cultures for children who aren't familiar with them and "mirrors" that allow students to see themselves and their lives represented in text (Bishop, 1990). However, as Tschida et al. (2014) note, if teachers simply provide one or two books (or stories) about a group of people, there is a "danger of the single story" (Adichie, 2009). Adichie (2009) says that offering a single story about a culture or group of people can lead to a viewpoint of others as monolithic or stereotypical, and instead of students learning and appreciating new cultures, they can become more entrenched in negative misunderstandings.

Thus, when a teacher or classroom offers texts as "windows" and "mirrors," the teacher also must offer critical facilitation, so students do not think the "*one* story is the *only*" story (Tschida et al., 2014). To conclude, in choosing LGBTQ+ books for the classroom, it is important to combine the windows and mirrors idea while considering the danger of providing students with a one-dimensional viewpoint or perspective. Instead, teachers should choose diverse texts within the category of LGBTQ+ families, individuals, and lives. As Hermann-Wilmarth and Ryan (2019) note, it is "particularly helpful to identify books that show characters of different races, classes, religions, and gender expressions" (p. 20).

Finally, the simple physical presence of these books in a classroom is not enough to challenge dangerous heteronorms or narratives about how gender should look or what gender is (Hermann-Wilmarth, 2010; Kedley, 2015;

Ryan & Hermann-Wilmarth, 2019). Parents, community members, and even state governments may reject the presence of books with LGBTQ+ themes in schools; the 2019 COVID pandemic put parents in closer contact with the materials and texts their children were using, as children spent more of the school day in the house, and their materials were scanned or put online (Winter, 2022). This is why an active engagement, facilitation, and participation from the teacher are necessary when talking about literature with LGBTQ+ themes in the early grades. Teachers must also take an active role in advocating for their presence in the K–3 classroom, and challenge those—from parents and administrators to lawmakers—who would remove these books from the classroom.

USING AUTHENTIC LGBTQ+ LITERATURE IN THE CLASSROOM WITH YOUNG CHILDREN

Many books about LGBTQ+ topics are best read with elementary students with some sort of critical facilitation by a teacher or adult. Because LGBTQ+ people and communities are frequently marginalized, students may bring negative stereotypes and feelings about the themes and people in the books; a teacher can help children students work through these topics, unpack stereotypes, and humanize characters. Having the books in the classroom, and given them space to be read a visibly, shows students that the teacher values this community and these topics.

But having a book available in the classroom is only one step; choosing a book with LGBTQ+ themes or characters for a classroom read aloud allows students to "literally and figuratively hear voices that have too often been silenced in schools" (Ryan & Hermann-Wilmarth, 2019, p. 313). Read aloud "work well for exploring LGBTQ+ topics because they are teacher-mediated" (p. 313). With read aloud, teachers can model honest thinking, share background knowledge, and scaffold for new or challenging ideas. Think aloud, additionally, can model a teacher thinking about reading, predicting, questioning, or applying prior experiences (Block & Israel, 2004).

As noted earlier in this chapter, Tschida et al. (2014) suggest that if supplying a limited number of stories about LGBTQ+ themes, communities, and people, a teacher runs the risk that students see the LGBTQ+ community as monolithic. Thus, it is important to offer a variety of stories about LGBTQ+

people—books with different types of families, people, adventures, and challenges, so students see the LGBTQ+ community as dynamic and diverse. Include on the classroom shelf books with LGBTQ+ characters who are of different races, genders, and classes, from different regions, and with different themes.

LGBTQ+ CHILDREN'S BOOKS TO START WITH

Baldacchino, C., & Malenfant, I. (2014). *Morris Micklewhite and the Tangerine Dress*. Groundwood Books.

Morris—an early elementary-grade student—has a favorite piece of clothing during playtime and from the dress-up box: a tangerine-colored dress. He likes the way it sounds and feels and looks on him. Morris' classmates remark on Morris' choice in a negative way, and Morris is sad and embarrassed. He spends a day at home with his mom. His mom encourages Morris to be who he is, and when he returns to school, he challenges the idea that dresses are only for girls. Morris' peers see how happy he is and realize clothes don't have a gender. **Recommended for grades 1–3.**

Ford, J. R., Ford, V., & Harren, K. (2021). *Calvin*. G.P. Putnam's Sons Books for Young Readers.

Calvin is a boy who was assigned a girl at birth. But soon he realizes he is a boy, and he tells his parents about his desire for new clothes, a new haircut, and a new name. His family, friends, and school celebrate these changes in Calvin's life as an exciting step forward while supporting him and helping him feel comfortable sharing his news. **Recommended for K–3.**

Gonzalez, M. C. & S. G. M. (2020). *They, She, He Easy as ABC*. Reflection Press.

Maya Cristina Gonzalez has many radical picturebooks and is well-known as an author. This book covers a topic that is frequently in the news but rarely talked about in early elementary classes: pronouns. This collaboration with Matthew SG on pronoun use and gender fluidity is a great way to introduce the words used to refer to other people in a picturebook with rhymes. Introducing pronoun use as flexible—and not automatically linked to sex assigned at birth—is a way to familiarize young children with gender fluidity. Students can also learn to use parts of speech in a practical way. **Recommended for K–3.**

Hall, M. (2015). *Red: A Crayon's Story.* **Greenwillow Books.**

Red: A Crayon's Story is a go-to gift for elementary teachers and young children alike. Red is a blue crayon that is labeled red. Although all the other crayons believe Red will color on paper with the color red, Red knows he is really blue. After lots of suggestions from the other colors on how to draw in the color red, they eventually accept and celebrate that Red is actually a blue crayon. This is a great book for teaching classes at the university level, and to perform a think aloud or read aloud with. **Recommended for K–3.**

Hernandez, M., & Gomez. (2020). *Federico and All His Families.* **NubeOcho.**

This story about a street (or in this case, a roof) cat named Federico will appeal to younger children. Federico spends his day visiting all the families in the neighborhood where he lives and loves. The families he visits are made up of all sorts of combinations of adults, children, and generations. The families love Federico, and Federico loves the families, and this story shows how love exists in all sorts of relationships. This is a board book, and thus the recommendation is for the early grades or before. **Recommended for K–1.**

Herthel, J., Jennings, J., & McNicholas, S. (2014). *I am Jazz.* **Dial Books.**

I Am Jazz is an older text but is on this list because it has been a frequent recipient of book bans and book challenges (https://bannedbooksweek.org/banned-spotlight-i-am-jazz/). Thus, it is important to promote this book and the story of Jazz Jennings. The book is based on Jazz' real life—from being assigned a boy at birth, but knowing she was a girl. Jazz also had a reality television show and she and her family are spokespersons and activists for the movement. **Recommended for grades 1–3.**

LaCour, N., & Kaylani, J. (2022). *Mama and Mommy and Me in the Middle.* **Candlewick.**

Young adult books are what Nina LaCour usually writes, but here she ventures into the realm of children's picture books. This book features a family with two moms. One of the moms must be away from home for a week, and the daughter in the family misses her terribly. She is relieved when she comes home that the family is back together again. This book is notable because it is a family story. **Recommended for K–3.**

Lil Miss Hot Mess & De Dios Ruiz, O. (2022). *If You're a Drag Queen and You Know It.* **Running Press Kids.**

In 2015, Drag Queen Story Hour (DQSH) was started in San Francisco. DQSH "captures the imagination and play of the gender fluidity of childhood and gives kids glamourous, positive, and unabashedly queer role models" and allows children to "see people who defy rigid gender restrictions and imagine a world where everyone can be their authentic selves" (https://www.dragqueenstoryhour.org/). Because drag queens (and kings) represent fun, bold gender play, the book *If You're a Drag Queen and You Know It* will be fun in a classroom with active and energetic elementary students. The book uses drag performers as characters to get students to dance, shake, twirl, and laugh. **Recommended for K–3.**

Lukoff, K., & Kaylani, J. (2019). *When Aidan Became a Brother.* **Lee & Low Books.**

This 2019 selection was a Stonewall Book Award Winner from the American Library Association, among other accolades. As Aiden, the main character, grows, he realizes he is a boy (and not a girl, as he was labeled at birth). Then his parents tell Aiden he is going to be a brother, and Aiden embraces the new and exciting role. This is a great representation of gender-affirming parents in a classic "new baby" story. **Recommended for K–3.**

McGinty, A. B., & Roberts, D. (2022). *Bathe the Cat.* **Chronicle Books.**

Any child who has ever played with a cat will enjoy reading *Bathe the Cat*. In a biracial family led by two dads, the family cat needs a bath and the house needs to be cleaned. But the cat refuses and finds ways to both avoid the bath and disrupt the cleaning. This story presents the gay dads as just another fun and loving family. Teachers looking for ways to present authentic LGBTQ+ families in literature through picturebooks and in the classrooms would appreciate this book. It would also be a great gift for your family members and friends looking to diversify and build homebook collections. **Recommended for K–3.**

Sullivan Wild, C., & Chua, C. (2022). *Love, Violet.* **Farrar, Straus, ad Giroux.**

Valentine's Day in many spaces across the country celebrates heterosexual love and homosocial friendship. This book, however, celebrates elementary student Violet's sweetness and love for classmate Mira and expands definitions of what friendship and love can look like for children; the story offers an alternative to the boy-girl dynamic that is ever-present in typical Valentine's Day celebrations. This book is a 2022 Lambda Literary Award Finalist. **Recommended for K–3.**

Twill, J., Bundo, Marlon, & Keller, E. G. (2018). *Last Week Tonight With John Oliver Presents a Day in the Life of Marlon Bundo.* **Chronicle Books.**

This book details the life of the Vice President's bunny who lives in Washington DC. Soon, Marlon Bundo—the pet bunny—falls in love with another boy bunny and they want to get married. However, there are some people in the government who want to stop boy bunnies from marrying other boy bunnies. Marlon and his friends work to get acceptance for all, and eventually, he marries the boy bunny he loves. This book has a back story, but it isn't necessary to know the back story to enjoy the book (google it!). There is also an audio recording of the book that is useful for read aloud. Adults may like the story as much as younger kids. **Recommended for grades 1–3.**

Instructional Activity: with *Red: A Crayon's Story* (Hall, 2015)

Red: A Crayon's Story is a perfect picture book for a "think aloud" activity with younger students, especially in kindergarten or first grade. However, this book certainly does not be excluded from older elementary-grade classrooms. To perform the think aloud with this text, follow the steps outlined below:

- Read through *Red: A Crayon's Story* and become familiar with the story. Especially think about how this story relates to gender identity and gender roles.
- Choose a focused question to "think aloud" with your group of students.
    - For the purposes of this example, the think aloud question will be: *What does this remind you of in real life? Can you think of any times in your*

life where someone feels different inside than how other people think they are or should be?
- Designate three to four places in *Red: A Crayon's Story* where you can stop the read aloud with your class and have a brief discussion. Ideally, these spots are places in the book that will generate discussion from your group of students if you ask them to answer the question: *What does this remind you of in real life? Can you think of any times in your life where someone feels different inside than how other people think they are or should be?*
- As you read aloud, stop at the designated spots to ask the students the question. Share your own "thinking" first to prompt the students to share. Students may share their own incidences when they were told they were one thing, but they believe they are another thing. Perhaps students believed they are old enough to do something, but adults believed they were not. Or perhaps children liked a certain type of clothing, but their parents or guardians required them to use different clothing. Repeat this discussion at the three to four designated spots of the book, tailoring the question and discussion to the students' responses.
- If students don't bring up gender identity in the discussion, that is OK. However, teachers may ask students if they have heard of gender roles and gender diversity and can prompt students to think about what it means when a child might feel like one gender, but others believe and treat the student as if they are something else. From past experience, students frequently are able to share examples of times they were expected to act a certain way ("like a boy" or "like a girl") even though they didn't feel it was natural or how they wanted to act.
- Continue critically discussing this theme—of feeling one way but being treated another, of gender roles, and of gender diversity—throughout the year, and revisiting the theme of *Red: A Crayon's Story*.

RESOURCES ON LGBTQ+ CULTURE AND LITERATURE FOR CHILDREN

An easy way for a teacher to keep up with the current relevant news on LGBTQ+ children's books is by following the chatter on social media (Twitter, Instagram). This is a quick way to engage in the topics teachers are currently talking about, find out what books are newly published, and follow along with what books are being targeted for challenges. This also allows the teacher to be informed enough to advocate for books and topics at their own school and in their own classroom.

Second, there are many award lists and websites to keep up with what book activists and experts are saying. "We Need Diverse Books" offers a blog and other materials on contemporary publishing and text issues (https://diversebooks.org/). Lambda Literary (https://lambdaliterary.org/history-mission/) is an organization that "has championed LGBTQ+ books and authors" for over thirty years and offers books lists annually. The American Library Association (https://www.ala.org/awardsgrants/stonewall-book-awards-mike-morgan-larry-romans-children%E2%80%99s-young-adult-literature-award) also offers annual recommended reading lists and awards for books with LGBTQ+ topics, including the Stonewall Book Award.

Finally, there are a number of literacy scholars who do research on the topic of LGBTQ+ books, literacy, and elementary classrooms. These book activists and teachers can be followed on social media. Teachers can request copies of their books or articles through a local or school library, and keep up with the latest LGBTQ+ children's literature news and research through these channels.

REFERENCES

Adichie, C. N. (2009, July). The danger of a single story. *TED Talks.* https://www.ted.com/talks/chimamanda_ngozi_adichie_the_danger_of_a_single_story/transcript?language=en.

Bishop, R. S. (1990). Mirrors, windows, and sliding glass doors. *Perspectives*, *6*(3), ix–xi.

Block, C., & Israel, S. (2004). The ABCs of performing highly effective think-alouds. *The Reading Teacher*, *58*, 154–67. DOI: 10.1598/RT.58.2.4.

Hermann-Wilmarth, J. M. (2010, January). More than book talks: Preservice teacher dialogue after reading gay and Lesbian children's literature. *Language Arts*, *87*(3), 188–98.

Hermann-Wilmarth, J. M., & Ryan, C. L. (2019). Reading and teaching the rainbow: Making elementary school classrooms LGBTQ-inclusive. *American Educator*, *43*, 17–22.

Kedley, K. E. (2015). Queering the teacher as a text in the English language arts classroom: Beyond books, identity work and teacher preparation. *Sex Education: Sexuality, Society, and Learning, 15*(4), 364–77. DOI: 10.1080/14681811.2015.1027762.

Lavietes, M. (2022). Florida house passes 'Don't say gay' bill. *NBC News*. https://www.nbcnews.com/nbc-out/out-politics-and-policy/florida-house-passes-dont-say-gay-bill-rcna17532.

Najarro, I. (2021). Teachers are divided on teaching LGBTQ topics. *EdWeek*. https://www.edweek.org/leadership/educators-divided-on-whether-schools-should-teach-about-lgbtq-topics-survey-finds/2021/12.

Rhodan, M. (2016). Why do we have men's and women's bathrooms anyway? *Time*. https://time.com/4337761/history-sex-segregated-bathrooms/.

Rhoden, G. (2022). Florida isn't the only state pushing legislation that could harmful to LGBTQ students. *CNN*. https://www.cnn.com/2022/03/10/us/states-anti-lgbtq-legislation-florida/index.html.

Ryan, C., & Hermann-Wilmarth, J. M. (2019). Putting read-alouds to work for LGBTQ-inclusive, critically literate classrooms. *Language Arts, 96*(5), 312–17.

Thein, A. H. (2013). Language arts teachers' resistance to teaching LGBT literature and issues. *Language Arts, 90*(3), 169–80.

Tschida, C. M., Ryan, C. L., & Ticknor, A. S. (2014). Building on windows and mirrors: Encouraging the disruption of "Single Stories" through children's literature. *Journal of Children's Literature, 40*(1), 28–39.

Weise, J. (2021). Queer. In Strunk, K. K., & Shelton, S. A. (Eds.), *Encyclopedia of queer studies in education* (pp. 484–489). Brill.

Winter, J. (2022). What should a queer children's book do? *The New Yorker*. https://www.newyorker.com/news/annals-of-education/lgbt-books-kids-ban.

Chapter 10

Sharing Lived Dis/ability Experiences with Young Children through Picturebooks

Monica C. Kleekamp

UNDERSTANDING LIVED DIS/ABILITY EXPERIENCES

"I know they're not little. That's just how I think of them." Spoken by a school principal, these words referred to high school-aged students with complex support needs who primarily accessed special education services in an isolated classroom within her school building. How did fourteen- to twenty-one-year-old students arrive within their secondary setting and come to be described as "little"? What leads to dis/abled young adults and adults being infantilized, or perpetually positioned as child-like?

Considering how dis/ability is positioned in schools is an important place to begin in answering these questions. Though this example occurred in a secondary setting, the importance of unpacking what dis/ability is, how it is represented in picturebooks, and in what ways it can be shared with children in PK–3 settings is a timely and relevant justice-oriented discussion to support children who will later be the adolescents filling these secondary halls.

What is dis/ability? The ever-evolving answer(s) to this question depend widely on an individual's experience with dis/ability. Historically, dis/ability has often been described from the medical model as an abnormality located within an individual person (e.g., early childhood student) objectively described by a neutral party (e.g., medical doctors, school psychologists).

This dis/abled part may be within the person's mind (e.g., intellectual dis/abilities, autism) or body (e.g., physical dis/abilities) (or both). The goal of the medical model is to remediate that which is ailing inside the dis/abled person (Haegele & Hodge, 2016; Shakespeare, 2017). This process may include any wide range of professionals including doctors, nurses, therapists, special education teachers, and the like with the ultimate goal of supporting the individual in becoming as close to *normal* as possible.

When described this way, dis/ability sounds like something to be pitied. Dis/ability is positioned like a disease, evoking feelings of sympathy for those unfortunate enough to have been *infected.* Often unconsciously, and perhaps benevolently intended, these ideologies seep into every part of society, including the school system. Comments like the one the principal made in the opening paragraph may look egregious, but these ideas are not uncommon. That principal's words represent a lifetime of being socialized into thinking that dis/ability was something that keeps an individual perpetually child-like. Each of the students she referenced had been unable to arrive at some version of *normal* according to society's standards.

While this description of dis/ability remains dominant within educational spaces, there is also an alternative view of dis/ability worth considering. Everything in society from grocery stores to schools to playgrounds has been designed and constructed over time with certain people in mind—*normal* people. From the start, ways of moving around and communicating within these spaces have been pre-defined without dis/abled people in mind.

The social model of dis/ability argues that while the lived experiences of being dis/abled may result in daily challenges, the reason so many barriers to participation exist for dis/abled people results from the ways society was initially constructed (Meekosha & Shuttleworth, 2017). In other words, if, from the outset, educational spaces had been designed with every possible student who might move through the space in mind, inclusion would be a much easier process. Instead, because all facets of society were socially constructed based on normalized expectations for the body and mind (or bodyminds) (Price, 2015), inequities for those who live on the *disabled* side of the able/disabled dichotomy enter every facet of daily life.

Throughout this chapter, readers will notice the use of the slash (i.e., "/") within the word dis/ability. The use of the slash is intentional to draw readers' attention to the way *ability* and *disability* are always being socially constructed. Readers will also notice that identity-affirming language (i.e., dis/abled, autistic) is regularly used as opposed to person first language (i.e., person with a disability, person with autism) (Andrews et al., 2019). This is intentional.

For some time, dis/abled people and scholars have written about the importance of recognizing dis/ability as an integral aspect of one's identity. For example, autistic individuals often describe autism as central to one's personhood. There is not a person and then autism sitting next to a person, but rather, the two are interwoven. With the rise of social media in the twenty-first century, there continue to be more and more dis/abled people sharing their lived experiences through various platforms championing this language. Therefore, to honor those perspectives, the same language will be used here.

The remainder of this chapter will focus on what these ideas about dis/ability mean when sharing literature with young children. Though dis/ability is a complex topic, much like racism, homophobia, and the array of other isms and phobias discussed in this book, young children have proven time and time again that they are capable of navigating complex social topics (Beneke et al., 2022; Vasquez, 2014; Vehabovic, 2021; Wargo, 2019). Therefore, this chapter will focus on the *what* and the *how* of those conversations, centering sample texts for teachers to share as well as examples of these texts in action in classrooms.

EVALUATING AND SELECTING CHILDREN'S BOOKS FEATURING DIS/ABILITY

Having positioned dis/ability from a complex social perspective, the next section of this chapter offers four questions teachers might consider when deciding whether a text is a valuable addition to a classroom library and/or might serve as a shared literacy experience within the classroom. While a wide array of criteria for selecting texts with dis/ability experiences exist (see Kaiser, 2007; Kleekamp & Zapata, 2018; Pennell et al., 2018; Rieger & McGrail, 2015; Taylor et al., 2020), this section presents a condensed set of practical questions that teachers can take up in-the-moment.

Before reading the questions provided below, it is noteworthy that texts featuring dis/ability experiences continue to be overwhelmingly white and male in their representations (Bell, 2017; Adomat, 2014; Solis, 2004). Therefore, considering what intersectional opportunities for diverse representation exist within texts serves to demonstrate to children that people move through the world with complex experiences that are often marked by a society that multiply marginalizes people. While the chapters of this book, for ease of organization, are arranged by distinct diverse *categories*, teachers should look to select texts that address topics of diversity in the intersecting ways they appear in the real world (e.g., dis/abled, Black, and trans-women's experiences).

What Purpose Does the Book Serve?

When teachers begin reflecting on whether a text featuring dis/ability is a high-quality addition to a classroom library, they might begin by asking what purpose this book would serve for young children. In other words, what will children likely take away from a shared reading of this book? For decades, Bishop (1990) has reminded educators that texts serve as mirrors (i.e., a representation of a shared lived experience), windows (i.e., a look into someone else's world), and glass doors (i.e., a metaphor for one's ability to step into someone else's world through literature). This sentiment holds true when considering texts featuring dis/ability experience(s).

Is the motivation behind the text to explain what a particular dis/ability is? While young children's curiosity for learning about the world may lend itself well to discussions of diverse bodies and minds, texts that solely define dis/ability, without also including other plot lines, tend to present a flat storyline that Others a dis/abled character as abnormal. Without attending to other aspects of a character's life, these narratives tend to seek pity from the reader, recreating harmful tropes around dis/ability experiences already widely circulated in society and in schools.

Instead, teachers might hold up texts that attempt to share a character's full-lived existence with readers, including, but not limited to, dis/abled identities and experiences. These texts feature dis/ability as something that *just is*. Dis/ability is presented as neither good nor bad but rather from a neutral standpoint—another aspect of human diversity. However, these texts may also grapple with the social construction of dis/ability, by naming how humans respond to dis/ability experiences that continue to marginalize dis/abled people (see Aho & Alter, 2018).

In this way, young children with lived dis/ability experiences might see themselves represented in the pages of a book (i.e., a mirror). Students without dis/abilities observe someone else's experience (i.e., a window) and potentially develop empathy for the realities of existing in a world where variations of bodies and minds are often not welcomed.

Teachers can look to *I'm Here* by Peter Reynolds (2011) as a mentor text when critically examining the purpose behind a text featuring dis/ability. In *I'm Here*, a young boy (who isn't named) is the main character. Through a combination of image and text, readers experience a single day on the playground at school with this child. While his classmates play loudly across the playground, the main character sits alone, describing in child-friendly detail that the sensory experiences of the playground are aversive for him. The text ends with one classmate approaching the boy, stepping away from the noise of the playground, to play together.

While this text is written about an autistic experience, the word autism does not appear in the book. However, Reynolds does not shy away from the disconnect that is experienced between neurotypical and neurodivergent people. Rather, the text addresses this directly, speaking to the boy's experience without serving the purpose of making the reader feel sorry for the main character.

Who Authored and/or Illustrated the Text?

Next, teachers can investigate who wrote and illustrated potential books. What connection do these individuals have to dis/ability? What is their motivation for writing/illustrating this text? Dis/abled people writing and illustrating about their own lived experiences should be prioritized when adding representations of dis/ability to a classroom library.

Many children's books about dis/ability are often written by parents, interventionists, or educators. While these texts may present humanizing representations of dis/ability experiences, dis/abled authors and illustrators continue to be largely underrepresented in the field of children's literature. Therefore, the available books that have been published by these authors and illustrators should be centered as the most authentic representations of dis/ability given their connection to individuals' realities.

Texts that are written from the perspective of someone without a lived dis/ability experience often present stereotypical representations of dis/ability. These may include texts that feature dis/ability as a misfortune, positioning the reader to feel sorry for dis/abled characters. Texts that portray dis/abled characters in superhero roles can also further ostracize dis/abled people by exoticizing their experiences, as though dis/ability(ies) provide(s) special powers.

While these tropes have long been criticized by dis/abled people, they continue to be regularly published. This is largely due to the *lack* of experience authors, illustrators, and publishers have with dis/ability. Therefore, looking to dis/abled authors and illustrators serves as a strong indicator for high-quality texts.

As an example, teachers can look to *What Happened to You?* Written by James Catchpole (2021) and illustrated by Karen George, this picturebook describes James' childhood, which includes complexities related to a visible physical dis/ability. Throughout the beginning of the text, children incessantly ask Joe, the main character who is just trying to play a pretend pirate game, "what happened to you?"

Joe is aggravated by this question and gives an array of answers until he finally explodes in frustration. The children then resume playing pirates without Joe ever explaining what *actually* happened to him. This text deals with consent around highly personal information in a way that is both accessible to young children and speaks to a lived dis/ability experience.

From Whose Perspective Is the Story Told?

In addition to looking at who wrote and illustrated a text, teachers must also consider (especially for texts not written from a first-person experience) from whose perspective the story is written. Is the story about a dis/abled character written from the perspective of another character, such as a sibling, friend, or parent? Texts written from first-person perspectives or told by third-person unidentified narrators tend to be of higher quality. While texts written from someone else's perspective could potentially be valuable contributions, these approaches often describe the role of primary characters (e.g., sibling, friend) as *helpers* for the dis/abled person to participate in daily life.

This perspective does not center dis/abled characters' experiences but rather reifies treating dis/abled people as individuals who are overwhelmingly helpless, needing to be doted over by others. While addressing interdependence (i.e., the ongoing combination of self, technologies, and other people) within texts as a relevant part of daily life for dis/abled people is not untrue, positioned this way, readers are asked to have empathy for *helpers* and sympathy for dis/abled people.

Teachers can look to *My Three Best Friends and Me, Zulay,* written by Cari Best (2015) and illustrated by Vanessa Brantley-Newton, as an example of a text written from a first-person perspective. Zulay, the main character, describes her daily life as a student, best friend, Blind person, dancer, and runner. She explains her journey navigating her school building and the community through touch and a sight cane. There is no other character in the book that can speak to Zulay's experiences better than she can as she prepares to run a race at school.

What Is the Role of Dis/ability Within the Story?

Dis/ability is an important layer of identity. However, all identities are messy, interwoven, and layered. The same is true for dis/ability. Therefore, when selecting texts, teachers should investigate the role dis/ability plays in the story. Is dis/ability the only feature readers learn about the dis/abled character? These stories tend to be one-dimensional without accounting for other identity characteristics. High-quality texts present characters as multidimensional with multifaceted experiences. (Auto)biographical picturebooks can serve as productive sites for deep character development.

A sample biographical picturebook is *Emmanuel's Dream: The True Story of Emmanuel Ofosu Yeboah,* by Laurie Ann Thompson and Sean Qualls (2015), which provides a representation of Emmanuel's life as a dis/ability advocate from Ghana. While this text largely features Emmanuel's journey advocating for dis/abled people all over the world (particularly in Africa), this is not the only dimension of Emmanuel's life presented. Emmanuel is a son, athlete, and hard worker. He is dynamic, smart, and loving with a complicated existence in the world and within his family. He is never just one thing, and readers follow this thread as they examine his interactions across much of the world.

SHARING AUTHENTIC LITERATURE FEATURING DIS/ABILITY IN THE CLASSROOM WITH YOUNG CHILDREN

Having utilized the guiding questions in the previous section, teachers may next wonder how to share selected stories with young children. In the following section, teachers will find accessible entry points into literature (particularly picturebooks) with young children.

Specifically designed to feature examples of teacher talk and facilitation during shared readings, this section is divided into what teachers can say/do before a shared reading, during a shared reading, and after a shared reading with a conclusion that speaks to the importance of featuring diverse literature, including texts that feature lived dis/ability experiences, throughout the schoolyear.

Before a Shared Reading: Introducing a Touchstone Text

When inviting children to begin considering how texts might serve as windows, mirrors, and/or gliding glass doors, teachers might begin by selecting a touchstone, or mentor, text. A touchstone text is a book preselected and pre-read by the teacher to be shared with students from a mentoring (or modeling) perspective. Having thought deeply and critically about what texts qualify as high quality, a teacher will likely choose a picturebook that clearly conveys a wide array of the high-quality features described in the previous section.

Teachers can begin a shared reading by inviting students to enter the literacy invitation with a purpose (e.g., guiding question). The teacher activates students' prior knowledge around the content that will appear in the story, grows connections between the characters in the story and students, and invites students to share their own lived experiences and affective responses related to the upcoming narrative (Keene & Zimmerman, 1997).

In this way, students step into the story already oriented to key ideas, guided by the teacher. It is imperative here to note that the purpose of setting a shared intent or goal when stepping into a piece of literature featuring a lived dis/ability experience is *not* solely to teach about what a dis/ability is but rather to invite children to think about the sociopolitical multilayered aspects of the picturebook about to unfold (Bomer & Bomer, 2001).

For example, a teacher might choose to share *I'm Here*, by Peter Reynolds (mentioned in the previous section), as a touchstone text. Since this text features a main character who finds the rambunctious conventions around school recess to be overwhelming, the teacher might first talk with students about individual preferences for play. Here, the teacher leaves space for students to share about their own play, including where and when they like to play, with whom they like to play, aspects of play they don't like, times when they prefer to play alone, and so on. Before entering the shared reading, the teacher might say, "As we read, I'd like us to think about how different characters in the story play. We'll stop along the way as we read to think more about play."

During a Shared Reading: Creating Informed Guided Questions

Having set an intention for shared reading, teachers and students next step into the touchstone/mentor text together. During the prereading of the text, teachers might find it helpful to craft guiding questions inviting students to think deeply about the social complexities of dis/ability. Selecting specific spreads within texts ahead of time for asking these questions (by utilizing sticky notes or another visual representation to children) will provide space to invite students to pause and reflect with intention (Farell et al., 2010).

While guiding questions will likely vary by the shared intent set by the teacher at the beginning of a shared reading, examples of general questions within texts featuring a lived dis/ability experience might include:

- Tell me about someone you know or have met like [main character].
- How are you like [main character]? How are you not like [main character]?
- If you could draw yourself into this illustration, where would you put yourself? Why? What would you be doing? How would you be feeling?
- Would you be friends with [the main character]? Why or why not?

Teachers may notice that these questions invite students to consider connections they have with a main character that are designed to evoke initial ideas from children, likely with follow-up discussion needed from the teacher.

For example, an early childhood teacher in a recent research study chose to share *The Girl Who Thought in Pictures: The Story of Dr. Temple Grandin* by Julia Finley Mosca (2017). This picturebook is a biographical account of Temple Grandin, an autistic animal rights scientist and activist. The text tackles Grandin's successes as well as moments of social exclusion.

The intention for this touchstone text invited children to consider the social construction of *normal* versus *different* and times when students had been made to feel *different*. After developing guiding questions, the teacher placed sticky notes of each question on specific spreads of the text. One spread within the picturebook specifically addressed issues of social isolation in schools as Temple is bullied by her peers who throw objects at her while she is seated at her desk. This spread represents the marginalization many dis/abled individuals will likely experience at some point during their education.

When the teacher reached this spread, she asked, "I'm wondering . . . if you could draw yourself anywhere in this picture, where would you be?" Elizabeth, a first-grade student, stood up, and touched a page on the picturebook between the flying objects and Temple. She said, "I would probably put myself over here trying to stop them because I don't like when people are mean to other people."

"What would you be doing?" asked the teacher.

"I would be, um, telling them to stop and probably blocking the paper balls that they're throwing. I would be blocking them from getting to her," Elizabeth responded.

"How would you be feeling?" the teacher inquired.

"I would be feeling angry and sad at the same time," Elizabeth answered.

"Why?" the teacher pressed.

"Because I really don't like whenever people are mean, and it makes me think of a time when somebody's been mean to me, and it makes me angry that they're doing it to them and sad that it reminds me of something that happened to me," Elizabeth finished.

Elizabeth shared experiences that demonstrated that she too has felt isolated. Her shared experiences, not pity, drove her reasoning for stepping between harsh spoken words and flying objects. Elizabeth illustrated that young children are ready to enter into discussions related to social isolation and to critically consider the implications this has for an individual.

She situated her response as an initiative toward social justice in an effort to resist bullying. Because the teacher crafted guiding questions ahead of time, this text served as a moment for Elizabeth (and her peers) to consider their own lived experiences (mirror) and the experiences of others whose lives may look different than their own (window).

After a Shared Reading: Responding with Craft Making

Following a shared reading, teachers might next invite young children to respond to the group discussion with craft materials. Students who may not have entered the conversation via spoken language might be able to access another modality as they process the information they have just shared.

Teachers can incorporate a wide array of student-choice in this response invitation to provide inclusive avenues of participation. For some students, painting, drawing, or coloring might be desired craft-making response choices. For others, searching for images online, cutting them out, and taping them to the rest of their craft may be a preferred option. In sum, *making* in response to literature should serve the purpose of helping students process information rather than demanding the specific tools they use to do so.

For example, the early childhood teacher who shared *The Girl Who Thought in Pictures: The Story of Dr. Temple Grandin* followed the reading with an invitation for students to consider how they felt connected (or not) to the main character, Temple. She approached one student, Chase, who had not yet chosen any tools for craft making. "Tell me about someone you know like Temple," the teacher requested.

Chase looked up and said, "me."

"How are you like Temple?" the teacher asked.

"She was different, and people made fun of her. And that happens to me," Chase answered.

"When is a time you've felt different?" the teacher responded.

"I'm like different from everybody else," Chase answered.

"Tell me what that looks like at school or at home," the teacher continued.

"Uh, everybody's just normal and I'm different and some people make fun of me. Not in our class but some people make fun of me because my favorite color's pink," Chase continued.

Chase explained that other children sometimes laugh at him which makes him feel sad. Rather than distancing himself from someone (i.e., Temple) seen as different, Chase identified himself as someone like Temple. He demonstrated that children have the capacity to relate to dis/abled characters in texts based on shared lived experiences and interests when characters are multidimensional.

After sharing the connections Chase made with the main character, the teacher asked Chase if he wanted to express his feelings with art materials. Chase agreed but decided that rather than focusing on being sad, he wanted to choose the character connections he shared with Temple that made him happy. Chase chose a large pink piece of construction paper and drew himself and Temple smiling on the page.

Following the Lesson: Creating Ongoing Connections

As with all diverse literature, the sharing of dis/abled lived experiences through picturebooks is not just something to be shared on a particular day (e.g., International Day of Persons with Disabilities), during a particular month (e.g., Autism Acceptance Month), or when a new dis/abled student enters the classroom. Rather, these texts are meant to be shared throughout the school year through thoughtful pairings that bring multiple dis/abled perspectives into view alongside and with one another (Zapata et al., 2019).

In this way, teachers promote representations of people with diverse bodyminds as valued members of society. Beyond the ideas suggested in this section, teachers might look to create independent reading time that incorporates an array of dis/ability experiences displayed in featured texts, on bookshelves, in book boxes, and the like.

HUMANIZING CHILDREN'S BOOKS FEATURING DIS/ABILITY

Bailey, J. (2019). *A friend for Henry*. Chronicle Books.
Recommended grades: K–2
Awards: Schneider Family Honor Book

This picturebook features Henry, a student who attempts to follow the rules at school and interact with other students. Other children consistently break the rules by being too loud and using Henry's carpet square. Henry, who is identified as autistic on the dust jacket of the book, feels frustrated by the unspoken rules he does not understand. Written from the narrator's third-person perspective, this text centers on the challenges autistic students encounter in neurotypically designed spaces. Rather than featuring groups of children who pity Henry, this text instead features Henry's journey toward friendship with a peer who accepts and honors the way Henry moves through the world.
Churnin, N. (2016). *The William Hoy story*. Albert Whitman & Company.
Recommended grades: PK–3
Awards: New York Public Library Best Books for Kids, Storytelling World Resource Honor Book

This biographical picturebook provides an overview of William Hoy's life, a famous baseball player who was also D/deaf. In the late 1800s, calls by umpires during baseball games were made verbally (without hand signals). As an athlete on the field, Hoy did not have access to this information. Alongside others, Hoy helped introduce many of the baseball signs still used today (e.g., "out," "safe"). This text serves as a powerful connection to access, equity, and universal design in classrooms. For example, the historical context of Hoy's life demonstrates an accessibility option that he required to participate (i.e., access to signs) from which all baseball players benefit (i.e., access to universally accepted visual symbols when an umpire's verbal call is not heard).

Finison, C. (2021). *Don't hug Doug (He doesn't like it)*. G. P. Putnam's Sons.

Recommended grades: PK–2

    This picturebook, written from a third-person narrator perspective, is about Doug, a young boy who enjoys doing lots of things with his friends but does not enjoy hugs. The text presents alternatives to hugs (e.g., high fives) for interactions with Doug. This text includes dynamic and visual imagery while also describing realities for students who find sensory experiences related to certain kinds of touch (e.g., hugs) aversive. This picturebook invites students and teachers into discussions of sensory preferences, needs, and body autonomy.

Khan, R. (2014). *King for a day*. Lee & Low Books.

Recommended grades: PK–2

Awards: Best Books, Kirkus Reviews, Junior Library Guild Selection, and Best Multicultural Books, Center for the Study of Multicultural Children's Books.

    Malik is a wheelchair rider who is competing in a kite battle on the Hindu celebration of Basant, a tradition that originated in Pakistan and now transcends a variety of religions and cultures. Malik is the main character, and the story is written from his first-person perspective. Malik, with the help of his siblings, wins the kite battle, even though he has only brought one kite to the competition. This text centers on multiple intersectional layers of diversity including race, religion, culture, and dis/ability.

Newman, T. (2020). *Itzhak: A boy who loved the violin*. Abrams Books for Young Readers.

Recommended grades: PK–2

Awards: Schneider Family Honor Book

    This biographical picturebook tells the story of Itzhak Perlman, the world-renowned Israeli American violinist, who, as a child, contracted polio, resulting in physical disabilities affecting all of his limbs. The arc of the text follows the trajectory of Perlman's life from a young child to perform at the Ed Sullivan Theater at age thirteen. This text serves as a comprehensive look at Perlman's childhood and as an opening to discuss the multifaceted components of the life of a musician, including but not limited to his lived dis/ability experience.

Pimentel, A. B. (2020). *All the way to the top: How one girls' fight for Americans with disabilities changed everything.* Sourcebooks eXplore.

Recommended grades: PK–2

Awards: Schneider Family Honor Book

This picturebook portrays the protests led by dis/abled people prior to the passing of the Americans with Disabilities Act in 1990. The text is written from the perspective of Jennifer Keelan, a wheelchair rider born with cerebral palsy who joined the protests for disability rights at six years old and famously pulled herself up the Capitol steps in Washington DC using only her arms because there was no ramp access at this time. This text serves as an accessible opportunity to learn about dis/ability rights and activism movements in the United States.

Scott, J. (2020). *I talk like a river.* Neal Porter Books.

Recommended grades: PK–3

Awards: Schneider Family Book Award, Boston Globe-Horn Book Award Winner

This picturebook describes the pressure the main character, a school-aged unnamed boy who stutters, feels when interacting with classmates and his teachers. After a particularly difficult "speech day" during which the main character was put on the spot in front of his peers, his father takes him to the river and compares the bumbling, busy, fast river to his son's speech. This simile serves as a catalyst for building the boy's confidence as he goes back to face school the next day. Written from the author's first-person perspective as a stutterer, this text invites students into discussions of social exclusion and empathy.

Rahman, B. (2021). *A sky-blue bench.* Pajama Press.

Recommended grades: K–2

Awards: Schneider Family Honor Book

This text is intersectional in its representation of culture, gender, and dis/ability. Aria, the female main character living in Afghanistan, returns to school after an acquired physical injury resulting in the need for a prosthetic leg. When she arrives back at school, she finds that she must sit on the floor all day because there are no tables or desks for the students (due to years of warfare). Sitting on the floor all day causes significant pain. The text discusses Aria's perseverance in locating materials to build a bench for herself and her classmates so that she can access education. Collectively, this text invites students and teachers into an intersectional experience of marginalization and persistence through a window into a culture that may look very different than the United States.

Lebeuf, A. (2021). *My city speaks.* Kid Can Press.
Recommended grades: PK–2
Awards: Schneider Family Book Award

This picturebook is written from the first-person perspective and features an unnamed girl as the main character navigating her city with her white cane. The cane features a red bottom, indicating low vision (i.e., meaning the user has some usable vision). Each spread of the text explores different aspects of the city through senses other than sight (e.g., touching or hearing parts of the city). This text does not explicitly name blindness or low vision but features the white cane as a representation of diverse ways of experiencing the city. This text provides openings for students to see blind and visually impaired people present in children's literature.

Talbott, H. (2021). *A walk in the words.* Nancy Paulsen Books.
Recommended grades: PK–3
Awards: Schneider Family Honor Book

Written from the first-person perspective and based on the author's lived experience, the main character, an unnamed boy in the text, describes his journey learning to read. The main character describes his strengths in visualizing and drawing but difficulty with reading in the traditional ways he sees his classmates excelling. The arc of the narrative follows the main character's journey in discovering what works best for him while confronting feelings of shame when he watches his peers read with ease in class. This text is particularly relevant for students labeled as "struggling readers" to see their journey, strengths, and personal experiences represented in the pages of a text that confronts feelings of exclusion in nuanced and respectful ways.

RESOURCES ON DIS/ABILITY ADVOCACY AND LITERATURE FOR CHILDREN

Schneider Family Book Award
Website: https://www.ala.org/awardsgrants/schneider-family-book-award

Disability Visibility Project
Website: https://disabilityvisibilityproject.com/

Disability in Kid Lit
Website: https://disabilityinkidlit.com/

Judy Heumann
Website: https://judithheumann.com/project/about/

Autistic Self-Advocacy Network (ASAN)
Website: https://autisticadvocacy.org/

National Association of the Deaf
Website: https://www.nad.org/

American Foundation for the Blind
Website: https://www.afb.org/

National Stuttering Association
Website: https://westutter.org/

Crip Camp: A Disability Revolution (Netflix Documentary)
Website: https://www.netflix.com/title/81001496

REFERENCES

Adomat, D. S. (2014). Exploring issues of disability in children's literature. *Disability Studies Quarterly*, 34(3), 1–17. https://doi.org/10.18061/dsq.v34i3.3865.

Aho, T., & Alter, G. (2018). "Just like me, just like you": Narrative erasure as disability normalization in children's picture books. *Journal of Literacy & Cultural Disability Studies*, 12(3), 303–19. https://online.liverpooluniversitypress.co.uk/doi/abs/10.3828/jlcds.2018.24.

Andrews, E. E., Forber-Pratt, A. J., Mona, L. R., Lund, E. M., Pilarski, C. R., & Balter, R. (2019). #Saytheword: A disaility culture commentary on the erasure of "disability." *Rehabilitation Psychology*, 64(2), 111–18.

Bell, C. (2017). Is disability studies actually white disability studies? In L. J. Davis (Ed.), *The disability studies reader* (5th ed., pp. 406–15). New York, NY: Routledge.

Beneke, M. R., Machado, E., & Taitingfong, J. (2022). Dismantling carceral logics in the urban early literacy classroom: Towards liberatory literacy pedagogies with/for multiply-marginalized young children. *Urban Education*. Advance online publication. https://doi.org/10.1177/00420859221091235.

Bishop, R. S. (1990). Mirrors, windows, and sliding glass doors. *Perspectives: Choosing and Using Books for the Classroom*, 6(3), ix–xi.

Bomer, R., & Bomer, K. (2001). *For a Better World: Reading and Writing for Social Action*. Heinemann.

Farrell, M., Arizpe, E., & McAdam, J. (2010). Journeys across visual borders: Annotated spreads of *The Arrival* by Shaun Tan as a method for understanding pupils creating of meaning through visual images. *American Journal of Language and Literacy*, 33(3), 198–210.

Haegele, J. A., & Hodge, S. (2016). Disability discourse: Overview and critiques of the medical and social models. *QUEST*, 68(2), 193–206.

Kaiser, C. E. (2007). Is your early childhood literature collection disability-inclusive and current? *Children & Libraries*, 5(3), 5–12.

Keene, E. O., & Zimmermann, S. (1997). *Mosaic of thought: Teaching comprehension in a reader's workshop*. Heinemann.

Kleekamp, M. C., & Zapata, A. (2018). Interrogating depictions of disability in children's picturebooks. *The Reading Teacher*, 72(5), 589–97.

Meekosha, H., & Shuttleworth, R. (2017). What's so "critical" about critical disability studies? In L. J. Davis (Ed.), *The disability studies reader* (5th ed., pp. 175–94). Routledge.

Pennell, A. E., Wollak, B., & Koppenhaver, D. A. (2018). Respectful representations of disability in picture books. *The Reading Teacher*, 71(4), 411–19. https://doi.org/10.1002/trtr.1632.

Price, M. (2015). The bodymind problem and the possibilities of pain. *Hypatia*, 30(10), 268–84.

Rieger, A., & McGrail, E. (2015). Exploring children's literature with authentic representations of disability. *Kappa Delta Pi Record*, 51(1), 18–23. https://doi.org/10.1080/00228958.2015.988560.

Shakespeare, T. (2017). The social model of disability. In L. J. Davis (Ed.), *The disability studies reader* (5th ed., pp. 195–203). Routledge.

Solis, S. (2004). The disabilitymaking factory: Manufacturing "differences" through children's books. *Disability Studies Quarterly*, 24(1), 1–13. https://doi.org/10.18061/dsq.v24i1.851.

Taylor, T. M., Moss, K., Brundage, K. E., & Prater, M. A. (2020). Selecting and using children's books with authentic representations of characters with developmental disabilities. *DADD Online Journal*, 7(1), 10–30.

Wargo, J. M. (2019). Sounding the garden, voicing a problem: Mobilizing critical literacy through personal digital inquiry with young children. *Language Arts*, 96(5), 275–85.

Vasquez, V. M. (2014). *Negotiating critical literacies with young children*. Routledge.

Vehabovic, N. (2021). Picturebooks as critical literacy: Experiences and perspectives of translingual children from refugee backgrounds. *Journal of Literacy Research*, 53(3), 382–405.

Zapata, A., Crisp, T., Wargo, J., Kleekamp, M., & Bostic, Q. (2019). *On the importance of critical selection and teaching of diverse children's literature (Inclusion, diversity, and equity policy statement)*. https://www.childrensliteratureassembly.org/uploads/1/1/8/6/118631535/inclusiondiversityandequitypolicystatement.pdf.

ADDITIONAL CHILDREN'S LITERATURE CITED

Best, C. (2015). *My three best friends and me, Zulay.* Margaret Fergus Books.

Catchpole, J. (2021). *What happened to you?* Faber and Faber Limited.

Mosca, J. F. (2017). *The girl who thought in pictures: The story of Dr. Temple Grandin.* The Innovation Press.

Reynolds, P. H. (2011). *I'm here.* Atheneum Books.

Thompson, L. A., & Qualls, S. (2015). *Emmanuel's dream: The true story of Emmanuel Ofosu Yeboah.* Schwartz & Wade Books.

About the Editor and Contributors

EDITORS

Xiufang Chen, PhD, is associate professor of literacy education in the Department of Language, Literacy, and Sociocultural Education at Rowan University in New Jersey. Her research centers on literacy teacher education, online literacy instruction, and integration of technology and sociocultural dimensions of literacy instruction. She has received the Build-A-Bear Workshop Foundation and RU Seed Funding grants for her projects on nurturing preschool children's multicultural awareness through reading and responding to multicultural children's books. Findings of her studies on using multicultural children's books in preschool classrooms have been presented at several highly esteemed national and international educational conferences and have been published in refereed academic journals.

Susan Browne, EdD, is associate professor in the Department of Language, Literacy, and Sociocultural Education at Rowan University. Dr. Browne teaches undergraduate and graduate reading courses. She serves as a research advisor to Master's and EdD candidates and teaches in the Language and Literacy PhD Program. She is a codirector of the Rowan University Writing Project. Dr. Browne's research interests and publications are in the areas of critical pedagogy, urban education, and diverse literature for children and adolescents and reader response.

About the Editor and Contributors

CONTRIBUTORS

Deborah Greenblatt is assistant professor of multicultural education at Medgar Evers College, The City University of New York. She has a PhD in Urban Education with a focus on educational policy and leadership from The CUNY Graduate Center. Prior to pursuing her doctorate, Dr. Greenblatt was a public elementary school teacher for many years. Dr. Greenblatt's research focuses on social justice, equity, and democracy in teaching and teacher education. Dr. Greenblatt is the coauthor of *Reimaging American Education to Serve all our Children: Why do we Educate in a Democracy?* She is also the author of several journal articles including Conflicting perspectives: A comparison of edTPA intended outcomes to actual experiences of teacher candidates and educators in New York City Schools in *Journal of Inquiry and Action in Education*; Neoliberalism and teacher education in *Policy Futures in Education*; and several articles in *Education in a Democracy*. Dr. Greenblatt is on the Board of Directors for the National Network for Educational Renewal, the Board of Directors and Advisory Board for Community of Volunteer Educators, and the Advisory Committee for PBS THIRTEEN Educational Services.

Doctor Julia López-Robertson is professor in the Department of Instruction and Teacher Education at the University of South Carolina. She is the author of *Celebrating our Cuentos: Choosing and Using Latinx Literature in Elementary Classrooms*, published by Scholastic.

Kate E. Kedley is assistant professor at Rowan University. Dr. Kedley is a former secondary English Language Arts and Drivers Education teacher in Iowa, Arizona, and the Central American country of Honduras. Dr. Kedley's research centers around critical literacy and education, public engagement, LGBTQ+, and young adult literature, language education, and social and educational movements in Honduras. Kate has published work in various journals such as the *English Journal, Sex Education*, and the *Journal of Lesbian Studies*.

Melanie D. Koss is professor of literacy in the Department of Curriculum and Instruction at Northern Illinois University. She teaches courses in children's and young adult literature with an emphasis on diversity, equity, and inclusion. Her research interests include examining representations of diversity in children's and young adult literature and literature awards, exploring ways children's and young adult literature can effectively be used in the teaching of English Language Learners, the role of teacher autonomy in the selection of children's and young adult literature for the curriculum and classroom, and the implication of censorship and book banning in the classroom. Recent publications can be found in Journal of Children's Literature, The Reading Teacher, The ALAN Review, and Journal of Language and Literacy Education.

Melissa García Vega teaches at CUNY–Lehman College. Her research interests examine Children's literature with emphasis on the Caribbean region, multilingual learners, and the global context.

Monica C. Kleekamp, PhD, CCC-SLP (she/her/hers), is assistant professor of speech-language pathology at Maryville University in St. Louis, Missouri. Kleekamp's research focuses on disrupting deficit orientations to dis/ability and literacy within education and therapeutic spaces by honoring interdependent neuroqueer literacies produced by/with diverse bodyminds. Recent publications featured in scholarly journals include peer-reviewed articles in *Research in the Teaching of English, Journal of Literacy Research, Reading Teacher*, and *Literacy Research: Theory, Method, and Practice*.

Shanetia P. Clark, Ph.D., is an Associate Professor of Literacy in the Department of Early and Elementary Education at Salisbury University. Her research and teaching interests include children's literature and the exploration of aesthetic experiences within reading and writing classrooms.

Tim Swagerty (Muskogee/Choctaw) is instructor of social studies in the West College of Education at Midwestern State University in Wichita Falls, Texas. His previous publication "Digital Access to Culturally Relevant Curriculum: The Impact on the Native and Indigenous Student (IGCGlobal)" highlighted the proliferation of culturally insensitive online classroom curricular materials and the impact of undependable broadband service in Native rural and Reservation communities during COVID-forced distance learning.

Zeynep Isik-Ercan is professor of early childhood education and the codirector of Early Childhood Leadership Institute at Rowan University, New

Jersey. Her research regularly appears in academic journals on topics such as culturally and linguistically diverse children, teachers, families and communities, immigrant families with young children, culturally responsive teaching and intellectual development, and professional development of educators and leaders. She actively works with state organizations, schools, and educators through coaching and training programs.

www.ingramcontent.com/pod-product-compliance
Lightning Source LLC
Chambersburg PA
CBHW020124240426
43673CB00038B/587